A SOURCE BOOK
OF
SCOTTISH HISTORY

VOLUME TWO

A SOURCE BOOK
OF
SCOTTISH HISTORY

VOLUME TWO
1424 to 1567

Edited by

William Croft Dickinson D.Lit., LL.D.

Gordon Donaldson M.A., Ph.D.

Isabel A. Milne M.A.

THOMAS NELSON AND SONS LTD
LONDON EDINBURGH PARIS MELBOURNE
TORONTO AND NEW YORK

THOMAS NELSON AND SONS LTD
Parkside Works Edinburgh 9
3 Henrietta Street London WC2
312 Flinders Street Melbourne C1
5 Parker's Buildings Burg Street Cape Town

THOMAS NELSON AND SONS (CANADA) LTD
91–93 Wellington Street West   Toronto 1

THOMAS NELSON AND SONS
19 East 47th Street New York 17

SOCIÉTÉ FRANÇAISE D'EDITIONS NELSON
25 rue Henri Barbusse Paris Ve

———

First published March 1953

CONTENTS

CONTENTS

ABBREVIATIONS

A.P.S.	Acts of the Parliaments of Scotland
E.R.	The Exchequer Rolls of Scotland
Knox	John Knox, *History of the Reformation in Scotland*, ed. Dickinson
Nat. MSS Scot.	The National Manuscripts of Scotland
R.M.S.	Register of the Great Seal of Scotland
R.P.C.	Register of the Privy Council of Scotland
R.S.S.	Register of the Privy Seal of Scotland
S.H.R.	*Scottish Historical Review*
T.A.	Accounts of the Lord High Treasurer of Scotland

CHAPTER ONE

DESCRIPTIONS OF SCOTLAND

The contrast between the account of Scotland given by Aeneas Sylvius (later Pope Pius II) and that given by Pedro de Ayala undoubtedly reflects a steady improvement in the standard of living in the fifteenth century. The second half of that century saw the foundation of many collegiate churches, a considerable development in domestic architecture, and the erection of many ' burghs of barony '—all indicative of an increase in wealth. The period was one of an ' expanding economy,' which is also revealed in the recurring ' currency crises ' of the reign of James III (cf. pp. 216–20). But we must also remember that Aeneas Sylvius, on his way to Scotland, had been so severely storm-tossed that he had vowed to make a pilgrimage, barefoot, to the nearest shrine if he were spared to reach land. Unfortunately, to fulfil his vow, he had to walk barefoot for ten miles over frozen ground and, according to one of his biographers, suffered ' aches in his joints ' for the rest of his life. His account may well be an embittered one. Ayala, on the other hand, was anxious to give as favourable a description of Scotland as possible. Spanish diplomacy was then intent on wooing Scotland away from the ' auld alliance ' with France, and Ayala concludes by suggesting that if the third daughter of Ferdinand and Isabella be not yet engaged it would be a service to God to marry her to the King of Scots. His account, written to impress the Spanish Court, is certainly exaggerated (as is his summation of the royal revenues). Nevertheless, even allowing for the facts that Aeneas Sylvius did not enjoy himself while Pedro de Ayala obviously did, it is clear that there had been considerable advance during the reigns of James II and James III : though it is noticeable that the national economy was still a primitive one based upon the export of wool, hides and fish.

Major's descriptions, taken from his *Historia Majoris Britanniæ* (first published in Paris in 1521), are probably reliable. The short lease was certainly the curse of Scottish agriculture—though, strangely, Major makes no reference to the enactments for setting lands in feu (cf. pp. 220–3), a system which was fast developing

I

with the growth of a ' money-economy.' Excerpts taken from Major's other writings and throwing light on social conditions in Scotland in the late fifteenth and early sixteenth centuries (including some comments on feu-holdings) have been printed in *Innes Review*, ii, pp. 65–76.

AENEAS SYLVIUS

(1435)

Here [in Scotland] I once lived in the season of winter, when the sun illuminates the earth little more than three hours. At that time James was king, robust of person, and oppressed by his excessive corpulence. . . .

I had previously heard that there was a tree in Scotland, that growing on the banks of rivers produced fruits in the form of geese, which as they approached ripeness dropped off of their own accord, some on the ground and some into the water ; that those which fell on the ground rotted, but that those submerged in the water immediately assumed life, and swam about under the water, and flew into the air with feathers and wings. When I made enquiries regarding this story, I learned that the miracle was always referred to some place further off, and that this famous tree was to be found not in Scotland but in the Orkney Islands.[1]

. . . In this country I saw the poor, who almost in a state of nakedness begged at the church doors, depart with joy in their faces on receiving stones as alms. This stone . . . is burned instead of wood, of which the country is destitute. . . .

The towns have no walls, and the houses are for the most part constructed without lime. The roofs of the houses in the country are made of turf, and the doors of the humbler dwellings are made of the hide of oxen. The common people are poor, and destitute of all refinement. They eat flesh and fish to repletion, and bread only as a dainty.

[1] A visitor like Aeneas was not likely to know the treeless reputation of the Orkneys.

The men are small in stature, bold and forward in temper ; the women, fair in complexion, comely and pleasing, but not distinguished for their chastity, giving their kisses more readily than Italian women their hands.

There is no wine in the country unless what is imported. All the horses are amblers, and are of small size. . . . Hides, wool, salted fish and pearls are exported to Flanders. Nothing pleases the Scots more than abuse of the English. . . .

Hume Brown, *Early Travellers in Scotland*, pp. 25 et seq.

DON PEDRO DE AYALA

(1498)

The king . . . is of noble stature, neither tall nor short, and as handsome in complexion and shape as a man can be. . . . He speaks the following foreign languages : Latin, very well ; French, German, Flemish, Italian, and Spanish. . . . The king speaks, besides, the language of the savages who live in some parts of Scotland and on the islands. . . . He is courageous, even more so than a king should be. . . . I have seen him often undertake most dangerous things in the last wars. I sometimes clung to his skirts and succeeded in keeping him back : On such occasions he does not take the least care of himself. He is not a good captain, because he begins to fight before he has given his orders. . . .

I will give an account of his revenues. Although I do not know them to a certainty, I do not think that I shall be far wrong. I shall estimate them a little below their real amount.

He has a revenue from arable and pasture lands, which are let by leases of three years. The farmers pay a fine upon entry. This rent is said to amount to 50,000 pounds Scots. . . .

Another revenue is that from the customs. The import duties are insignificant, but the exports yield a considerable sum of money, because there are three principal articles of export, that is to say, wool, hides and fish. The customs

3

are worth about 25,000 ducats a year [i.e. £20,000].[1] They have much increased, and still continue to increase. Another revenue is that derived from the administration of the law. His predecessors farmed it to certain persons called justices (*justiciarios*), like our *corregidores*. This king does not like to farm the administration of the law, because justice is not well administered in that way. It is said that this revenue amounts to more than 30,000 ducats, but I will put it down at only 25,000 ducats.

He has another revenue from his wards, which is very considerable, and which offers good opportunities for rewarding his servants. If lords, or gentlemen of the middle class, in whatever part of the kingdom they may be, die and leave children under twenty-two years of age, the king is the guardian of them. He receives all their revenues till they come of age. He lets or sells such guardianships. He even sells the marriages of his wards, male and female. When the ward comes of age, and the king gives him the title of his father, or brother, or testator, he pays the amount of one or two year's rent, or any other sum that is agreed upon, into the exchequer of the king. I am told that this is the richest source of revenue, but I will estimate it at only 20,000 ducats. . . .[2]

He has a rent from the fisheries, not in money, but in kind, for his kitchen, and likewise from meat and poultry etc. . . . He is in want of nothing, judging from the manner in which he lives, but he is not able to put money into his strong boxes.

. . . The Scots are not industrious, and the people are poor. They spend all their time in wars, and when there is no war they fight with one another. It must, however, be observed, that since the present king succeeded to the throne they do not dare to quarrel so much with one another as formerly, especially since he came of age. They

---

[1] The actual value of the customs was about £3,000.
[2] There is no evidence to support any large income from the feudal casualties of ward, relief and marriage ; all too often these casualties were given away by the king. The age of majority is twenty-one.

4

have learnt by experience that he executes the law without respect to rich or poor. . . .

It is impossible to describe the immense quantity of fish. The old proverb says already ' piscinata Scotia.' Great quantities of salmon, herring and a kind of dried fish, which they call stock fish, are exported. The quantity is so great that it suffices for Italy, France, Flanders and England. They have so many wild fruits which they eat, that they do not know what to do with them. There are immense flocks of sheep, especially in the savage portions of Scotland. Hides are employed for many purposes. . . . The corn is very good, but they do not produce as much as they might, because they do not cultivate the land. Their method is the following : they plough the land only once when it has grass on it, which is as high as a man, then they sow the corn, and cover it by means of a harrow, which makes the land even again. Nothing more is done till they cut the corn. I have seen the straw stand so high after harvest that it reached to my girdle. . . .

On the islands there are many flocks, and great quantities of fish and of barley. The inhabitants are very warlike and agile. I saw them in the last war. They do not know what danger is. The present king keeps them in strict subjection. . . . None of the former kings have succeeded in bringing the people into such subjection as the present king. He went last summer to many of the islands and presided at the courts of law.

The prelates are very much revered ; they have the larger share in the government. Spiritual as well as secular lords, if they have a title or a dignity, belong to the General Council. It meets four times a year in order to administer justice. It is a very good institution. . . .

The kings . . . do not remain long in one place. The reason thereof is twofold. In the first place, they move often about, in order to visit their kingdom, to administer justice, and to establish police where it is wanted. The second reason is, that they have rents in kind in every province, and they wish to consume them. . . .

The women are courteous in the extreme. I mention this because they are really honest, though very bold. They are absolute mistresses of their houses, and even of their husbands, in all things concerning the administration of their property, income as well as expenditure. They are very graceful and handsome women. They dress much better than here [England], and especially as regards the head-dress, which is, I think, the handsomest in the world.

The towns and villages are populous. The houses are good, all built of hewn stone, and provided with excellent doors, glass windows, and a great number of chimneys. All the furniture that is used in Italy, Spain, and France, is to be found in their dwellings. It has not been bought in modern times only, but inherited from preceding ages. . . .

There is not more than one fortified town in Scotland, because the kings do not allow their subjects to fortify them. . . . .

Ibid., pp. 39 et seq.

PEDER SWAVE

(1535)

I enquired if there were any trees in Scotland from which birds were produced. All replied that no doubt was possible on the matter, that it was a fact they were so produced, that those which fell into the water became alive, and that those which fell on the land had no principle of life. . . . There is a certain floating island in Scotland, which deflects from one shore to the other with the ebb and flow of the tide. . . . The bird called the gannet lays no more than one egg, and hatches it under its foot in a standing position.[1]

[1] Sir William Brereton, who travelled in Scotland in 1636, wrote: 'These solem-geese (as it is reported of them), when their eggs are sufficiently sitten, they stamp upon them with their feet, and break them.' Thomas Morer, in 1689, improved on the account of incubation given by Swave by deriving 'solan' from 'sole on.'

The wild Scots live in the manner of the Scythians, they are ignorant of the use of bread ; when they are hungry they outstrip a stag in swiftness of foot, overtake it and kill it, and so sustain life ; they eat the flesh raw, only squeezing out the blood. Not far from Edinburgh there is a mountain that constantly smokes like Etna. . . .

Ibid., pp. 56–7

JOHN MAJOR
(1521)

In Scotland the houses of the country people are small, as it were cottages, and the reason is this : they have no permanent holdings, but hired only, or in lease for four or five years, at the pleasure of the lord of the soil ; therefore they do not dare to build good houses, though stone abound ; neither do they plant trees or hedges for their orchards, nor do they dung the land ; and this is no small loss and damage to the whole realm. If the landlords would let their lands in perpetuity, they might have double and treble of the profit that now comes to them—and for this reason : the country folk would then cultivate their land beyond all comparison better, would grow richer, and would build fair dwellings that should be an ornament to the country ; nor would those murders take place which follow the eviction of a holder. If a landlord have let to another the holding of a quarrelsome fellow, him will the evicted man murder [1] as if he were the landlord's bosom friend. Nor would the landlords have to fear that their vassals would not rise with them against the enemy—that is an irrational fear. Far better for the king and the common-weal that the vassal should not so rise at the mere nod of his superior ; but that with justice and in tranquillity

[1] It should be noted, however, that pursuers in criminal actions frequently state that they have been ‘ slaughtered ’ when only too clearly they are still ‘ on life ’ to bring their actions for ‘ invasion and assault.’

7

all cases should be duly treated. Laws, too, can be made under which, on pain of losing his holding, a vassal must take part in his lord's quarrel. This readiness on the part of subjects to make the quarrel of their chief their own quarrel ends often, of a truth, in making an exile of the chief himself.

England excels Scotland, by a little, in fertility . . . but in fish Scotland far more abounds. . . .

In both of the British kingdoms the warlike strength of the nation resides in its common people and its peasantry. The farmers rent their land from the lords, but cultivate it by means of their servants, and not with their own hands. They keep a horse and weapons of war, and are ready to take part in his quarrel, be it just or unjust, with any powerful lord, if they only have a liking for him, and with him, if need be, to fight to the death. The farmers have further this fault : that they do not bring up their sons to any handicraft. Shoemakers, tailors, and all such craftsmen they reckon as contemptible and unfit for war ; and they therefore bring up their children to take service with the great nobles, or with a view to their living in the country in the manner of their fathers. Even dwellers in towns they hold as unfit for war ; and in truth they are much before the townsfolk in the art of war, and prove themselves far stouter soldiers. . . . Though they do not till their land themselves, they keep a diligent eye upon their servants and household, and in great part ride out with the neighbouring nobles.

Among the nobles I note two faults. The first is this : If two nobles of equal rank happen to be very near neighbours, quarrels and even shedding of blood are a common thing between them ; and their very retainers cannot meet without strife. . . . The second fault I note is this : The gentry educate their children neither in letters nor in morals—no small calamity to the state. They ought to search out men learned in history, upright in character, and to them intrust the education of their children, so that even in tender age these may begin to form right habits, and act when they are mature in years like men endowed with reason. Justice, courage, and all those forms of temperance which may be put to daily use they should pursue, and have in abhorrence the corresponding vices as things low and mean. The sons of neighbouring nobles would not then find it a hard thing to live together in peace ; they would no more be stirrers up of sedition in the state, and in war would approve themselves no less brave. . . .

Further, just as among the Scots we find two distinct tongues, so we likewise find two different ways of life and conduct. For some are born in the forests and mountains of the north, and these we call men of the Highland, but the others men of the Lowland. By foreigners the former are called Wild Scots, the latter householding Scots. The Irish tongue is in use among the former, the English tongue among the latter. One-half of Scotland speaks Irish, and all these as well as the Islanders we reckon to belong to the Wild Scots. In dress, in the manner of their outward life, and in good morals, for example, these come behind the householding Scots—yet they are not less, but rather much more, prompt to fight ; and this, both because they dwell more towards the north, and because, born as they are in the mountains, and dwellers in forests, their very nature is more combative. It is, however, with the householding Scots that the government and direction of the kingdom is to be found, inasmuch as they understand better, or at least less ill than the others, the nature of a civil polity. One part of the Wild Scots have a wealth of cattle, sheep, and horses, and these, with a thought for the possible loss of their possessions, yield more willing obedience to the courts of law and the king. The other part of these people delight in the chase and a life of indolence ; their chiefs eagerly follow bad men if only they may not have the need to labour ; taking no pains to earn their own livelihood, they live upon others, and follow their own worthless and savage chief in all evil courses sooner than they will pursue an honest industry. They are full of mutual dissensions, and war rather than peace is their normal condition. The Scottish kings have with difficulty been able to withstand the inroads of these men. From the mid-leg to the foot they go uncovered ; their dress is, for an over garment, a loose plaid, and a shirt saffron-dyed. They are armed with bow and arrows, a broadsword, and a small halbert. They always carry in their belt a stout dagger, single-edged, but of the sharpest. In time of war they cover the whole body with a coat of mail, made of iron rings, and in it they fight. The common folk among the Wild Scots go out to battle with the whole body clad in a linen garment sewed together in patchwork, well daubed with wax or with pitch, and with an over-coat of deerskin. But the common people among our domestic Scots and the English fight in a woollen garment. For musical instruments and vocal music the Wild Scots use the harp, whose strings are of brass and not of animal gut ; and on this they make most pleasing melody. Our householding Scots, or quiet and civil-living people—that is, all who lead a decent and reasonable life— these men hate, on account of their differing speech, as much as they do the English.

A History of Greater Britain (Scot. Hist. Soc.), pp. 30–1, 47–50

CHAPTER TWO

GOVERNMENT

THE AUTHORITY OF THE CROWN

Acts of Parliaments of James I

Owing to the weak rule of Robert II and Robert III, followed by the weak regencies of Robert, Duke of Albany, and Murdoch, Duke of Albany, James I, on his return to Scotland in the spring of 1424, found that certain of the nobles had become ' over mighty,' that lawlessness was passing unchecked and unpunished, and that the authority and finances of the Crown had been seriously impaired. According to Bower, James is said to have exclaimed, ' If God give me life, though it be but the life of a dog, then throughout all Scotland, with His help, will I make the key keep the castle and the bracken bush keep the cow.'

Some indication of what James I found upon his return and some indication of his immediate steps to restore law and order and to strengthen the authority and the finances of the Crown are revealed in the first nine acts of his first parliament, held at Perth in May 1424. Oppression is to be put down ; there is to be firm administration of the law under responsible royal officers ; and the revenues of the Crown are to be inbrought wholly for the use of the Crown.

The Act of 1426 is likewise a declaration of the king's determination to enforce his own law in his own kingdom. As recently as 1384 the Earl of Fife and Archibald Douglas, Lord of Galloway, had ' reserved ' their rights to certain special laws in Fife and in Galloway. Such special laws naturally hindered the execution of the laws of the realm, and might be used to gainsay justice.[1]

But James did not rest content with legislation. The Exchequer Rolls reveal that immediately upon his return the many annuities which had been paid from the customs and the burgh fermes to

[1] Although the transcript of these acts is unofficial there is no reason to doubt its accuracy.

members of the nobility during the reigns of Robert II and Robert III and during the regency were swept away, and that the king insisted upon a close examination of any claims for payments from the Crown finances. This is illustrated by the extract from the Exchequer Rolls for 1425 (see also *Scottish Historical Review*, xxix, 4–5).

1424. The Parliament of the most serene prince lord James, by the grace of God illustrious king of Scots, was held at Perth 26th May 1424 . . . the three estates of the realm having been summoned and assembled there, certain persons were elected to determine the articles given by the lord king and licence was given to the others to go home.

1 In the first to the honour of God and halikirk that the halikirk and the minsteris of it joise and bruk thar aulde privilegis and fredomys and that na man let thame to set thar landis and teyndis under all payne that may folowe be spirituale law or temporall.

2 Item that ferme and sikkir pece be kepit and haldin throu all the realme and amangis all and sindry liegis and subjectis of our soveran lorde the kyng. And that na man tak on hande in tyme to cum to amuff[1] or mak weire aganis otheris under all payne that may folowe be course of common lawe.

3 Item it is statut and ordanyt that na man opinly or notourly rebell aganis the kyngis persone under the payne of forfautour of lif landis and guidis.

4 Item it is statut and ordanyt that gif ony disobeyis till inforse the kyng aganis notoure rebellouris aganis his persone quhene thai be requiryt be the kyng and commandit thai salbe chalangit be the kyng as fautouris of sik rebellyng bot gif thai haif for thame resonable excusacioun.

5 Item it is statut that na man of quhat estate degre or condicioun he be of rydande or gangande in the cuntre leide nor haif ma personis with him na may suffice him or till his estate and for the quhilkis he will mak full and redy payment. And gif ony complaynt be of sik ridaris

[1] i.e. move

or gangaris the kyng commandis his officiaris of the lande
that quhar thai happin to be till arest thame and put thame
under sikkir borowis [1] quhill the kyng be certifyit tharof
and haif saide his will quhat salbe done to sic trespassouris.
6 Item it is ordanyt that thar be maide officiaris and
ministeris of lawe throu all the realme that can and may
halde the law to the kingis commonis and sik as has
sufficiently of thar awin quhar throughe thai mai be punyst
gif thai trespass. And gif ony be infeft of sik officis of befor
and ar not sufficient to minister to thame in propir persone
that utheris be ordanyt in thar stedis for the quhilkis thai
that has sik officis of the king in fee be haldin to answer
to him gif thai trespass.
7 Item the parliament statutis and the kyng forbiddes
that ony cumpanyis pas in the cuntre lyand apone ony the
kingis liegis or thig [2] or sojorne horsis outher on kirkmen
or husbandis of the lande. And gif ony complaynt be maid
on sic trespassouris to the scheref of the lande that he arest
sic folkis and chalange thame as brekaris of the kyngis pece
taxand the kingis scathis apone thame. And gif thai be
convyct of sic trespassis that thai be punyst and fynde
borowis bath till assithe the kyng and the party plenyeande.
And gif sik trespassouris takis ony skaythe in the aresting
of thame it salbe imput to thame self and in case that na
complaynt be maide to the schref the schref sall inquyre
at ilke hede court that he haldis gif ony sik faltouris be
within his schrefdome. And gif ony beis fundin that thai
be punyst as is befor writtyne.
8 Item it is consentyt throu the hail parliament that all
the gret and smal custumys and buroumaillis of the realme
byde and remane with the king till his leving. And gif
ony manner of persone makis ony clame till ony part of the
saide custumis that he schawe to the king quhat he has for
him and the king sall mak him ansuer with avisment of his
counsall.
9 Item anentis the landis and rentis the quhilkis war of

---

¹ sure pledges   beg : presumably with violence

befor tyme our soverane lorde the kingis antecessouris it is sene speidful that the king charge all and sindrie schrefis of his realme to gar inquyre be the best eldest and worthiest of thar bailyereis quhat landis possessionis or annuell rentis pertenys to the king or has pertenyt in his antecessouris tymes of gude memour David Robert and Robert his progenitouris and in quhais handis thai nowe be and at ilk schref gar retour the inquest under his seil and thair seilis that beis apone it. And gif it likis the king he may ger summonde all and sindry his tenandis at lauchfull day and place to schawe thar charteris and evidentis and swa be thar haldingis he may persave quhat pertenys to thame.

A.P.S., ii, 3–4

1426.

It is ordanit be the king with the consent and deliverance of the thre estatis that all and sindry the kingis liegis of the realme leif and be governyt undir the kingis lawis and statutis of this realme alanerly and undir na particulare lawis na speciale prevalegis na be na lawis of uther cuntreis nor realmis.

A.P.S., ii, 9, c. 3

RESTORATION OF THE CROWN FINANCES

1425. Memorandum : That the bailies of Kinghorn compeared in exchequer, before the auditors of accounts, and showed a charter of the late lord David de Brus, illustrious king of Scotland, relating to the setting of the said burgh in feu-ferme for fifty shillings to be paid annually ; from which [fifty shillings], they stated on oath, the constable of Kinghorn, who holds his office in fee, was wont to receive, and at present receives, annually and heritably, forty shillings from the said fermes, and the lord John Lyon receives ten shillings from the said fermes in a like way. Accordingly orders are given to the aforesaid bailies that henceforth no payment shall be made to anyone from the said fermes, but that the bailies in office for the time shall inbring to the exchequer of our lord king the whole of the burgh fermes ; and if any are infeft [in payments] from the same, they shall show their charters to our lord king and his council, otherwise no payment shall be made to them from the fermes.

E.R., iv, 396

ACT OF ANNEXATION

With the overthrow of the Black Douglases in 1455 their vast estates were forfeited to the Crown, and thereupon Parliament passed this important ' Act of Annexation.' If the king were unable ' to live of his own ' (i.e., support the expenses of government, and his own personal expenses, out of the revenues of the Crown lands, the burgh fermes, the great customs and the profits of justice and feudal casualties) many ' inconvenients ' (and notably taxation) would ensue. Therefore, in order to ensure that the king can ' live of his own,' certain ' lordships and castles ' are henceforth to be ' annexed ' to the Crown, and are to be inalienable save with the consent of Parliament, and then only for ' great and reasonable causes.' Significantly the list of ' lordships and castles ' which accompanies the act begins with ' the whole customs of Scotland ' (cf. vol. i, pp. 171–2), and includes strategic points like Edinburgh Castle and Stirling Castle.

Previous attempts to prevent the alienation of Crown lands had been made in 1357 and 1367—but those attempts had covered *all* the Crown lands, none of which were to be alienated without ' mature advice ' (1357) or without ' the consent of the three estates ' (1367) ; and the attempts had been unsuccessful (see vol. i, pp. 162 et seq.). Henceforth, however, the Crown lands were to be of two categories—' annexed lands,' which were inalienable and were to be retained with the Crown for the support of the Crown, and ' unannexed lands,' of which the king could dispose at his pleasure. The king, moreover, is to swear, and his successors at the time of their coronations are to swear, to observe and to keep this statute (cf. vol. i, pp. 143, 163, 165).

In England regular taxations, arising out of the Continental commitments of English kings, led to the development of a constitutional check, ' No supply without redress of grievances.' In

Scotland, where taxations were few and exceptional, the constitutional development was an endeavour to ensure that the king could and did ' live of his own ' without oppression of his people.

1455.

Forsamekill as the poverte of the crowne is oftymis the cause of the poverte of the realme and mony uther inconvenientis the quhilkis war lang to expreyme, be the avyse of the full consale of the parliament it is statute and ordanyt that in ilk part of the realme for the kingis residence quhar it sall happyn him to be thar be certane lordschippis and castellys annext to the crowne perpetualy to remane, the quhilk may not be giffyn away nother in fee nor in frank-tenement till ony persone of quhat estate or degre that ever he be but avyse, deliverance and decret of the haill parliament ande for great seande [1] and resonable causis of the realme, and albeit it happyn our soverane lorde that now is or ony of his successouris kingis of Scotlande till analy or dispone apon the lordschippis and castellys annext to the crowne as is befor saide, thai alienacionis or disposicionis salbe of nane avale, sa that it salbe lefull to the king beyng for the tyme to ressaif thai landis quhen ever him likis till his awne use but ony process of law and the takaris sall refunde all profettis that thai haif takin up of thai landis agane to the king for all the tyme that thai hade thame ande that our soverane lorde that now is be sworne and in lik maner all his successouris kingis of Scotlande in to thar coronacione to the keping of this statute and all the poyntis tharof.

A.P.S., ii, 42

SAUCHIEBURN. THE DEATH OF JAMES III AND THE ACCESSION OF JAMES IV

The forfeiture, in 1484, of Lord Crichton and of a number of those who, with him, had supported James III's brother, Albany, in

[1] fitting

opposition to the king, had caused many others of the nobility to fear for their own estates ; and when, in January 1488, James III secured an Act of Parliament endorsing his annexation of the revenues of Coldingham Priory to the Chapel Royal at Stirling, Scotland was soon divided into two opposing camps. In the north the nobility and prelates were, in general, on the side of the king ; in the south the Humes (who regarded the revenues of Coldingham as their own) and the Hepburns (who were in alliance with the Humes) were quickly joined by many of those who had earlier supported Albany. Following an indecisive skirmish at Blackness, in May 1488, both sides agreed to an interchange of their ' debates and causes ' ; but the ' Pacification of Blackness,' which was then accepted, was unstable, and particularly so in that the king's son, James [IV], was to remain in the hands of ' wise lords and honourable persons of wisdom and discretion ' —namely, the opposition. In June the two sides again met at Sauchieburn, near Stirling, those in opposition to the king having the prince James in their midst. James III fled the field but, being thrown from his horse, was carried into a nearby building and there murdered.

The articles of the ' Pacification of Blackness ' were recorded in the proceedings of the first parliament of James IV when, after discussion of the causes leading to ' the field of Stervilin [Sauchie-burn] in the quhilk umquhile James, king of Scotlande . . . happinit to be slane,' it was ' declared and concluded ' that the late king's death was due to the ' perverse counsel ' of those around him, and that his son, ' our sovereign lord that now is,' and those who were with him in the field were ' innocent, quhyt and fre.'

For the constitutional historian, however, there is significance in James III's reliance upon his council, in opposition to the big feudatories who, from time to time, might have control of parliament. James III appears to have been using his ' chosen ' or ' privy ' council in an attempt to curb the power of the nobility ; and not all his councillors were ' perverse,' nor were they all ' new men.' Significantly Elphinstone, bishop of Aberdeen, was consistently on the side of the king. There appears to be no truth in the charge that James III had been ' inbringing . . . Inglismen . . . to the perpetuale subieccione of the realme.'

1488.

ITEM in this present perliament oure soveran lord beand present togidder with his thre estatis of the realme wes proponit the debaite and cause of the feild of Stervilin in the quhilk umquhile James, king of Scotlande, quham God assolye, faider to our soveran lord, happinnit to be slane and the cause and occasioune beand thar of commonit, oppynnit and arguit amangis the lordis of the thre estatis, Jhonne, Lord Glammys present and schew certane articulis subscrivit with the forsaid umquhile king James hand, the tenour of the quhilk folowis :

THIR ar the articulis uppone the quhilkis our soveran lord sall gif commissioune under his gret sele to thir lordis under writtin, that is to say the bischop of Aberdene, chancellar, the erlis of Huntlie, Erole, Marschiale, Lord Glammys and Alexander Lindesay to comone, conclude and end with thir lordis followand, that is to say the bischop of Glasgw, the erlis of Anguss, Ergile, Lord Halis, Lord Lile, the quhilkis lordis sall haffe full commissioune of my lord prince and of all the lordis being with him.

IN the first to comone and conclude that the kingis hie honour, estate, riale autorite be exaltit, conservit and borne up at he may exhers justice universally to all his liegis in all the partis of his realme.

ITEM at his maist noble persone be at all tymes in honour, securite and fredome and at thar be prelatis, erlis, lordis and baronis and utheris personis of wisdome, prudence and of gud disposicioun and unsuspect to his hienes [1] and evinly to all his liegis dayly about his nobill persoun to the gud giding of his realme and liegis.

ITEM that all the personis being about my lord prince that has in tyme by gane done displessour to his hienes mak honorabile and aggreabile amendis to his hienes be the wisdome and discrecione of the said lordis thar liffis heretage and honouris except.

ITEM that the kingis hienes sall gif honorabill susten-

[1] highness

tacioun and levin to my lord prince his sone at the consideracione of the said lordis.

ITEM at wise lordis and honorabill personis of wisdome and discrecioun evinly and of gud disposicione salbe dayly about my lord prince for the gud governance of him and securite of his person in his tender age.

ITEM to avise commone and conclud how my lord prince sall in all tymes tocum be obedient to his faider the king and how that faiderly luff and tendernes sall at all tymes be had betuex thame.

ITEM how the lordis and uthir personis being about my lord prince sall haf our soverane lordis favouris and grace, favouris and hertly forgevinnys, and thar personis to be in securite as best can be devisit be the said lordis for ony displessour done to the kingis hienes in ony tyme by gane.

ITEM at my lord prince sall tak in hertlie favouris all lordis spirituale and temporale and all uthir personis that has bene with the kingis hienes in consale or uthir service now in this tyme of truble.

ITEM at all discencionis and discordis now standand or beand betuex ony lordis or gret baronis of baith the partis salbe drawin be the wisdome of the said lordis to unite concord sa that luf and favour may stand ymangis oure soverane lordis liegis and peax to be had and justice to procede and specialy betuix the erle of Buchain and Lorde Lile.

The quhilkis beand rede and schewin that the saidis articulis wes diverse tymes grantit to and brokyne be the perverst counsale of diverse personis beand with him for the tyme quhilkis counsalit and assistit to him in the inbringing of Inglissmen and to the perpetuale subieccione of the realm and under dissate and colour maid and refusit and that our soverane lord that now is ever consentit to for the commoun gude of the realme, for the quhilkis the erle of Huntlie, the erle of Erole, the Erle Marschell, the said Lord Glammys and utheris diverse baronis and utheris the kingis trew liegis left him and his dissaitful and perverst counsale and anherdit to our soverane lord that now is and his trew opynyoun for the commone gud of the realme : the quhilk mater beand schewin, commonit, examinit and understanding be the thre estatis and haile body of the parliament thai riply avisit declarit and concludit and in thar lawtey and allegeance ilk man for him self declaris and concludis that the slauchteris committ and done in the feild of Striviline quhar our soverane lordis faider happinnit to be slane and utheris diverse his baronis and liegis wes aluterly in thar defalt and colourit dyssate done be him and his perverst counsale diverse times befor the said feild, and that our soverane lord that now is and the trew lordis and baronis that wes with him in the samyn feild war innocent quhyt and fre of the saidis slauchteris feild and all persute of the occasioun and cause of the samyn and that a parte of the thre estatis forsaid, bischopis, prelattis, gret baronis and burgesis gif thar selis hereapoun togidder with our soverane lordis gret sele to be schewin and producit to our haly faider the paipe, the kingis of France, Spanye, Denmark and utheris realmes as salbe sene expedient for the tyme.

A.P.S., ii, 210–11, c. 15

ADMINISTRATION OF JUSTICE IN THE ISLES

The administration of justice by sheriffs and justiciars had never reached the western isles which, under the Macdonalds, ' Lords of the Isles,' had long been virtually independent of the Crown. In 1491 a large force of Islesmen, under Alexander of Lochalsh, nephew of John, Lord of the Isles, had seized Inverness and harried the lands of Cromarty. The ' invasion ' was eventually repelled by the Earl of Huntly, and although John, Lord of the Isles, was probably innocent of complicity therein, he was forfeited in 1493 and made a full surrender to the king. Immediately thereafter James IV proceeded to the west highlands to receive the submissions of the vassals of the Lord of the Isles, and he was again in the west highlands in 1494, 1495, 1497 and 1499. Then, in 1504, the following act was passed in an endeavour to carry the king's law into these outlying parts. We do not know how far the act was effective, if it was effective at all ; certainly it would become a dead letter with the death of James IV at Flodden; but it is nevertheless of importance in its intent.

1504. Item becaus thair hes bene greit abusioune of justice in the north partis and west partis of the realme sic as the northt Ilis and south Ilis for lak and falt of justice airis justicis and schreffis and tharthrou the pepill ar almaist gane wilde, it is tharfor statute and ordanit for the acquietting of the pepill be justice that thair be in tyme tocum justicis and schreffis depute in thai partis as eftir folowis ; that is to say that the justicis and schreffis of the northt Ilis haif thair sait and place for administratioun of justice in Invernes or Dingwale as the materis occurris tobe decernyt be the saidis officiaris, and that ane uther justice and schreff be maid and deput for the south Ilis and thai partis, and to haif his place and sait for administratioun of justice in the Tarbart [1] or at Lochkinkerane [2] at the will and plesour of the saidis officiaris as the materis occurris.

A.P.S., ii, 249, c. 3

FACTION AND FEUD. FRANCE AND ENGLAND

The early years of the reign of James V witnessed a contest between opposing factions for the control of the king and the government. Now, too, the opposing factions tend to favour an alliance with France or with England, though personal hatreds and ambitions affect men on both sides, and during this period the nobility, almost without exception, appear to have placed their own interests before the interests of their country.

Immediately after Flodden the Queen-Mother, Margaret Tudor, was appointed as guardian of the young king and regent of the kingdom. But there were many who distrusted her as the sister of Henry VIII ; and her marriage to Archibald Douglas, sixth Earl of Angus (August 1514) deepened, through jealousy and fear, the cleavage in the nobility. In 1515 John, Duke of Albany (son of Alexander, Duke of Albany, the exiled brother

---

[1] Tarbert, Loch Fyne   [2] Later Campbeltown

of James III) arrived from France, by invitation, to take over the regency which, with intervals when he returned temporarily to France, he held until 1524. Albany stood for a strong pro-French policy ; and throughout his regency Henry VIII persistently strove to have him removed from office and equally persistently fomented the factions and feuds of the nobility, particularly the feud between Angus and Arran. Moreover, to add to the confused picture, Margaret Tudor, who had at first intrigued with her brother, Henry VIII, quarrelled violently with her husband, Angus, and in 1518 strove to align herself with Albany.

Twice, during this period, in 1522 and 1523, Albany had led a Scottish army to the Borders in fulfilment of the ' auld alliance ' and the treaty of Rouen (*infra*, p. 67), and, in 1523, in answer to a devastating raid by England ; but twice the Scots, remembering Flodden, had refused to invade England. Feeling the impotency of his position, Albany left Scotland for France in May 1524 on the understanding that if he did not return before 1 September 1524 his regency would be regarded as at an end.

Almost immediately thereafter, in July 1524, Margaret Tudor and Arran, temporarily in power, and representing the ' pro-English ' party, arranged for the ' Erection ' of the king. James V, aged 12, was brought from Stirling to Edinburgh and was publicly raised on to a throne and invested with crown, sword and sceptre ; the officers of state were removed from office ; and in November 1524 (Albany not having returned from France) a Parliament held by the Queen-Mother and Arran declared Albany's regency at an end and confirmed the appointments which they had made of officers of state chosen from members of their own faction.

1524.

Change of Ministry. *1 August 1524*

In presens of the kingis hienes comperit James, archibischop of Sanctandrois, chancelare, and at the command [and] desire of his grace dischargit him of the cure and office of chancellary and deliverit to him the greite seile, protestand that how it war usit in tyme tocum he suld nocht be haldin to answer tharfore, and als renuncit and dischargit all commissiouns and auctorite grantit and gevin to him be the governour.

The abbot of Halirudhous, prive seile, resignit the said office in our soverane lordis hand and promist to deliver the prive seile to his hienes eftir none.

The secretar resignit his office in the kingis handis and promyst inlikwis to deliver to his grace the signetis.

The thesaurar and comptrollar resignit thar officis in the kingis handis sa that his hienes may dispone tharupon.

The erle of Levinax gaif our his office and commissioune of lieuetenentry grauntit and gevin to him be the governour, sa that our soverane lord may dispone tharupoune as sall pleis his grace.

The lord Borthuik presentlie dischargit him of the cure gevin to him of the keping of the kingis maist noble persoune.

The lord Flemyng renuncit and dischargit him of the office of chalmerlanrie, and our soverane lord to dispone tharupoune as he pleis.

The lard of Tulialloun dischargit him of the office of ischareschip to be disponit as it sall pleas our soverane lord.

Maistir Johnne Cantlie, archidene of Sanctandrois and clerk of the expens, dischargit him of the said office to that effect that the kingis grace may dispone tharupoune as he pleis.

Attour our soverane lord with avis of the hale lordis of his consale declaris all offices pertenyng to his grace to be vaikand in his handis, and dischargis all intromettouris tharwith fra using tharof, to be gevin grauntit and disponit be our said soverane lord with avis of his consale, offices of heretage allaneralie except.

[*On the same day a number of lords subscribe a declaration that* ' the departing of our soverane lord the kingis grace furth of Striveling to Edinburgh is for the gude and weile of his maist noble persoune and commone weile of his realme ' ; *they affirm their loyalty to the king* ' nochtwith-standing our promittis or bandis maid be us or ony of us to Johnne duke of Albany or ony uthiris in the contraire ' ; *and revoke the power, authority and governance of the said duke.*]

Acts of the Lords of Council in Public Affairs, 204–5

1524.

Acts of the Parliament of November 1524

In the first for the honour of God and halikirk it is statute and ordanit in this present parliament that the fredomes and liberteis of halikirk with all privilegis and emenyteis thairof and of all spirituale personnis be observit and kepit in honour worschip and fredome for the tyme of our soverane lord that now is, lik as has bene in tymes of his maist noble progenitouris of gud mynde of before, and revokis, cassis and adnullis all actis and statutis maid in the contrare and in speciale the actis maid in the last parliament and will at the samyn be cancellat and deleit out of the bukis of parliament and counsale.

ITEM in the first our soverane lord with avise of his derrest modere the quenis grace and the lordis thre estatis of his realme understandand that Jhone, duke of Albany, than tutour and governour to our said soverane lord the kingis grace, at his last departing furth of this realm, promittit to haif returnit to the samyn at the first day of September last bipast for dew execucioun of his office and administration of justice to oure soverane lordis liegis enduring the tyme of his said office with supportacioun of the king of Francis for defence of this realm as efferit and was promisit, quhilk he has nocht kepit, bot absentis him agane the tenour of his said promitt and office of tutory abusand and negleckand the samyn to the gret hurt and scaith of our said soverane lord his liegis and subditis, quherfore the saidis thre estatis has decernit his said office of tutory and governance to be expirit and he secludit thairfra, and has statute and ordanit that our said soverane lord sall use and exerse his awne auctoritie and haif the full reule and governance of his realm, liegis and subditis in tyme tocum be avise of his said derrest modere the quenis grace and lordis of his counsale and that honest writtings in this mater be divisit and send to the king of France and the said duke to the excuse of our said soverane lord his lordis and realm and thare accusatioun.

ITEM because the quenis grace be naturale lufe affection and inclinatioun is maist tendir, sure and traist for the gude and weil of our soverane lord, hir derrest sonnis persoun, it is statute and ordanit that sche sall haif the keping and reule of his maist noble persone with wyse vertuis men of gud inclination and conversatioun that may and will instruct him in vertewis, bountie and gud maners, to be chosin be avise of the quenis grace and lordis of counsale, and that all officiaris of his maist noble persone houshald with utheris his officiaris be chosin sufficient abill and convenient men thairto be avise of the quenis grace and lordis of counsale scho beand principale.

ITEM it is statute and ordanit that our soverane lord, with avise of his derrest modir the quene, sall dispone apon all wardis, mariagis, relevis, nonentressis, beneficis and all utheris his casualiteis and that na dispositioun thairof be of avale without the subscriptionis of our said soverane lord and his derrest moder the quenis grace.

A.P.S., ii, 286

1524.

Letter of King James V to Henry VIII, 5 August 1524

Richt excellent, rycht hie and michty Prence, oure derrest and richt interlie weil-belovit uncle, we recommend ws on to yow in our maist effectuouse and hertlie maner, certifying yow, richt dere uncle, we ressavit youre lettres datit at Greynewiche the 12 day of Junii, quharby we persave cleirlie the gret luf, tendir and naturall affectioune ye have hade and has all tymes to the surete and weilfair of our persounne, exaltacioun of oure estait, and that ye will concure with ws in the governance of oure self and realme, gevande on to ws all requisyte supportacioun, manteinance and assistance, with diverse gude and vertuise exortaciouns and counsalis ; of the quhilke we thank yow in oure maist hertlie maner.

Richt dere uncle, we have sadlie and profundlie weyit the effecte of youre said lettres, havande the samyn in every worde deiplie prentit in oure hart, and fallowande youre entent, desyre and counsall as oure maist tendir eme, nerest in proximite of blude and maist speciall freynde, in quhais lawte, kyndnes and frendschip we have put all oure confidence, has also actyflie, with the help of oure derrest modir, takin on ws the governance of our reaulme and put oure selfe to fredome and liberte, expellande all autorite of the Duke of Albany, under quhais governans oure realme and lieges has bene richt evill demanyt. Prayng yow, oure derrest uncle, till continew youre gude mynde till ws, our realme and lieges, nocht dowting bot as we encrese in yers and vertuise condicionis, we sall equalie encrese in frendschip, lawte and kyndnes unto yow, as oure gretest freynde and maist tendir uncle, fortefyar and supplear of ws in oure tendir aige ; and sall reule ws and our realme be your avise and counsall in syk sort that ye sall tak occasioun to encrese dalye in youre help, supple and kyndnes on to ws your derrest nepho quhilk intendes evir to follow your counsall. Rycht excellent, richt hie and michtie Prince, oure derrest and richt intirlie weilbelovit uncle, the Blissit Trinite haif yow in His haly preservacioune. Gevin undre oure signet at oure Palyse of Edinburghe the fyft day of the monethe of August.

your lovyng nywo   JAMES R.

(*Addressed*) To ane richt hie and mychty Prince, our derrest and richt inteirlye weilbeluffit uncle, the King of Inglande
gif.

Facsimiles of National Manuscripts from William the Conqueror to Queen Anne, ii, No. XIV

The Ascendancy of Angus

But Angus was soon able to defeat the measures taken by the Queen-Mother and Arran, and in 1526 he became virtually the ruler of Scotland.

1526. Item the three estatis of the realme gaderit in this present parliament seing and understanding that oure soverane lorde is be the grace of Gode now cumin to his aige of xiiij yeris Therfor declaris and decernis that his auctoritie riale is in his awne handis and to be exercit & usit be his hienes in tyme tocum out throw his realme liegis and subditis And decernis all uther auctoritie gevin and usit in tymes bipast now to be expirit & ceise in tymes cuming etc.

A.P.S., ii, 301, c. 2

This means something quite different from what it says, and shows how the Scottish Parliament, as in 1524, was the tool of the faction then in power.

In July 1525 certain lords had been chosen ' to remane with the kingis grace quarterlie ' in rotation ; and the lords for the first quarter were Archibald Douglas, sixth Earl of Angus, and Gavin Dunbar, Archbishop of Glasgow, with certain others, lay and spiritual, to be ' with thaim in cumpany ' (*A.P.S.*, ii, 294*b*). Angus, however, having secured the person of the king, ' would in no wise part with him,' and, being in opposition to the other main faction—that of Margaret, the Queen-Mother—kept the king in his own hands. Thus, when the Estates in 1526 declared that the royal authority was in the hands of the king, they virtually declared that royal authority was in the hands of Angus.

In this same Parliament of June 1526, moreover, the king took all offices into his own hands ' to be disponit to sic personis as his graice and counsale sall think expedient ' (*A.P.S.*, ii, 301*a*)—and that meant as Angus thought expedient. Forthwith all the principal offices again changed hands and were filled by supporters of the Red Douglas. He himself assumed the office of Chancellor ; his brother, George, was Master of the Household ; his uncle, Archibald Douglas, was Treasurer ; James Douglas of Drumlanrig was Master of the Wine-cellar ; James Douglas of Parkhead was Master of the Larder ; and Erskine of Halton was Secretary— all of these offices enabling their holders to keep close watch on the king. This was the time of which Pitscottie wrote, ' The Earle of Angus gydit all. . . . And nane at that tyme durst stryve with ane Douglas nor yeit ane Douglas man.'

In May 1528, however, the king escaped from the Douglas hold ;

and now it was the turn of the king and the opposing faction to hold a Parliament by which Angus was forfeited (September 1528).

1528. This court of parliament schewis for law and I geif for dume that forsamekle as it is fundin be the sensment of parliament that Archibald Erle of Angus, George Douglas his bruther and Archibald Douglas his eyme [1] hes committit and done tresoune aganis our souerane lorde in the inobedience and refusing to fulfill our souerane lordis command maid and devisit be the lordis of consale And in convocatioune of our souerane lordis liegis within the burgh of Edinburcht viij dais continualie And in munitioune of the castell of Temptalloune [2] Newerk [3] with men and artalyerie aganis his hienes with artalyerie & vittalis And in the assistence and manteinance gevin to the lard of Johnstoun to hery and byrne with cumpanyis of thevis bath be day and nycht And in halding of our souerane lordis persoune aganis his will continualie be the space of twa yeris aganis the decret of the lordis of his parliament and in exponying [4] of his persone to battell [5] he being of tendir age For the quhilkis causis thai have forfaltit thair lyfis landis and gudis to remane with our souerane lorde and his successouris in tymetocum. And that I geif for dume.

A.P.S., ii, 326*a*

For a while Angus held Tantallon in defiance of the king, but he was eventually compelled to seek refuge in England.

REPRESSION

Not unnaturally during these and similar periods the maintenance of law and order languished and, in the words of Lesley, ' justice appeared to be ruggit up by the roots.'

---

[1] uncle   [2] Tantallon   [3] Newark   [4] exposing
[5] On the occasions when, firstly, Sir Walter Scott of Buccleuch strove to free the king (near Melrose, 25 July 1526), and, secondly, John Stewart, 3rd Earl of Lennox, strove to free him (near Linlithgow, 4 September 1526).

In an endeavour to secure some form of order, and to meet the failure of the system of regular justice-ayres, the government began to resort to the unhappy expedient of ' commissions of justiciary ' whereby it granted to local lords who were both well-affected and strong full powers to hold justice courts for particular causes or particular periods, or over particular persons or particular areas. Such commissions were often grossly abused. In their fullest form they were granted as ' commissions of lieutenandry,' when the ' lieutenant ' had virtually all the powers of the king. Huntly, in the north, and Argyll, in the south, frequently held such commissions of ' lieutenandry ' ; significantly the one became ' Cock o' the North,' and the other ' Maccailean Mor.'

A commission, however, might also take the form of ' Letters of Fire and Sword,' similar to the one here printed. A late example of such commissions was that issued for the extirpation of the MacIan MacDonalds which led to the well-known ' Massacre of Glencoe ' (1692).

Not only in the Highlands but also on the Borders (and especially in the ' Debateable Land ') the government could often be put to defiance. Lesley speaks of the Borderers as living ' in the greatest liberty and licence ' ; and James V's expedition against the Armstrongs was but one example of strong action taken by the Scottish and English governments alike (cf. *Scottish Historical Review*, xxx, 109–25).

1528. *Letters of Fire and Sword against the Clan Chattan*

James, be the grace of God, King of Scottis, To our shirreffis of Kincardin, Abirdene, Banf, Elgen, Fores, Narne, and Inuernyss ; and to our derrest bruthir, James, Erle of Murray, our lieutenant generale in the north partis of our realme, and to our louittis consignis [   ] Erle of Suthirland ; Alexander, Maistir of Sutherland ; Johne, Erle of Cathnes ; Johne, Lord Forbes ; Hew, Lord Fraser of Lovet ; Johne Grant of Freuchy ; Ewin Alansone, capitane of the Clan Cammeroun ; Johne M'Kainze of Kintaill ; Wellem Chesholme of [   ] Vrquard, our shirref of Cromerty ; Johne M'Ky of Strathnaver ; and all vthiris, frehaldaris, baronis, capitanis of Clannys, and gentilmen, oure trew liegis, within our shirefdomis and

boundis abouewrittin, oure shirreffis in that parte, coniunctlie and seuerallie, specialie constitute, Greting : Forsamekill as Johne M'Kinla, Thomas Makkinla, Ferquhar
M'Kinla, brethir, Donald Glass, Anguss Williamsone, his
bruthir William, Lauchlane M'Kintoschis son, throcht
assistance and fortifying of all the kin of Clanquhattane,
duelland within Baienach, Petty, Brauchly, Strathnarne,
aud vther partis thairabout, committis daly rasing of fire,
slauchtir, murthur, heirschippis, and waisting of the cuntre,
sa that oure trew liegis in thair partis about thaim may
nocht leif in peace, and mak ws seruice. And in speciale,
the saidis personis and thair complices hes cumm laitlie
to the landis pertening to James Dunbar of Tarbert, in the
Bray of Murray, and thair hes rasit fire, slane, and murtharit
vj men and two wemen, and mutilate vthir v men, and
maid plane heirschip of nolt, scheip, hors, gait, swyne,
cornis, and insycht gudis, layand the land waist, and makand
depopulation of the cuntre, and tendis in contemption of
oure autorite to ourthraw all landis about thaim with thair
maisterfull oppressioun, heirschippis, and destruction, and
suffir na man to brouk landis that thai may wyn to, and
will na wayis obey to our lawis. And we and oure consale
avisitlie considerand the grete harmys and contemptionis
done be the said kin of Clanquhattane, and thair assistaris,
aganis the commoun wele, hes concludit and determit to
mak vtir exterminatioun and destructioun of all that kin,
thair assistaris, and parte takaris. And thairfore it is our
will, and we charge straitlie and commandis yow, our said
lieutenent, and shirreffis foirsadis, and your deputis, and
vtheris, our shirreffis in that parte aboue exprimit, that
incontinent thir oure lettres sene, ye pass all at anys, or
as ye may cum to, as salbe ordourit be yow, our said lieutenant, with all your powaris and convocatioun of our liegis
in thai partis, in feir of weir, vpon the said Clanquhattane,
and invaid thame to thair vter destructioun, be slauchtir,
byrning, drowning, and vthir wayis ; and leif na creatur
levand of that clann, except preistis, wemen, and barnis.
And that ye tak to your self, for your laubouris, all thair

gudis that may be apprehendit, and hald the symyn to your avne vse ; and thair attour ye sall haue reward of ws for your gude seruice in the premissis. And gif ony personis assistis to thame, that is nochte of thair kin, or takis thair parte, that ye invaid thai assistaris, in lykewyse as the principale, to thair vtir destructioun. For the quhilkis inuasionis, slauchteris, birningis, taking of gudis, or vthir skathis, done or to be done vpon the said Clanquhattane, or thair assisteris, thair sall neuir actioun nor cryme be impute to you, nor vtheris, our trew liegis, doaris, or committaris thairof ; nor accusatioun, nor restitutioun follow thairupon in the law, nor by the law, in tyme to cum. Bot all schairpnes done and to be done vpon thame salbe haldin and repute lauchfull and richtuuslie done, be command of ws and oure consale, for the common wele of oure realme ; and als that ye tak the wemen and barnis of the said clan to sum partis of the sey, nerrest land, quhair schippis salbe forsene on our expenssis, to saill with thame furth of our realme, and land with them in Jesland, Zesland, or Norway ; becaus it were inhumanite to put handis in the blude of wemen and barnis. This ye do, and ilkane of yow for your awne parte, as ye lufe the commoun wele of our realme, and will haue thank of ws thairfore and ansueir to ws thairvpoun. The quhilk to do we committ to yow, coniunctlie and seueralie, our full powar be thir our lettres. Gevin vnder our signete, at Edinburgh, the x day of Nouember, and of our regne the xvj yeir.

Ex deliberatione dominorum consilii, &c.

J. CHEPMAN.

Spalding Club Miscellany, ii, 83–4

Johnnie Armstrong

The well-known story of Johnnie Armstrong comes from the chronicle of Lindesay of Pitscottie. The only record evidence for the incident comes from the Justiciary Records and the Register of the Privy Seal.

1530. 1 April—John Armestrang, 'alias Blak Jok' and Thomas his brother convicted of common theft, and reset of theft etc.—HANGED.

Pitcairn, *Criminal Trials*, i, pt. i, 154

1530. 8 July—Ane letter maid to Robert Lord Maxwell, his airis and assignais ane or ma, of the gift of all gudis movabill and unmovabill, dettis, takkis, obligationis, soumes of money, giftis of nonentres and utheris quhatsumevir, quhilkis pertenit to umquhile Johnne Armstrang bruthir to Thomas Armstrang of Mayngertoun and now pertenyng to our soverane lord be resoun of eschete throw justifying of the said umquhill Johnne to the deid for thift committit be him etc.

R.S.S., ii, 702

James V's Act of Revocation

It had become customary for a sovereign upon reaching the age of twenty-five to revoke all grants, made during his minority, which could be regarded as in any way harmful to his 'estate and living.' In 1537, while still at Rouen, and soon after his marriage to Madeleine de Valois, James V, having then attained the age of twenty-five, issued a wide Act of Revocation including a clause revoking anything done 'by evil and false suggestion' —wording which would enable the king to revoke any grants which had been made to the nobility, including grants made during the period of his own 'personal' rule since 1528. This Act of Revocation was subsequently ratified by Parliament in 1540. Not unnaturally it led many of the nobility, even those loyal to the Crown, to doubt the security of their possessions; without a doubt it was James V's intention to use the Act in his policy of breaking up the large estates of the nobility.

1540. WE James, be the grace of God king of Scottis, understandand clerlie the privilege of the canoun law, actis and statutis of our realme providit and gevin to the succours of all maner of personis to revoik, cass and adnull all thingis done be thame in thare youthheid and less aige quhare

throw thai ar gretlie and hevilie dampnagit and scaithit
in thair heretagis be imprudent alienationis donationis and
venditionis of the samyn and that thai may at thair perfite
aige revoik the samin of all thingis done be thame prejudiciale in thare menorite and less aige, and thairfor oure
predecessouris kingis of Scotland at thair perfite aige of
xxv yeris past hes in tymes bigane maid revocatioun of all
sic thingis that hes bene done be thame in hurt and detriment of thare crown, landis, rentis and possessionis pertening to the samin and uther thingis quhare intill thai be
circumventioun war dampnagit and scaithit maid thair
revocatioun cassand and adnulland all sic giftis alienationis
and donationis, herefor we at oure perfite aige of xxv yeris
byrunnyn beand for the tyme furth of oure realme in the
partis of France maid oure generale revocatioun schortlie
at Rowane the thrid day of Aprile the yeire of God i^{m}v^{c}xxxvii
yeris as at mare lenth is contenit in ane instrument maid
thairupoun subscrivit with the hand of maister George Cuk
notar publict off the quhilk the tenour followis:

We for certane grett and resonable caussis moving us and
haifand respect to the welle of oure croune and commoun
wele of our realme revokis all maner of giftis, infeftmentis
and dispositionis quhatsumevir we haif maid or hes bene
maid be our tutouris and governouris for the tyme during
our minorite and less aige in quhatsumevir cause or caise
that thai may cum under revocatioun be the commoun law
or consuetude of our realme, protesting solempnitlie that
our absence furth of the samin at this tyme and the solemp-
niteis requirit on that behalf nocht being done be to us
na prejudice anentis the said revocatioun with the quhilkis
we dispense and suppleis all faltis thairwith be our kinglie
power and auctorite riale and will that this stand for oure
generale revocatioun of all maner of thingis done be us or
our saidis tutouris and the samin to be extendit in the
maist ample and large forme as ony utheris revocationis
maid be our maist nobill fader or our progenitouris kingis
of Scotland, the quhilkis our said generale revocatioun we
in this present parliament with the avise and consent of

our thre estatis ratifiis and apprevis and yit as eftir followis revoikis cassis and annullis in generale and als in speciale . . .

Item We revoik all giftis and confirmatiounis gevin be ws of quhatsumevir landis and heretages be evill and fals sucgestioun be the expreming of ane fals cause quhare gif thai had bene expremitt ane trew cause and the verite we had nocht gevin the samin And tharthrow we ar gritumlie and enormlie hurt . . .

AND generalie we revoike cassis and adnullis all and quhatsumevir thingis done be us in our less aige in detriment and harme of oure saule and conscience hurting of the privilege of our crowne prejudiciale to the samin and to us in our patrimonie thairof, and quhat the commoun law and consuetude of our realme levis us to revoik, and this our revocatioun to be of als grett effect and als largelie extendit in generale and in speciale as ony revocationis maid be ony oure progenitouris kingis of Scotland of befor and specialie be our darrest fader of gude mynd (quhem God assolye) and king James the secund, and protestis suppois we of our favoris and benevolence suffer ony persoun or personis to use or posside ony privilegis or possessionis of landis, rentis and offices that ar fallin under our revocatioun it sall mak na rycht to the usaris or halderis thairof bot it sall be lefull to us to put our handis thairto quhenevir it sall pleise us but ony contradictioun be vertu of our said revocatioun actis and constitutionis of our realme maid of befor.

A.P.S., ii, 357–8, c. 4

CHAPTER THREE

PARLIAMENT

COMPOSITION

The duty of ' suit and service ' to the lord's court was a burden inherent in the holding of land (cf. vol. i, pp. 68–9). The tenant of the lord was bound to render suit to his lord's court, and that service was part of the return which he made for his enjoyment of the issues of his land. But such a duty, if it entailed a long journey or a long absence, might be a heavy burden ; and gradually most of the smaller tenants-in-chief of the king, who owed suit to the king's court (and notably in its sittings as a ' parliament ') had ceased to attend. Parliament had become a sitting of the big lords, spiritual and temporal. Yet, theoretically, all who held direct of the king, even the smallest freeholder, owed suit to the king's court. And James I endeavoured to enforce their attendance *in person*. Possibly it was part of his intention to exact fines from those who stayed away ; probably he hoped to secure support from the small barons and freeholders to counterbalance the influence of the ' big men.'

The Act of 1426, however, was apparently not observed. The small men could not, or did not, come. Accordingly, two years later, James I endeavoured to secure, not the attendance in person of *all* the ' smal baronis and fre tenandis,' but the attendance of their elected representatives. Even this endeavour appears to have failed. Representatives of the shires did not sit in Parliament until after the ' County Representation Act ' of 1587 which, in its preamble, recited James I's Act of 1428.

That James may have been imitating English practice is suggested by the provisions in the Act of 1428 for the election of a ' speaker ' and for the summoning of the big lords by special precept. The special summons (which alone took effect) led to the ' lords of parliament '—men below the rank of dukes and earls, and above the rank of barons. Hence arose such titles as Lord Crichton, Lord Ochiltree, Lord Somerville.

1426. Item the king and the hail parliament hes ordanit ande statute that all prelatis erlis baronnis and frehaldaris of the king within the realme sen thai are haldyn to geif thare presens in the kingis parliament ande general consale fra thin furth be haldyn till appere in propir persone ande nocht be a procuratoure bot gif that procuratour allege ande prufe lauchfull cause of his absens.

A.P.S., ii, 9, c. 8

1428. Item the king with consent of his hail consal general has statute and ordanit that the smal baronnis and fre tenandis nede nocht to cum to parliamentis nor general consalys swa that of ilk schrefdome thare be sende chosyn at the hede court of the schrefdome twa or ma wismen efter the largeness of the schrefdome, outetane the schrefdomis of Clakmannan and Kynross of the quhilkis ane be sende of ilk ane of thaim, the quhilk salbe callit commissaris of the schire.

Ande be thir commissaris of all the schiris sall be chosyn a wise and ane expert mann callit the common spekar of the parliament the quhilk sal propone all and sindry nedis and causis pertening to the commonis in the parliament or generall consal. The quhilkis commissaris sal haf ful ande playn powere of al the laif of the schrefdome under the witnessing of the schreffis sele and with the selis of divers baronnis of the schire to here treit ande finally to determyn all causis to be proponit in consale or parliament.

The quhilkis commissaris and spekaris sal have thare costage of thaim of ilk schire at aw comperance in the parliament or consal. And of thare rentis ilk punde sal be utheris fallowe to the contribucioun of the said costis.

All bischoppis abbotis prioris dukis erlis lordes of parliament and banrentis, the quhilkis the king wil, be reservit and summonde to consalis and to parliamentis be his special precep.

A.P.S., ii, 15, c. 2

The Committee of the Articles

In medieval times, with major difficulties of communication and access, attendance at Parliament was, for many, bound to be burdensome. Moreover it was equally burdensome to have to remain in attendance for any length of time. An attempt to meet the latter of these two difficulties had already been made in the reign of David II when ' certain persons were elected by the said Estates to hold the Parliament, and leave was given to the rest to return home.' But this device of the *licentia redeundi* and of conferring the whole power of Parliament upon a commission (cf. vol. i, pp. 173–86), although apparently becoming a matter of course, and used in the first parliament of James I (*supra*, p. 12), was not without its dangers.

James I recognised the difficulties of securing and maintaining the attendance of the small barons and freeholders, and the Act of 1428 was an attempt to limit their burden, and yet to secure adequate attendance, by allowing them to elect representatives (*supra*, p. 36). But apparently James also realised that the work of Parliament could be expedited, and the burden of long attendance relieved, if matters came before Parliament in a prepared form. And out of this concept of preparing the work of Parliament in advance arose the committee which became known as ' The Lords of the Articles.'

In the preambles to the statutes of the first two parliaments of James I we have reference to the ' articles ' (*articuli*, that is, ' points ') put forward by the king, and in the preamble to the statutes of the third of his parliaments the articles put forward by the king are ' to be determined by certain persons thereto chosen by the Three Estates.' [1] Probably, though we have no evidence, these ' certain persons ' produced some form of draft legislation which was then considered by the whole House ; certainly that was the later development of the ' Committee of the Articles.'

In the reign of James II and the early part of the reign of James III the Estates still continued to ' commit the full power

---

[1] It is to be remembered that these preambles do not come from the official register of Parliament (which does not begin until 1466) but from the printed edition of 1566 which, however, is probably trustworthy.

of the whole Parliament ' to commissions, though the device of a Committee of the Articles may also have been used without evidence of its use appearing. In the Parliament of October 1467, however, a small committee was appointed *ad formandum articulos et pro moneta* ; and the Parliament which met on 20 November 1469 elected a committee of the ' artikillis ' on 21 November, and the statutes of the Parliament were passed on or about 27 November. Clearly the work of Parliament was being expedited, and significantly this same Parliament of November 1469 appointed a small committee, different in membership from its Committee of the Articles, to ' avise commone and refer again to the next parliament or generale consail of thir materis underwritten.'

The Committee of the Articles was henceforward regularly employed. In the reign of James V we find it closely associated with the king's Privy Council and with the afforced sittings of the Privy Council known as General Councils. Upon occasion Parliament appears to have granted the full powers of a commission to the members of the Privy Council ; in February 1525 the Lords of the Articles elected the members of the Privy Council from among their own number ; and in 1535 (and 1543) the Lords of the Articles were constituted as a commission with ' full power of parliament ' to devise and make ' acts, statutes and constitutions for good rule, justice and police to be had within the realm.'

The commission of 1543 was the last commission to be appointed with full power of Parliament until the expedient of the commission was again adopted during the civil war of the seventeenth century ; but the device of the Committee of the Articles was now established, and gradually closer and closer approximation in the membership of the Privy Council, the Committee of the Articles, and the College of Justice (see *infra*, pp. 43–51) put all power, legislative, executive and judicial, into the hands of a select few : and the select few could be instruments of a faction or of the king.

With the reign of James VI the position was reached where Parliament met and appointed the Committee of the Articles ; Parliament dispersed ; Parliament met again, after an interval rarely longer than a fortnight, and the legislation drafted by the Lords of the Articles was passed *en bloc* in one day. The Scottish Parliament had become the ' registrar of conclusions reached elsewhere.' (See, in general, R. S. Rait, *Parliaments of Scotland*, pp. 358 et seq.)

Preambles to the Statutes of the early Parliaments of James I

1424. Parliamentum . . . Jacobi . . . regis Scotorum . . . tentum apud Perthe xxvi die mensis Maii a.d. mccccxxiiii. . . . Convocatis tribus regni statibus et ibidem congregatis electe fuerunt certe persone ad articulos datos per dominum regem determinandos data ceteris licencia recedendi.[1]

1425. In the parliament . . . haldin in the town of Perthe the xii day of Marche the yer of God mccccxxiiii yeris . . . to the thre estatis of the realme thar gaderyt war proponit sindry articulis for the quiete and gud governance of the realme, to the quhilk it was anseuryt in maner as efter folowys. . . .

1426. In the parliament . . . haldin at Perth the xi day of the moneth of Marche with continuacioun of dais and of tymis folowande in the yere of grace mccccxx and v yeris . . . to the articulis present be the saide lorde the king to the prelatis, mychty lordis of the parliament, erlis and baronnis to be determynit be certane persounis thairto chosyne be the thre estatis it is answeryt, ordanyt, statute and decretyt in maner and forme as efter folowis. . . .

1427. Parliamentum tentum apud Perthe . . . primo die mensis Julii a.d. mccccxxvii . . . summonitis et vocatis more solito et debito episcopis, abbatibus, prioribus, comitibus, baronibus et aliis regni libere tenentibus qui de dicto domino nostro rege tenent in capite et de quolibet burgo regni certis burgensibus qui ad hoc summoniti fuerunt[2]

[1] This is the last time this formula appears (cf. vol. i, p. 185)

[2] This is the last time this formula is used for the burgh representatives, and it is probable that it is here used owing to the clerk copying from an earlier document. In 1401 burgh representatives are stated to have been summoned 'debito et more solito' (cf. vol. i, p. 175; and see Rait, *Parliaments of Scotland*, p. 247).

comparentibus omnibus illis qui debuerunt et voluerunt commode interesse, absentibus quibusdam aliis quorum quidem aliqui legittime excusati fuerunt alii vero quasi per contumaciam se absentarunt quorum nomina patent in rotulo sectarum quorum quilibet adjudicatur in amerciamento decem librarum.

A.P.S., ii, 3, 7, 9, 13

1467. *Committee ad formandum articulos*

[Parliament met on 12 October.] Die vero xiiii dicte mensis electi fuerunt ad formandum articulos et pro moneta ex clero episcopus Sanctiandree, episcopus Glasguensis, episcopus Aberdonensis, pro baronibus dominus Lyle, dominus de Caldorwood, magister David Guthre, pro burgorum commissariis Thomas Olifant, Andreas Charteris, Georgeus Girnelaw.

A.P.S., ii, 88

1469. *Committee of the Articles*

[21 November]

To the artikillis

for the prelatis

The bischop of Saintandrois
The bischop of Glasgow
The bischop of Dunkeldin
The bischop of Abirdene

for the barounis

The erle of Orknay
The lord Hammiltone
The lorde Gray
The lord Lindsay

for the commissaris

Sir Alexander Naper provost of Edinburgh
Alexander Chaumer alderman of Aberdene
Henry Levinstone
Adam Cosoure

A.P.S., ii, 93

1469. *Committee to advise and report*

Item the hail thre estatis has committit ful power to thir personis underwrittin of the haill parliament to avise commone and refer again to the next parliament or generale consail of thir materis underwritten : [*import and retention of bullion, coinage, compilation of an authorized law book*, ' reformatione for mane sworne athis and to set punytion thairupon ']. And thir personis to convene togiddir in Edinburgh the first Monunday of Lenterne etc. [*Four prelates, four barons and four burgh commissioners.*]

A.P.S., ii, 97, c. 20

1535. *Lords of the Articles with full power of Parliament*

. . . The kingis grace, with the avise and consent of his thre estatis in parliament, hes ordanit and ordanis this present parliament to stand under continuatioun in the samin forme, force and effect as it is now, without ony uther particular continuatioun, ay and quhil the samin be dissolvit be his grace or at his command. And becaus thair is mony actis, statutis and constitutionis to be maid for gude reule, justice and police to be had within this realme and amang all our soverane lordis liegis bay[th] spirituale and temporall, quhilkis can nocht be haistely done, and it ware bayth tedious and sumptuous to the haile estatis to byde and remane thairupoun, heirfore oure said soverane lord, with the avise and consent of his thre estatis in plane parliament, hes gevin to the lordis of articulis fornamyt full power of parliament to devise and mak sic actis, statutis and constitutionis for gude reule, justice and police to be had within the realme conforme to the articulis

to be gevin be the kingis grace and as sall plese ony utheris
to give and present to thame, and als upoun all uther materis
that sall pleise the kingis grace to lay to thame concernyng
his awin materis and effaris ; and quhatever thai ordane
or statutis to have the samyn forme, strenth and effect as
the samin war maid and statute be all the thre estatis
beand personaly present, and to be pronuncit in presens
of the kingis grace quhat day and place sall pleise his grace.
And gif ony gretare matere occuris that plesis his grace to
have the gretest of his prelatis and barounis counsale, he
shall advertise thame thairof be his speciall writtingis to
convene sic day and place as he sall think maist expedient.
And als that nochtwithstanding this perpetuate continuatioun of sete of parliament it salbe lesum to all jugis within
this realme to hald thair courtis and ministir justice to all
our soverane lordis liegis without ony spirituale dispen-
satioun and the kingis grace with consent of his thre estatis
presentlie in plane parliament dispense thairwith etc.

A.P.S., ii, 340

*In March 1543 the same procedure was followed, and it is described
in almost identical language* (ibid., 423).

CHAPTER FOUR

THE COURT OF SESSION

The failure of justice in medieval Scotland was largely due to the failure of the ordinary courts, particularly the sheriff courts and baron courts. As we have seen, James I, immediately upon his return from England, endeavoured to ensure that ' thar be maide officiaris and ministeris of lawe throu all the realme that can and may halde the law to the kingis commonis '(*supra*, p. 13), but he soon found that he was endeavouring to do something that was then impossible. Petitions and complaints of lack of justice continued to pour in, and burdened the king and council, including ' council in parliament,' with a load of judicial work. But the king and council, concerned with affairs of state, were unable to spare the time required for this mass of complaint and litigation. As a result, James I established in 1426 a new court consisting of the chancellor and ' certain discreet persons of the Three Estates ' to sit three times a year ' where the king likes to command them ' to hear and ' finally determine ' all and sundry complaints and causes. We know nothing of the working of this new court, but that it did function, at least occasionally, is clear from an ordinance of 1439 reducing the sittings (which are now those of ' the lord lieutenant and the king's chosen council ') to ' twa sessionis yerly ' —and, from its ' sessions,' the court came to be known as ' the session.'

The reduction to two ' sessions ' yearly was made during James II's minority, but in 1450 the act of James I was re-enacted in almost identical words (*A.P.S.*, ii, 34, c. 5). The re-enactment, however, was apparently not effective. In 1456 it was suggested that nine lords [of session], three from each estate, should ' minister the lawe justly and ewynly ' in three rotas of one month each (*A.P.S.*, ii, 46, c. 8) ; and in 1458 we have an enactment for putting the suggestion into practice. Again, in 1465, a similar arrangement was thought ' speedful ' (*A.P.S.*, xii, 31), but shortly thereafter the ' sessions ' appear to have been abandoned ; causes and complaints were again referred to the king and council, who, as before, found themselves overburdened owing to the failure of the ordinary courts. The real difficulties were already making themselves manifest : a shortage of trained personnel and a lack of finance to compensate the ' lords ' for the heavy calls made upon their time.

In 1491, in the opening years of the reign of James IV, certain lords of council were appointed as ' lords of session ' to attend to civil causes and to sit three times a year. This was very like a return to James I's attempt of 1426—save that now the members of the court were to be chosen from the council and not from the Estates. But although this arrangement led to the emergence of the ' lords of council and session,' and although thereafter certain members of council were regularly detailed to assist with civil causes, these ' lords of council and session ' were never able to devote themselves wholly to judicial work. In 1504, in an attempt to dispatch the heavy arrears of causes and to avoid future accumulations, a special ' council ' was to be chosen by the king, to have ' the same power as the lords of session,' to sit ' continually in Edinburgh or where the king makes residence or where it pleases him,' and ' to decide all manner of summons in civil matters, complaints and causes.' This ' council ' did not supersede the ' lords of session '—indeed, we find both bodies sitting concurrently and both hearing civil causes. By 1511, however, Edinburgh had become the normal place for the sittings of the lords of session, and the concept of a central civil court, composed of certain appointed ' lords of session,' was emerging.

But there was still no hard and fast division between the judicial work of the lords of session and other ' council work ' to which they might have to attend to the detriment of their judicial functions ; nor were the troublous years following Flodden conducive to constitutional development. Above all, a permanent central civil court could be satisfactorily established only if finance could be made available to provide it with a paid judicial bench.

At last, taking advantage of the local situation created by Henry VIII's breach with Rome, and of the general political and ecclesiastical situation in Europe, James V obtained from Pope Clement VII, in 1531, a bull whereby the church was to provide finance for a College of Justice ; in 1535 Pope Paul III issued a bull confirming the erection of the College and the taxation of church benefices for its maintenance ; and in 1541 the new College of Justice (or Court of Session) received formal parliamentary ratification. (See R. K. Hannay, *The College of Justice*, pp. 1–78.)

44

1426. Item oure soverane lorde the king withe consent of his parliament has ordanit that his chancellare and with him certane discret personis of the thre estatis to be chosyn ande depute be oure soverane lorde the king sall syt fra hyne furthe thre tymis in the yere quhare the king likis to commande thaim, quhilk sal knaw, examyn, conclude and finally determyn all and sindry complayntis, causis and querellis that may be determynit befor the kingis consal. The quhilk personis sal hafe thare expensis of the partiis fundyn fautyce and of thar unlawis or uthir ways as beis plesande to our soverane lorde the king.

A.P.S., ii, 11, c. 19

1439. [*In the Council held at Stirling*] It was sene spedfull and deliverit that thar suld be twa sessionis yerly in the quhilkis the lord lieutenant and the kyngis chosyn consal sall sit, the first begynande on the morn efter the exaltacioun of the haly cross [1] next to cum ande the tother to begyn apone the first monunday of Lenteryn [2] nixt thereftir folowande.

A.P.S., ii, 32, c. 1

1458. Inprimis as to the artikill of the Sessione it is seyne speidfull to the king ande the thre estatis that it be contynuit to the nixt parliament in maner as eftir folowys. That is to say the lordis of the Sessione sall syt thryse in the yere ilk tyme xl dais in this thre placis Edinburghe Perthe and Abyrdene ; The nowmer of the personis that sall sit salbe ix, haifande power and votis in the deliverance of causis, of ilke estate thre and the Clerk of the Regester ; The Sessione nowe nixt to begin and be haldin at Abirdene the xv day of Junij and continuande xl dais, The secunde Sessione to begyne at Perthe thareftir the v day of october and continew uthir xl dais, The thride Sessione to begyn in Edinburghe the xiij day of Februare next thareftir and continew xl dais ; The lordis that ar chosyne to the first Sessione in Abyrdene ar thir, The Bischope of Ross Catness or Murray the abbot

---

[1] 14 September   [2] i.e. Lent

of Dere dene David Bane and maister Walter Ydyll for the clergy, the Erle of Errole the Lorde Glammys ande the Lorde Forbess for the baronnys, Jhone of Fyffe Andro Menzeis and Walter Thomsone of Invernes for the burowys; The lordis that sall sit in the secunde Sessione in Perthe the bischope of Dunkeldin the abbot of Lundoris the archdene of Sanctandrois for the clergy, the Lorde Gray Patrik of Rettray Thomas of Abyrcrummy of that ilk for the baronnis, Archebald Stewart Robert Mersser and David Spalding for the burrowis; The lordis for the thride Sessione in Edinburghe to be haldyne the bischope of Glasgw or Galloway or ane uthir bischope the quhilk the king sall charge tharto the abbot of Halyrudhouse the provest of Linclowdane for the clergy, the Lorde Lindissay and the Lorde Halys for the baronys, Williame of Cranstone Alexander Naper and Robert Narne for the burowis; And at the scheref of the schyre at the lordis sittis in be redy by thame for the tyme of thar sitting till undirgang sik chargis as thai sall put till him togidder with a masare to minister in his office.

A.P.S., ii, 47, c. 1

1491. It is statut and ordinit that the chancellare with certane lordis of consale or ellis the lordis of sessioun sit for the administracioun of justice thris ilke yere. . . . Sa that justice may be put to dew execucioun to all partiis complenyeand.

A.P.S., ii, 226, c. 16

1504. Item it is avisit statute and concludit in this present parliament becaus thair has bene greit confusioun of summondis at ilk sessioun sa that laser [1] nor space at a tyme of the yeir mycht nocht have bene had for the ending of thame and tharthrou pure folkis hes bene delayit and deferrit fra yeir to yeir throw the quhilk thay wantit justice, That tharfor for eschewing of the said confusioun thair be ane consale chosin be the kingis hienes quhilk sall sitt

---

[1] leisure

continually in Edinburgh or quhar the king makis residence, or quhar it plesis him, to decide all manner of summondis in civile materis, complantis and causis dayly as thai sall happin to occure, and sal have the samin power as the lordis of sessioun and quhen thai sall begin and in quhat place salbe notifyit to the pepill be oppin proclamatioun at the kingis plesure.

A.P.S., ii, 249, c. 2

A bull of Pope Clement VII, dated 13 September 1531, related that James V proposed to erect a College of Justice (to be composed half of ecclesiastics), and for its maintenance granted to him and his successors, as long as they were faithful to the apostolic see, an annual tax of 10,000 ducats *auri de camera* (equivalent to about £10,000 Scots), to be paid by the prelates. (Keith, *Affairs of Church and State in Scotland*, Spottiswoode Society, i, 464–6.)

In the two acts which follow, James fulfilled the two conditions attached to Clement's grant : (i) by undertaking to remain loyal to the papacy, and (ii) by publicly committing himself to the project of a College of Justice.

1532. Our soverane lord in this present parliament, the thre estatis of this realme beand gaderit, exponit sene he and his noble progenitouris, kingis of Scotland, and liegis of the samin, has bene first, or at the leist with the first, that evir acceptit the Cristin faith and bene maist obedient sonnis to our haly faderis the papis of Rome and the auctorite apostolik, without ony maner of smot, violacioun or defectioun, and our haly faderis the papis of Rome has been verray gracius and benevolent to his hienes and realme with all maner of privilegeis and benefitis, and maist of all Pape Clement now pape of Rome has been mair gracius and benevolent till his grace than to all his forbearis ; Quharfor to schaw him thankfull and obedient sone to his halynes and the kirk of Rome it is divisit statute and ordanit be his hienes with avise and consent of the thre estatis of parliament that he sall keip, observe, manteine and defend the auctorite, liberte and fredome of the sete of Rome and halikirk and sall never mak nor statute ony actis, constitucionis, do nor attempt nor suffir to be done nor attemptit ony thing in contrare thairof ; and geif in tymes past ony thing has bene done or in tymes cuming sall happin to be done incontrare the auctorite, fredome and liberte of halykirk annullis and decernis the samin now as than and than as now of nane avale force nor effect and that nain of our said soverane lordis liegis be bund or oblist to obey the samin, salfand alwayis the actis foundit apon our haly fader the papis privilegis or thaim that hes bene lang in lovable use kepit and observit in our soverane lord that now is and his maist noble progenitouris tymes.

ITEM . . . becaus our soverane is maist desyrous to have ane permanent ordour of justice for the universale wele of all his liegis and thairfor tendis to institute ane college of cunning and wise men baith of spirituale and temporale estate for the doing and administracioun of justice in all civile actionis, and thairfoir thinkis to be chosin certane persounis maist convenient and qualifyit thairfore to the nowmer of xiiij persounis, half spirituale half temporall, with ane president, the quhilkis personis sall be auctorizat in this present parliament to sitt and decyde apon all actiouns civile, and nane utheris to have voit with thame onto the tyme that the said college may be institute at mare lasare ; and thir persounis to begynn and sitt in Edinburgh on the morne efter Trinite Sonday quhill Lammes and thaireftir to have vacance quhill the xix day of October nixt thaireftir and than to begin and sitt quhill Sanct Thomas evin effore Yule and thaireftir to begin apon the morn efter the Epiphany [1] day and sitt quhill Palmsonday evin and thairefter to begyn on the morn efter *Dominica in albis* [2] and sitt quhill Lammes ; and thir persounis to be sworne to minister justice equaly to all personis in sic causis as sall happin tocum before thaim with sic uthir rewlis and statutis as sall pleise the kingis grace to mak and geif to thaim for ordouring of the samin :

[1] *New Yere* deleted   [2] First Sunday after Easter

the thre estatis of this present parliament thinkis this artikle wele consavit and thairfor the kingis grace with avise and consent of the saidis thre estatis ordanis the samin to have effect in all punctis and now ratifyis and confermes the samin ; and has chosin thir persounis underwrittin to the effect forsaid, quhais processis sentencis and decretis sall have the samin strenth, force and effect as the decretis of the lordis of sessioun had in all tymes bigane : providing alwayis that my lord chancelare being present in this toun or uther place he sall have voit and be principale of the said counsell and sic uther lordis as sall pleise the kingis grace to enjone to thaim of his gret counsell to have voit siclik to the nomer of thre or four, that is to say the abbot of Cambuskynneth, president, Mr. R. Bothuile, Schir Jhone Dingwell, Mr. Henry Quhite, Mr. Robert Schanwell, vicar of Kirkcaldy, Mr. William Gibsone, Mr. Thomas Hay, Mr. Arthour Boyis, the lard of Balwery, Schir Jhone Campbell, Mr. Adam Otterburn, James Colvile of Est Wemys, the justice clerk, Mr. Francis Bothuil, Mr. James Lauson, and thir lordis to subscrive all deliverancis and nane utheris eftir that thai begyn to sitt to minister justice.

A.P.S., ii, 335–6, cc. 1–2

The prelates naturally viewed with alarm a standing contribution of £10,000 a year, and, knowing the king's immediate need of money, they entered into an agreement with James V whereby, in place of £10,000 a year, they would pay (i) £72,000, in eight half-yearly instalments over the next four years, and (ii) £1,400 a year, in perpetuity, towards the expenses of the College of Justice—this annual payment to be a charge on certain stated benefices.

Thus, in place of £10,000 a year being available for the new court, James V pocketed £72,000 and only £1,400 a year was available for the court—approximately £100 Scots for each judge, a sum which was far too small.

Then, in March 1534/5 a bull of Pope Paul III narrated Clement VII's grant, stated that James had erected the College, and had come to an agreement with the prelates whereby their annual liability was reduced to £1,400 Scots (this money to be distributed for the profit of the president and fourteen judges in proportion to their daily attendance in court), imposed this tax of £1,400, to be uplifted from benefices in the patronage of the prelates, and further assigned—*rege in hoc consentiente*—benefices in the royal patronage to the value of not more than £200 sterling. (The execution of the bull, dated 31 March 1535, is in Keith, *Affairs of Church and State in Scotland*, i, 467–82.) Finally, in March 1540/1 the institution of the College of Justice was formally ratified in Parliament.

1541. The kingis grace, with avise of his thre estatis of parliament, understanding that the institutioun of his college of justice and actis maid thairupoun are rycht proffitable to his grace and all the haill realme, and thairfor, now eftir his perfite aige of xxv yeris, has ratifyit and apprevit, ratifyis and apprevis for him and his successouris the institutioun of the said college of justice and actis maid for administratioun of justice thairin, and als ratifyis and apprevis the confirmatioun, ratificatioun and approbatioun of our haly fader the pape of the erectioun of the said college and of the gift of all benefices rentis gevin and to be gevin, assignit and to be assignit, to the honest sustentatioun of the said college of justice and all previlegis grantit and to be grantit thairto be oure said haly fader the pape and his hienes ; and will and ordanis for the caussis forsaid that the said college and institutioun thairof remane perpetualie for the administratioun of justice to all the liegis of this realme and to be honowrit siclik as ony uthir college of justice in uthir realmis ; and attour gevis and grantis to the president vicepresident and senatouris power to mak sic actis statutis and ordinancis as thai sall think expedient for ordouring of processis and haisty expeditioun of justice, and in absence of president and vicepresident will that the eldest in ordour of the saidis senatouris be president for the tyme to the effect that thair be na stop of justice ony tyme throw absence of the saidis president and vicepresident.

A.P.S., ii, 371, c. 10

Subsequent enactments made various changes in the constitution of the new court. The more important of these are : By an Act of 1579 it was no longer necessary for a churchman to be President ; by an Act of 1640 all the judges were to be laymen (and although that Act was voided by the Rescissory Act of 1661, no churchman has since been appointed an Ordinary Lord, while Archbishop Burnet, who was appointed an Extraordinary Lord in 1664, was the last churchman to sit on the Bench, and following his retiral in 1668 the Court has been composed exclusively of lay judges) ; by an Act of 1723 no more Extraordinary Lords were to be appointed by the king ; by an Act of 1808 the Court was divided into two Divisions—the Lord President with seven of the Ordinary Lords forming the First Division, and the Lord Justice-Clerk with six of the Ordinary Lords forming the Second Division ; and by an Act of 1831 the number of judges was reduced from fifteen to thirteen, of whom four, presided over by the Lord President, constitute the First Division of the Inner House, four, presided over by the Lord Justice-Clerk, constitute the Second Division of the Inner House, and the remaining five sit as Lords Ordinary in the Outer House.

Chapter Five

FOREIGN RELATIONS

The Treaty of Westminster-Ardtornish, 1461/2

This treaty between Edward IV and the MacDonalds of the Isles was negotiated on Edward's behalf by the Earl of Douglas (exiled by James II in 1455). It was partly a Yorkist attempt to counteract the Lancastrian sympathies of the Scottish government; partly also it was an attempt by the Black Douglases to regain something of what they had lost, and action by the MacDonalds of the Isles to assert their independence. John of Ross was later accused of usurping ' royal authority and the royal crown,' [1] and according to the Auchinleck Chronicle he ' past till Inverness and tuke the kingis fermes and all wittalis of the kingis and proclamit all the gudis and the landis of the kingis intill his handis and gaf remissionis and respittis.' [2] The treaty revealed the problem of the Isles in its most dangerous form, and although John submitted to James III in 1464 there was no concentrated attempt to crush the power of the MacDonalds of the Isles until the reign of James IV. John, Lord of the Isles, was finally forfeited in 1493. Nevertheless, in the difficult period of the ' English wooing ' (pp. 126-8) the MacDonalds of the Isles again entered into treaty with the King of England (Henry VIII) in 1545, when they bound themselves to do all they could to the annoyance of the Regent Arran in return for pensions and pay from England. (Cf. Gregory, *History of the Western Highlands and Isles*, 169-73).

. . . It is appointed . . . that . . . John de Isle, erle of Rosse, Donald Balagh and John of Isles, son and heire apparent to the seid Donald, with all there subgettez, men, people and inhabitantes of the seid erldom of Rosse and Isles aboveseid, shall at feste of Whittesontide next commyng become and be legemen and subjettes unto the seid most high and Christen prince Kynge Edward the Fourthe, his

---

[1] *A.P.S.*, ii, 108-9   [2] *Auchinleck Chronicle*, pp. 23, 60

heires and successours, kynges of Englond . . . and do homage unto hym. . . . And in semble wyse the heires of the seid John, th'erle, Donald and John shall be and remaigne for ever subjettis and liegemen unto the seid kynge Edward, his heires and successours, kynges of Englonde. . . .

ITEM the seid John th'erle, Donald and John and eche of them shall be always redy after the seid feste of Whittesontide upon convenable and resounable warnyng and commaundement . . . to do diligente and effectuall service with and to all them [sic] uttermest myght and power in suche werres as the seid most high and myghty prynce, his heires and successours, kynges of Englond . . . shall move or arreise or [cause to be] moved or arreised in Scotlande or ayenste the Scottes in Irlande or ayenst the kynges ennemyes or rebelles there. . . .

ITEM the seid John, erle of Rosse, shall from the seid feste of Whittesontyde next comyng yerely duryng his lyf have and take for fees and wages in tym of peas, of the seid most high and Christen prince C merc sterlyng of Englysh money, and in tyme of werre . . . he shall have wages of CC li. sterlyng . . . yerely and after the rate [i.e., *pro rata*] of the time that he shall be occupied in the seid werres. [*Donald is to have £20 in peace and £40 in war, and John, his son, £10 and £20.*]

ITEM . . . if it so be that hereafter the seid reaume of Scotlande or the more part thereof be conquered, subdued and brough[t] to the obeissaunce of the seid most high and Christen prince and his heires or successours . . . be th'assistence . . . of the seid John . . . and Donald and of James, erle of Douglas, then (the seid fees and wages . . . cessyng) the same erles and Donald shall have . . . all the possessions of the seid reaume beyonde [the] Scottyshe See, they to be departed egally betwix them, eche . . . to holde his parte of the seid most Cristen prince. . . .

ITEM if so be that by th'aide . . . of the seid James, erle of Douglas, the seid reaume . . . be conquered . . . he shall have, enjoye and inherite all his owne possessions

. . . on this syde the seid Scottyshe See . . . to holde them of the seid most high and Christen prince. . . .

[*Sealed and signed at London on 13 February 1461/2* [1] *and ratified by King Edward at Westminster on 17 March following.*]

Rotuli Scotiae, ii, 405–7

THE ACQUISITION OF ORKNEY AND SHETLAND, 1468–71

Treaty of 1468

The Treaty of Perth, 1266,[2] (confirmed by the Treaty of Inverness, 1312) had provided that, in return for the cession of the Western Isles, Scotland should pay 100 merks annually to Norway. There is little evidence to show how regularly the ' annual ' of Norway was paid. James I apparently made some effort to pay off an accumulation of arrears, but the payment was finally ' extinguished ' in a treaty of 1468 which arranged for the marriage of James III to Margaret, daughter of Christian, King of Denmark, Sweden and Norway. By that treaty also Christian pledged his lands and rights in Orkney for part of his daughter's dowry and, as the pledge was never redeemed, Christian's lands and rights in Orkney passed to the Scottish crown. (Later, redemption was more than once offered but was always refused—see *infra*, p. 57.) The Scottish original document in the Register House is imperfect, but the missing words can be supplied from the Danish text which, although no longer extant, was printed by Torfaeus in *Orcades seu rerum Orcadensium Historia* (1697), pp. 191 et seq., and in Peterkin's *Rentals of the Earldom of Orkney*, Appendix II. A conflated text is given in *E.R.*, viii, lxxvii et seq., and a complete text and translation appear in *Kirkwall Burgh Charters*.

Christian . . . King of Denmark, Sweden and Norway . . . to all Christians . . . [*since the envoys of King James have contracted matrimony with Margaret per verba de futuro and also by virtue of a special procuratory (dated 28 July 1468) per verba de presenti*]. Therefore . . . we . . . (obtaining first

---

[1] In the *Rotuli Scotiae* the treaty is wrongly dated 1462/3 (see Annie I. Dunlop, *Life and Times of James Kennedy, Bishop of St Andrews*, 225n).

[2] See vol. i, pp. 21–3

54

the consent as well as the assent of the prelates, magnates and nobles of our kingdom of Norway and carefully considering, moreover, the profit and advantage of both kingdoms) do grant, deliver and by the tenor of the presents give, as part of the dowry of Margaret, our only daughter, to the foresaid Prince James . . . and Margaret, our daughter, his spouse, and their heirs and children only, the yearly pension of 100 merks sterling due every year to us and our heirs, kings of Norway for the time, in consideration of the islands of the Sudreys and Man ; wholly remitting, moreover, all and sundry sums of money, damages, reparations and compensations due by reason of the pension foresaid and upon occasion of the contracts entered into by our predecessors, the former kings of Norway and the kings of Scotland. . . .

For completion, moreover, of the whole dowry, we promise, undertake and pledge us, our heirs and successors, to the foresaid most excellent Prince James, most serene king of Scots, or his procurators, for the sum of sixty thousand florins of the Rhine, to be faithfully paid, of which sum we shall fully and faithfully pay ten thousand florins foresaid and give satisfaction thereof in counted money, readily and effectually, to the foresaid procurators before their return to the kingdom of Scotland from our kingdom of Denmark ; and for the sum of fifty thousand florins remaining of the whole sum foresaid we, Christian, king of Norway, with consent and assent of the prelates, magnates and greater nobles of our realm of Norway foresaid, give, grant, pledge and mortgage and place under assured pledge and security all and sundry our lands of the islands of the Orkneys with all and sundry rights, services and their rightful pertinents, pertaining or that in whatsoever manner may pertain to us and our predecessors, kings of Norway, by royal right ; to be held and had all and whole our lands of the islands of the Orkneys foresaid, with all and sundry customs, profits, freedoms, commodities and their other rightful pertinents whatsoever, as well named as not named, pertaining or that can rightfully pertain in any way in the future to the foresaid lands of Orkney, by the foresaid most excellent Prince James, king of Scots, our dearest son and ally, as part of the dowry with our foresaid daughter Margaret, ever and until whole and full satisfaction and payment is effectually made by us, our heirs and successors, kings of Norway, to the foresaid James, king of Scots, his heirs or successors, of the sum of fifty thousand florins of the Rhine remaining of part of the dowry. . . .

[*Margaret is to have the palace of Linlithgow, the castle of Doune, and her terce. If James predecease her, she may either leave Scotland within three years, or remain : if she leave Scotland, James's successors are bound to pay her 120,000 Rhenish florins for her terce, from which sum is to be deducted 50,000—the unpaid part of the dowry—and the Orkneys are to revert to Norway ; provided, however, that Margaret does not marry the king of England or any person of that country.*]

Further, . . . we, Christian, king of Norway, and we, the spokesmen and procurators of the most excellent Prince James, king of Scots, having power hereto, desiring to draw together in a stronger bond of alliance, for us, our heirs and successors and the magnates of our realms, scrupulously undertake on the word of a king to afford mutual friendship and the maintenance of the new alliance, help, aid and assistance, each in his turn, at the request of the other, against whatsoever prince or princes, nation or people (our allies before the date of the presents alone excepted), and by the tenor of the presents assuredly to maintain them, pledging hereto ourselves and our heirs and successors.

[*But in the event of the death of either James or Margaret before the solemnisation or consummation of the marriage, all the agreements made are to be wholly extinguished.*]

In faith and witness of all and sundry the foregoing we, Christian, . . . have had our seal appended, and we, spokesmen foresaid, have had our seals appended, in double form, to the presents, at the town of Havn [Copenhagen] . . . on 8 September 1468. . . .

The Pledging of Shetland, 1469

King Christian succeeded in raising only 2,000 of the 10,000 florins promised in the foregoing treaty, and on 20 May 1469 he pledged Shetland for the remaining 8,000. There is no record evidence for the transaction, which is related by Torfaeus (op. cit., p. 188) from a chronicle.

There is also a story, related by Ferrerius, the continuator of Boece (edn. 1574, f. 389), that on the birth of Prince James (afterwards James IV) in 1473 King Christian renounced his right to redeem the islands. That there is no truth in this appears to be proved by the fact that in 1485 one of the commissions of a proposed Scottish embassy to the pope was to seek confirmation of the conventions with Denmark ' of the donacioun and impigneracioun of the landis of Orknay and Scheteland ' (*A.P.S.*, ii, 171). It is quite possible that Christian himself had no thought of redeeming the islands, but his successors several times raised the subject, which they would hardly have done with such persistence if the right of redemption had in fact been renounced. Attempts to discuss the question of redemption were made at least down to 1667 (Torfaeus, op. cit., pp. 227–8), if not to 1749 (*Scott. Notes and Queries*, 3rd ser., i, 115–16).

Annexation of the earldom of Orkney and lordship of Shetland to the Scottish crown, 1472

It would appear that the transactions of 1468 and 1469 referred only to the Norwegian king's lands and rights in the islands, and did not include the lands of the earldom and lordship, which had been held (since 1379) by the Scottish family of St Clair and had been extensively Scotticised. In 1470, however, Earl William St Clair resigned his rights to the king of Scots in exchange for lands in Fife (*R.M.S.*, ii, Nos. 996–1002), and on 20 February 1471/2 the Scottish parliament passed the following act of annexation :

Our souverain lorde with deliverance of his thre estatis annext and uniit the erledome of Orkney and the lordschip of Scheteland to the croune, nocht to be gevin away in tyme to cum to na persoune nor personis except anerly til ane of the kingis sonnis of lachtfull bed.

A.P.S., ii, 102

And William Tulloch, bishop of Orkney, entered on a tack of the fermes of Orkney and Shetland on 22 August 1472 (*E.R.*, viii, 224–5).

Treaty of Perpetual Peace between England and Scotland, 1502

The marriage treaty of James IV and Margaret Tudor (*Foedera*, xii, 787–92) and the treaty of perpetual peace (ibid., 793–800) were sealed at Richmond on 24 January 1501/2. On 12 July 1502 James informed Henry that he was prepared to ' supersede ' or suspend the confirmation of the ancient league with France, which it was customary to renew on the accession of each king (*Foedera*, xiii, 12). The treaties were formally ratified by Henry VII on 31 October 1502 (ibid., xiii, 30–1) and by James IV on 17 December 1502 (ibid., 49–50) ; and the ' Indenture for Peace and Friendship ' was renewed with the accession of Henry VIII.

The bull of Alexander VI, dated 28 May 1503, confirming the treaty, is in the Register House (Papal Bulls, No. 42). It is to be noted that by the bull (and as requested in the treaty) either king (or his successors) breaking the treaty of perpetual peace would incur excommunication by the Church. James's invasion of England in the campaign which culminated in Flodden was held by the Pope (then anxious for the assistance of England in his ' Holy League ' against France) to be a breach of the treaty, and the Pope (Leo X) endeavoured to turn the situation to his own advantage (see *infra*, p. 88). See also J. D. Mackie, *Earlier Tudors*, 158–62.

Considering it to be agreeable to reason that those whom the bond of consanguinity or affinity has joined in the nearest degree should also be joined, united and tied by the greatest and strongest bonds of leagues, confederacies and friendships, and maturely considering and keeping in view the bond and amity, truce, friendship and alliance which presently exists between our said most illustrious princes for the term of their lives and that of the survivor and for a year after the survivor's death, and also the marriage [*between James and Margaret*] to be contracted before Candlemas next, we will (by authority and in virtue of sufficient commissions made and given to us by our foresaid princes . . .) that there be a true, sincere, whole and unbroken peace, friendship, league and alliance, not only for the term of the life of each of our said princes and for a year after the death of the survivor, but from this day forth in all times to come, between them and their heirs and lawful successors, heritably and lawfully succeeding . . .

It is agreed that neither of the kings foresaid nor any of their heirs and successors shall in any way receive or allow by their subjects to be received any rebels, traitors or refugees suspected, reputed or convicted of the crime of treason. [*And if such persons do come to either kingdom, it shall be forbidden to give them any countenance, but, on the request of their sovereign, they are to be put in ward and to be handed over within 20 days.*]

[*In the event of any king, prince or other person invading or disturbing either realm or attempting to usurp it, the prince of the other realm shall come to its assistance.*]

[*Provision is made for the comprehension of the existing allies of Scotland and England if they so desire.*] Although it happen the said king of England or his heirs and successors foresaid or any of them to levy war against any of the said princes comprehended herein, then the king of Scotland . . . shall wholly abstain from making any invasion of the kingdom of England, its places and dominions, as well by himself as by his subjects, but it shall be lawful to the king of Scotland to give help, assistance, favour and succour to that prince against whom war has been levied by the king of England, for his defence and not otherwise. [*And a reciprocal provision is made for the case of the king of Scotland making war on an ally of the king of England.*]

. . . It is agreed . . . that each of the foresaid princes

shall, before 1 July 1503, obtain at his own expense a
rescript or letters apostolic . . . whereby all and singular
the contents of the present treaty are by apostolic authority
approved and confirmed. And moreover each of the princes
foresaid, their heirs or successors, before the said 1 July,
shall . . . require the sacred apostolic see and the supreme
pontiff to impose sentence of excommunication . . . on
either of the said two princes and on their heirs and successors
who shall violate, or permit to be violated, the present peace
or any clause of the present treaty. . . .

Foedera, xii, 793–7

FLODDEN

A few days before the encounter with the English army at Flodden
a royal edict granted remission of the feudal casualties of ward,
relief and marriage to the heirs of those of the king's army killed
during the campaign. A similar remission had been granted a
century earlier at the time of the battle of Harlaw (1411)
(vol. i, p. 170), and was to be similarly granted to the heirs of
the slain at Pinkie.

24 August 1513. At Twesilhauch in Northumbirland the
xxiiij day of August the yere of God 1513 yeris it is statute
and ordanit be the Kingis hienes witht avise of al his lordis
being thar for the tyme in his ost in this forme as efter
follois that is to say gif ony man beis slane or hurt to deid
in the kingis army and ost be Inglissmen or deis in his
army enduring the tyme of his ost his aieris sall have his
ward reliefe and mariage of the king free dispensand with
his aige quhat yeild that ever he be of and ordanis the
kingis letteris to be direct hereapon to the effect foresaid
necessar as efferis.

A.P.S., ii, 278

The Battle

The following two letters from Thomas Ruthall, bishop of Durham,
to Thomas Wolsey provide a very close account of the battle,

written after a lapse of only a few weeks. Allowance must be made for exaggeration of the glory of the victory, but the first letter describes the equipment of the Scottish army and indicates one of the reasons for its overthrow. The Scots put their trust in their long spears with which a body of men made an admirable phalanx ; but the long spear proved useless against the English bill, which could cut through the spear-shaft ; and when the Scots, having lost the use of their spears, were compelled to fight hand-to-hand with only their swords they were unable to reach the English bill-men and were literally cut down at a distance (see W. Mackay Mackenzie, *The Secret of Flodden*, 91–3). The traditional account of the Scottish stand (e.g. in *Marmion*) is wrong in speaking of ' stubborn spearmen ' in the later stages of the battle ; nor can the Scots have formed a ' desperate ring ' round King James, who was probably killed early in the fight and in the forefront of the battle. For a recent discussion of the tactics of the battle and of the comparative strength and training of the English and Scottish armies, see J. D. Mackie, ' The English Army at Flodden,' in *Scottish History Society Miscellany*, vol. viii.

. . . For on the 9th daie of this instante monethe of Septembere after a mervelouse greate conflicte and terrible bataille the King of Scotes with the greatest parte of the lordes and nobles of his reame wer in playn bataille venquyshed, overthrowen and slayne. At whiche bataille my Lorde Tresourere like a noble, valiaunte and puysaunt capitain, by his greate wisdome, hardiesse and experience, with the assistence, goode conduyt and actyvenesse of his sonne the Lorde Haworde, Admiralle of Englande, so acquited hym self that for this moste famouse acte redounding to the inestimable honour, comforte, commoditie and suertie of the Kinges Grace, this his reame and subjectes of the same, they deserved asmoche lawde, renomme and thankefull remembraunce as ever anny noble men did. Specially remembring the multitude of theire enmyes, being ferre in nombre above the Kinges armye, conscidering also the grete nombre of mervelouse large peces of ordynaunce as courtauldys, culverins, sacres and serpentyns amounting in the hoole to 17 great peces, besides moche other smale

ordynaunce. Regarding also the greate and strong per-
sonnages of the Scotes being aswelle fournesched with
goodely harneys, wepons and other abilimentes of werre
as ever men were, with their abundaunce of vitails, wynes
of all sortes, brede, bere and ale, tentes and pavylions ferre
above our estimacion and not lightely credible ooneles it
had bene seen, tasted and vewed by our folkes to their greate
refreshing, and over that the hardinesse and sharp setting
on of the said Scotes with the discomforte and feblenes of
our people being destitute of vitails and having no thing
to drinke but oonely watere by the space of thre daies and
moche scacitie of that, with the mervelous greate payn and
laboure that they toke in going 8 myles that daye on fote
by daungerouse and paynfulle passages over hilles and hill
dales and yet, moste daunger of all, in ascending and
clymyng an highe and stipe hille to encountre and geve
bataill to the said King of Scotes being there campyd and
his ordynaunce set to his moste advauntage and annoysaunce
of our armye. And the said Scotes having the hill, the
wynde and the sunne with thaym ayeinst our folkes, all
whiche impedimentes, daungers and perells well con-
sciderde, it is to be thought this victorye procedethe more
by the veray hande of God, with the helpe and merites of
the gloriouse Confessour Seint Cutbert, thenne by anny
strenghte or power of menne, how be it after so greate
payn and labour there lakked no goode courage, strenghte
and herte in our folkes as it well appered by their
actes.

For besides the King of Scotes all the lordes of Scotlande,
excepte fyve, and the moste parte of the noble men of the
same which that day dyed, there were 10 thousande Scotes
slane, and as summe of thaym afferme they lacke 15 thousande in the hoole to the utter confusion of all Scotlande.

The said Scotes wer so surely harnessed with complete
harneys, jackes almayn, ryvettes, splentes, pavices and
other habilimentes that shote of arrowes in regarde did
theim no harme, and whenne it comme to hande strokes
of billes and halbardes they wer so myghtie, large, strong

and grete men that they wolde not fall whenne 4 or 5 billes strake on oon of thaym at oonys ; how be it our billes qwite them veray welle and did more goode that day thenne bowes for they shortely disapointed the Scotes of their long speres wherin was their greatest truste and whenne they came to hande stroke, though the Scotes faght sore and valiauntlye with their swerdes, yet they coude not resiste the billes that lighted so thicke and sore upon theym.

There were that day many goode and towarde capitains which did their partes righte welle, how be it the Lorde Howard was the firste setter on and toke moste payn in conduyting the vawarde of our armye to whome joyned Seint Cutbertes banner with the hoole retynewe of the bisshoprike ; and al be it the Scotes had moste dispecte to the said banner and set moste feresly upon it, yet what by the grace of God, the assistence of Seint Cutbert to his banner, and the valiauntnesse of the capitains and others being undre the same, there gate they noon advauntage but greate losse and damage of their folkes, and yet fewe or noon being under the same banner wer slayn thoughe many hurte. This with grete honour is Seint Cutbertes banner retourned againe to his churche, bringing with it the King of Scotes banner which for a memorial now standeth besides the shryne there. And the sayd Kyng was not farre from hys baner when he was slayne. And besides this all the grete ordinaunce of Scotlande is taken and resteth at Berwike with diverse prisoners, but not many, for our folkes entending to make all thing sure, toke little regarde in taking of prisoners, but rid all that came to hande, bothe King, bisshopes, lordes, knyghtes, nobles, or others what so ever came which wer not so soon slayn but forthewith dispoiled out of their ~~ordynaunce~~ harnais and array and lefte lying naked in the felde where men moughte have seen a mervelouse nombre of many goodely men well fedde and fatte, among which nombre was the King of Scotes bodye founde, having manye woundes and naked, and the same was broughte to my Lorde Tresourer thenne being in Berwike in whose keping the same bodye yet restethe.

And yet whenne our capitains and folkes had thus welle acquited them self, greate displeasure was doone unto theym, for in their absence from their tentes, they being occupied with the Scotes, all their goodes, horses and necessaries wer clerely taken awaye. But whether it wer doon by Scottes or bordourers I canne not saye, but the brute is that the borderours did full ill. I pray God amende theym for by this dealing our folkes wer wars discouraged at their departing thenne by all the harmes doon to them by the Scottes, and suche dealing hath and shall cause thame to have the wars wille to retourne thider again if necessite require.

Facsimiles of National MSS. [of Great Britain], ii, No. 4

Maistre Almosner this victory was the most honorable, happy and beneficialle for the Kynges Grace and this reame as ever came to the same or can be rememberyd in any cronicle. And ondoubtydly it was more myraculous than by power of man. . . . The Scottes lackyd no thyng necessary for the warrys but oonly the grace of God, for of elect men, harneys, ordinaunce and vitaylis thay had suche plentie that never the lyke hathe ben harde of in this parties, and I assure you alle Englande cowd not have vitaylid our host as thay wer vitaylid, every thing consideryd. And this by the helpe of God and Saynt Cutbert this malicyus provision made by the sayde Kyng for the warrys thys 7 yeris was overthrowen in half an howre so that I trust in God thay schalle never be hable to make the semblable whilis Scotlande standythe. My Lord Treasourer hathe the body of the Kyng of Scottes with hym to Yorke and I cowd in no wyse induce hym to leve it here at Duresme, howbeit my folkes undre Saynt Cutbertes baner browzt whom hys baner, hys sworde and his qwyschys, that is to say, the harneys for hys thyes, whiche be in Saynt Cutbertes churche. Maister Almoner, Sir William Bulmer hathe as hardylie acquytyd hym self as welle at the fyrst voyage ayenst the Scottes as at this batayle as ever manne dyd whereby he hathe welle deservyd a greate garamercy and summe honourable reward for by suche valiaunt actes princes have hertofore have of poore men made greate lordes. And suerly after my Lord Treasourer and my Lord Haward no man did better there that day and what he dyd at the fyrst voyage, when with 7 or 800 men he sette uppon and venquysched the Chamberlayn of Scotlande with 10,000 Scottes, and tooke 4 or 500 prisoners, it is manyfest and notorious. . . .

Communicacion hathe be had bytwyxt the Lorde Dacre and the Chamberlayne of Scotlande sens this conflict and an overture made for abstinence of warre, whereunto my Lorde Treasourer in consideracion of the weakenesse of our borders, lacke of men and vitaylis for the defence therof, is moche inclinyd, and hathe wretyn to the ~~Kyn~~ Qwene and the counsayle to know thayre myndes therin, wherof as yet we have had noone aunswere. Surely Maister Almoner if this victory mowzt be folowyd Scotlande were chastysid for ever. But suche capitayns and souldiours as wer at this businesse in mervoulous fowle wethyre, lackyng mete ~~and~~ drynke, and whiche have also lost thayr horses and goodes, had lever dye then to cumme thedyr agayn. And this I feare me, veray force for lacke of the premisses schalle dryve us to abstinence of warre, whiche wer so greate a pitie mervelous lacke and daunger, at lengthe as I have ~~at lengthe~~ wretyn to the Qwenys Grace and the counsayle, and rather then it schuld thus be left I had lever spend alle the goodes I have (if it be possible to be doon, as I trust it schalbe) if I may help thereto. The grettyst difficultie that I see therein is this that ~~the~~ suche men of warre as schalbe sent to the borders dare not trust the borderers, whiche be falser than Scottes, and have doon mor harme at this tyme to our folkes than the Scottes dyd, and therfor, if it were Goddys pleaser and the Kynges, I wolde alle the horsemen on the bordours were in Fraunce with you, for there schulde thay do moche goode, where as here thay doo noone, but moche harme, for, as I have wretyn byfore, thay never lyghtyd from thayr horses, but when the bataylis joynyd than felle thay to ryfelyng and robbyng aswelle on our syde as of the Scottes, and have taken moche goodes besides horses and catelle. And over that thay tooke dyverse prisoners of ours, and delyveryd thaym to the Scottes, so that our folkes asmoche feare the falshed of thaym as thay do the Scottes, and this I feare wolbe the stoppe of this goode mater. On our syde were slayne at this batayle by estimacion oon thousand men, howbeit no greate manne of name but Sir John Bothe of Lancaschire and two or thre other knyghtes and summe gentylmen. Howbeit there be many taken prisoners of ours to the nombre, as I am informyd, of 100 or 6 score, the specialties of whos namys I have not as yet. Neverthelesse I send unto you hereinclosyd the namys of suche lordes and others of Scotlande as were slayne at the felde, with the specialties of the gentylmen made knyghtes by my Lord Treasourer. ~~Howbeit~~ And albeit I suppose my Lord ~~and~~ Traisourer hathe sent thaym thedyr byfor, yet for my acquytayle I thowzt ye schulde have thayme by me and for lacke of layser I can not wrete the premisses to the Kynges Grace wherfore I have now wretyn a schort letter to hys Hyghnesse desiryng hys Grace to geve credence to you in alle the premisses. It may like you therfore at some convenient tyme to rede this rude letter to hys Grace, and to make my Lord Pryvie Seale pryvie thereunto to whome I have now wretyn a schort letter. Here I make my abode at Duresme, and I like the countray veraylie welle. Our Lorde send the Kynges Grace and you as goode spede there as we have had here. Wretyn hastylie at Duresme the 20 day of Septembre.

Your awn, T. Duresme.

Facsimiles of National MSS. [of Great Britain], ii, No. 5

Invasion Rumours

As news of the defeat at Flodden reached Edinburgh preparations were made for defence of the capital against invasion, and this

entry in the burgh records is indicative of the courage of the
magistrates and council at a desperate time.

10 September 1513. Forsamekill as thair is ane greit rumour
now laitlie rysin within this toun tuiching our Souerane
Lord and his army, of the quhilk we understand thair is
cumin na veritie as yit, thairfore we charge straitlie and
commandis in our said Souerane Lord the Kingis name,
and the presidentis for the provest and baillies within this
burgh, that all maner of personis nychtbouris within the
samyn have reddye thair fensabill geir and wapponis for
weir, and compeir thairwith to the said presidentis at
jowyng of the commoun bell, for the keiping and defens
of the toun aganis thame that wald invaid the samyn.

And als chairgis that all wemen, and specialie vaga-
boundis, that thai pas to thair labouris and be nocht sene
upoun the gait clamorand and cryand, under the pane
of banesing of the personis but fauouris, and that the uther
wemen of gude pas to the kirk and pray quhane tyme
requiris for our souerane Lord and his armye and nychtbouris being thairat, and hald thame at thair previe labouris
of the gait within thair houssis as efferis.

Edinburgh Burgh Records (Burgh Records Society), i, 143-4

The belief that the ' Flodden Wall ' around the burgh was
thrown up hastily when news of the disaster arrived is contrary to
the evidence. It was only on 17 March 1513/4, six months later,
that the town council imposed a levy for the ' furnessing and
defens ' or ' walling ' of the burgh (*Edinburgh Burgh Records*, i, 146) ;
even then progress was very slow, and council minutes suggest that
as late as 1560 the ambitious scheme had not been completed
(Royal Commission on Ancient Monuments, *Edinburgh Inventory*,
lxiv–lxv).

TREATY OF ROUEN, 1517

With the failure of the Treaty of 1502 and with the ' Franco-Scot '
John, Duke of Albany (son of Alexander, Duke of Albany, brother
of James III) acting as regent during the king's minority, it was

natural that the ' auld alliance ' with France should be renewed.
During a visit to France (1517–21) Albany, acting on behalf of
James V, and the Duc d'Alençon, acting on behalf of Francis I,
concluded the Treaty of Rouen. This was an offensive and
defensive alliance against England, much like the earlier treaty
of Corbeuil in 1316 (vol. i, p. 135); but also, by this treaty, James V
was to marry a daughter of Francis I and, in virtue of the treaty,
James V, nearly twenty years later, married Madeleine de Valois,
the eldest surviving daughter of Francis I.

. . . Firstly, the said lord kings being good, true and loyal
brothers and friends, united, allied, confederated, without
fraud or evil intention, for the safety, guarding and defence
of their realms . . . will each cherish . . . the honour and
estate of the other . . . and will not give passage, aid,
favour, assistance or welcome in their realms, country,
lordships, ports and coastal havens either with men,
artillery, money or other means to those who, by invasion,
could or would bring annoyance or burden to either. . . .

And firstly if the king of England assail or make actual
war against the king of Scotland, his heirs and successors,
or against the said lord [king of France] his heirs and
successors, from that moment the said lord [king of France]
or the king of Scotland, if he is of age, or his . . . regent
. . . during his minority, being duly informed by writing,
by sure account or by common knowledge, will assist each
other in the defence of their persons and countries, as
follows—

That is to say, that for the first and the second times that
the said king of England, his heirs and successors, makes
war against either of the kings, the said lord [king of
France] and his successors shall be bound to give to the
king of Scotland, his heirs and successors 100,000 écus du
soleil, 500 lansquenets,[1] 500 infantry and 200 archers of the
said lord's command, paid until they arrive in the ports
and harbours of Scotland, but, from the time they arrive,
the lansquenets . . . shall be paid by the king of Scotland

---

[1] mounted spearmen

. . . and the said archers shall live at the expense of the said lord.

And, further, if the king of England assail or make war on the said lord [king of France], as said is, as soon as the king of Scotland, his heirs and successors, his tutor, regent or governor has been duly informed, as above, they shall be bound, with all their power and with the aid which the said lord gives to them, to break and make war on the king of England, his realm and his subjects, and if the king of England assail and make war also on the king of Scotland, his heirs and successors, the said lord, as soon as he has been informed as above, and in addition to the help above-mentioned, shall be bound for his defence, and to divert the war, to make war with all his power on the land and subjects which the king of England holds and occupies beyond the sea.

If it happen that . . . for a third time and more the king of England assail the said lord and make war on him or on the king of Scotland, his heirs and successors, they shall arrange as follows for the defence of themselves and their realms—

That is to say that, if war is made against the king of Scotland, his heirs and successors, as soon as the king of France his heirs and successors are informed in the manner specified above, they shall be bound to break and make war upon the country, lands, lordships and subjects which the king of England holds and occupies beyond the sea. And, on the other hand, if the king of England make war on the said lord [the king of France], his heirs and successors, the king of Scotland, his heirs and successors shall be bound, as soon as informed as above, to break and make war upon the king of England, his realm and subjects with all their power.

Further, it has been agreed between us that whenever the king of England makes war on the said lords [the kings of France], the king of Scotland shall be bound to send him 6000 good soldiers of his realm at the expense of the said lord [the king of France], if required.

Further, it has been agreed that if it should happen that the said lord king of France etc. in making war on the land and subjects of the king of England for the defence of the king of Scotland, his heirs and successors, should conquer the said land beyond the sea, or if it come into his hands by other means, nevertheless he shall not leave the war before his army in all its power, and that of his successors, shall cross the sea to make war on the realm of England, which war the said lord [the king of France] and his successors shall sustain until the war made by the king of England on the king of Scotland or his successors shall be ended by a treaty made with the consent of both kings, their heirs and successors, or otherwise . . .

Above all, for the great love and most cordial affection in which the said kings hold one another, and to seal the alliance and compact made between them, it is agreed that, if the promise of his eldest daughter made by the king of France to the Catholic King [of Spain] or to his brother does not take place . . ., the king of France shall betroth and marry her to the king of Scotland ; and if the promise of his daughter made by the king of France to the said Catholic King, or to his brother does take place, and it pleases God to give to him another daughter, then, when she shall have reached the age to contract marriage, the said king of France shall, if the Holy Mother Church agrees, betroth and marry her to his brother and cousin [the king of Scotland]. . . .

Teulet, Papiers d'Etat (Bannatyne Club), i, 39–43n

CHAPTER SIX

ARMY AND NAVY

MILITARY TRAINING AND EQUIPMENT

The military proficiency of the lieges was important in fifteenth-century Scotland where defence of the realm and the reconquest of the area held by England were matters of constant concern. The following extracts bear witness to the government's efforts to encourage archery (for too often the English longbowmen had won the battle ' at a distance ') at the expense of football and golf, and to ensure that the lieges (who formed the ' host ') possessed arms and armour, each proper to his estate. But despite James IV's act of 1491, it is to be noted that the *Treasurer's Accounts* are a silent witness to the purchase of footballs for the king's own use.

1424.

Item it is statut and the king forbiddis that na man play at the fut ball under the payne of iiij d. . . .

Item it is ordanyt that all men busk thame [1] to be archaris fra thai be xij yeris of eilde And that in ilk x lib. worth of lande thar be maid bowmerkis and specialy nere paroche kirkis quhare upone haly dais men may cum and at the lest schute thrise about and haif usage of archary. . . .

A.P.S., ii, 5, c. 18 ; 6, c. 19

1430.

Item be the awyse of the haill parliament it is statute and ordanit that ilk man that may dispende yerly xx lib. or at has jᶜ lib. in movabil guidis that he be wele horsit and haill enarmyt as a gentill man aucht to be And uther sympillar of x lib. of rent or l lib. in gudis haif hat gorgeat

---

[1] prepare themselves

or pesanne with rerebrasaris [1], vambrasaris [1] and gluffis of plate, brest plate, panse and legsplentis at the lest or better gif him likis.

Item that ilk yeman that is of xx lib. in gudis haif a gude doublat of fence or ane habergeon, ane yrn hat with bow and schefe, suerde, buklar and knyfe And all uther yemen of x lib. in gudis haif bow and schefe, suerde and buklar and knyff And the yeman that is nane archer na can nocht deyll with a bow sall haif a gude souer hat for his hede and a doublat of fence with suerde and buklar and a gude ax or ellis a brogit [2] staff.

A.P.S., ii, 18, cc. 11, 12

1458.

Item it is decretyt and ordanyt that wapinschawingis be haldin be the lordis ande baronys spirituale and temporale four tymis in the yere And at the fut ball ande the golf be utterly criyt doune and nocht usyt Ande at the bowe merkis be maide at ilk parroch kirk a pair of buttis and schuting be usyt ilk sunday And that ilk man schut sex schottis at the lest under the payne to be raisit apone thame that cumis nocht at the lest ijd. to be giffin to thame that cumis to the bowe merkis to drink . . . And that thar be a bowar and a fleger [3] in ilk hede towne of the schyre And at the towne furniss him of stuf and graithe [4] efter as nedis him tharto that he may serve the cuntre wyth . . . And gif the parrochin be mekill that thar be iij or iiij or fyve bow merkis in sik placis as ganys tharfor And that ilk man within that parrochin that is within fyfte and passit xij yeris sall use schuting and that men that is outwith and past thre scoir yeiris sal use uther honest gammys as efferis.

A.P.S., ii, 48, c. 6

[1] armour for the arms, back and front
[2] spiked
[3] arrow-maker
[4] gear, equipment

1471.

Item it is thocht expedient that na merchandis bryng speris in this Realme out of ony uther cuntre bot gif thai conten sex eln and of a clyft[1] Na at na bowar within the Realme mak ony speris bot gif thai conten the samyn lentht . . .

A.P.S., ii, 100, c. 6

1491.

And attour that in na place of the Realme be usit fut bawis gouff[2] or uthir sic unproffitable sportis bot for commoun gude and defence of the realme be hantit bowis schuting and merkis tharfore ordinit in ilk parrochoun undre the pane of xls. to be Rasit be the schiref and bailyeis forsaid of ilke parrochoun ilke yere quhare it beis fundin that bow markis be nocht maid na schuting hantit as said is.

A.P.S., ii, 226, c. 13

1497.

Item [the xxij day of Aprile], giffin to Jame Dog to by fut ballis to the King, ... ij s.

T.A., i, 330

ARTILLERY

While skill in archery remained a military asset, the increasing use of artillery made governments less dependent upon the general host for their military force ; but artillery involved increasing public expenditure, nor could it be brought within the normal feudal services rendered for the holding of land. By the middle of the fifteenth century an attempt was made to place some of this burden upon the barons by asking them to provide guns

---

[1] i.e. of one cleft of wood
[2] An early reference to a golf club occurs in a precept of remission under the Privy Seal in 1507—Preceptum remissionis Johannis Thowles commorantis in Brechin pro interfectione quondam Alexandri Meill ex subito per ictum baculi viz. *golf club* commissa (*R.S.S.*, i, No. 1547).

and gun carriages, but, generally, artillery remained a royal monopoly and a constant drain upon the Treasury.

1384.

Et prouno instrumento dicto *gun* empto pro castro de Edynburgh, iiij li.

E.R., iii, 672

1430.

Eodem anno rex de Flandria adduci fecit immanem fundam bombardicam æris metallo fabrifactam.

Bower, *Scotichronicon*, XVI, xvi

1436.

And by payment made to Nicholas Plumbar to meet the wages of certain workmen engaged on bombards, engines, and other military machines and apparatus . . . £590 8s. 2d.

E.R., iv, 677

1456.

Item it is thocht spedfull that the king mak request to certane of the gret baronys of the lande that ar of ony mycht to mak cartis of weir and in ilk cart twa gunnys and ilkane of thame to haif twa chawmerys with the remanent of the graith [1] that efferis tharto and ane cunnande man to schut thame And gif thai haif na craft in the schuting of thame as now thai may leir or the tym cum that will be nedfull to haif thame.

A.P.S., ii, 45, c. 4

Conveyance of Artillery to the Border (*Raid of Norham*)

1497. Item, the xix day of Julij, thir men [and] hors feit to pas with the artailyery, and giffin to ilkane ane owkis wage in thair hand ; In the first, ij{c}xxj man with schule, spaid, pyk, and matok, and ilk man vj s. for his owkis wage ; summa . . . . . . lxvj lib. vj s.

[1] gear

Item, that samyn daye, feit foure score xiij cart hors to draw gunnis, and with ilk iij hors ij men ; the some of men is lxij men ; the hale some of men and hors is in the hale jᶜ fifti five hors and men ; and to ilk man for the vij dayis giffin vij s., and to ilk hors vij s. ; the some of thir togidder is . . . . . . liiij lib. v s.

Item, that samyn day, feit to pas to the raid with the King lxj quareouris and masounis, and giffin to ilk man his owkis wage, ix s. iiij d. ; summa of all togidder is

xxviij lib. ix s. iiij d.

Item, feit sic like, to pas with the artailyery, xij wrichtis and ane coupar for the powdir ; and giffin to ilk man ix s. iiij d. ; summa . . . . . vj lib. xvj d.

Item, that samyn day, giffin to foure smythis siclike, to pas with the artalyerj ; to ilk man for his owkis wage ix s. iiij d. ; summa of all is . . . . xxxvij s. iiij d.

Item, for iiij gret towis to Mons, weyand xvj stane five pund ; for ilk stane iiij s. ; summa

iij lib. v s. viij d.

Item, to the pynouris, to gang to the Castell to help with Mons doune . . . . x s.

Item, to the menstralis that playit before Mons doune the gait . . . . xiiij s.

Item, giffin for xiij stane of irne, to mak grath to Mons new cradill, and gavilokkis to ga with hir ; for ilk stane xxviij d. ; summa . . . . . . xxxs. iiij d.

Item, the xxix day of Julij, giffin to vij wrichtis for tua dayis and a half tha maid Mons cradil ; to ilk man on the day xvj d. ; summa . . . . xxiij s. iiij d.

Item, the last day of August [Julij] giffin to Robin Ker to fee jᶜ werkmen to pas with Mons, sic like as the laif wer feit ; to ilk man vj s. ; summa . . . xxx lib.

Item, for xxiiij pund of talloune to Mons . . vj s.

Item, for half ane galloune of tar to it . . . ij s.

Item, for xvij waw [1] viij stane of irne, to be irne pellokkis to send to the ost ; for ilk waw xxviij s.

xxiiij lib. xiiij s. viij d.

[1] waw = 12 stones of 8 lb. each

Item, for wirking of thaim, for ilk waw xiiij s. ; summa
xij lib. vij s. iiij d.

Item, for mare talloune to Mons . . . . ij s.

Item, that samyn day, giffin to Johne Mawar, elder, and
tua wrichtis with him to pas with Mons, for thair owkis
wage . . . . xxxij s.

Item, to tua smythis to pas with hir, for ane owkis wage
to ilkain of thaim, ix s. iiij d. ; summa . xviij s. viij d.

Extracts from *T.A.*, i, 346–9

The range of Mons Meg is revealed in the following entry from
the Treasurer's Accounts for July 1558 where, among the accounts
for rejoicings, bonfires and pageants to celebrate the marriage
of Mary Queen of Scots and the Dauphin, we read :

1558. Item, the thrid day of Julii, to certane pyonaris for
thair laubouris in the monting of Mons furtht of hir lair
to be schote, and for the finding and carying of hir bullet
eftir scho wes schot fra Weirdie Mure [1] to the castell of
Edinburgh . . . . x s. viij d.

T.A., x, 367

This salute, fired with an actual gun-stone, shows that the range
of Mons must have been rather less than two miles. The
following details are given in an official memorandum of 1734 :
The length of her chase [the cavity of the barrel] is 9 feet
$2\frac{1}{2}$ inches, and the length of her [powder] chamber 3 feet $8\frac{1}{2}$ inches:
her total length is 13 feet 4 inches. The diameter of her bore
is 1 foot 8 inches, and of her chamber 9 inches. Her whole weight
is 19,452 lbs., or about $8\frac{1}{2}$ tons. The weight of her shot in iron
is 1,125 lbs., or in stone 549 lbs. It took 105 lbs. of powder to fill
her chamber when rammed. Her greatest range when at an
elevation of 45 degrees was 1,408 yards with an iron shot, and
2,867 yards with one of stone. To travel these distances an
iron shot took 16 seconds, and a stone shot 22 seconds (*Proc. of the
Soc. of Antiq. of Scotland*, l [1915–16], 199).

[1] Wardie Muir, near Granton

1513. *Scottish guns lost at Flodden* [1]

No. of Pieces	Scottish Description	English Description ('Articles of Battle')	English Description ('Exchequer Accounts')	Shot in lbs
5	Cannons	Great Curtals	Demi-curtals	34
2	Gros Culverings	Culverins	Culverins	20
4	Culverings pikmoyane	Sakers	Demi-culverins	10
6	Culvering moyane	Serpentines	Sakers and Serpentines	4–5

W. Mackay Mackenzie, *Secret of Flodden*, p. 59

1549. *Guns of many kinds*

Gunnaris, cum heir and stand by your artailyee, euyrie gunnar til his auen quartar. Mak reddy your cannons, culverene moyens, culverene bastardis, falcons, saikyrs, [2] half saikyrs, and half falcons, slangis, [3] and half slangis, quartar slangis, hede stikkis, murdresaris, [4] pasvolans, [5] bersis, doggis, doubil bersis, hagbutis of croche, [6] half haggis, culverenis, and hail schot. And ye soldartis and conpangyons of veyr, mak reddy your corsbollis, hand bollis, fyir speyris, hail schot, lancis, pikkis, halbardis, rondellis, tua handit sourdis and tairgis.

Complaynt of Scotland (Early English Text Soc.), 41–2

[1] Cf. Thomas Ruthall's comments on the 'grete nombre of marvelouse large peces of ordynance' in the Scottish army (*supra*. p. 61).
[2] cannon smaller than a 'culverene moyen'
[3] cannon similar to culverenes
[4] large cannon   [5] small cannon
[6] small hand cannon, resting on a crook (croche) placed on the ground

THE NAVY

Ships and shipbuilding were always important to Scotland, but towards the end of the fifteenth century the increasing use of artillery brought a greater distinction between fighting ships and others. James IV's reign saw the most rapid development of the Scottish navy. Armed merchantmen gave way to ships of war, and with the building of the *Margaret*, the *Great Michael* and other powerfully armed vessels, Scottish sea-power became of international importance and contributed largely to James IV's strong position in Europe. It was also, under the command of the Bartons, a cause of friction with England. After Flodden the Scottish navy declined, and the *Great Michael* was sold to the king of France—only to rot away in the harbour of Brest.

Building the Scottish Fleet

1506. To the most illustrious, etc. For a long time past we have been busy with the building of a fleet for the protection of our shores, and to this day we labour at it with great zeal . . . Since there is a greater abundance of building material in your realm, we have sent our men thither to fetch beams and oakwood from a friendly nation, and to bring shipwrights to us. . . .

Letter of James IV to Louis XII, in *Epistolae Regum*
(1722), i, No. XVII

Raising the mast of the Great Michael

1512.

Item, to ane boit that brocht doun the greit mast fra the Blaknes to the New Havin . . . . . x s.
Item, for i dusan of schulis for the castin of the gait [1] to the mast . . . . iij s. iiij d.
Item, to xxij werkmen for the updrawin of the said mast, ilk man viij d. for ane day ; summa . . xiiij s. viij d.
Item, Setterday the xv day of November, to xxiij werk-

---

[1] For one dozen shovels to clear the road

men at the updrawin of the mast for ane day, ilk man
viij d. ; summa . . . . xv s. iiij d.
Item, Setterday, the xxij day of November, to xvj men
that helpit up with the greit mast ane day, ilk man viij d. ;
summa . . . . x s. viij d.

Extracts from *T.A.*, iv, 457–8

The Great Michael

In the same yeir [1512] the king of Scottland bigit ane
great scheip callit the Great Michell quhilk was the greattest
scheip and maist of strength that ewer saillit in Ingland or
France. For this scheip was of so greit statur and tuik so
mekill timber that scho waistit all the wodis in Fyfe except
Falkland wode, by [1] all the tymmer that was gottin out
of Noraway. Scho was so strang and wyde of length and
breid that all the wryghtis of Scottland ye and money
wther strangeris was at hir devyse be the kingis commande-
ment quho wroght werie bessielie on hir, bot it was yeir
and day or scho was compleit.

To wit, scho was xij scoir of futtis of length and xxxv
futte withtin the wallis ; scho was ten fute thik in the
waill, cuttit jeastis of aik witht hir wallis and burdis on
ewerie syde sa stark and thik that na canon could gang
throw hir. This great schipe cummerit Scottland to get
hir to the sie ; from tyme scho was aflott and all hir mastis
and saillis compleit, witht towis and ankeris effeirand
thairto scho was comptit to the king to be xxx thowsand
pund of expenssis by [1] hir artaillye quhilk was werie great
and costlie to the king by [1] all the laif of hir order. To wit,
scho buire mony cannons sex on everie syde witht thrie
great basselis,[2] tua behind in hir dock and ane befoir, witht
iij[c] schott of small artaillyie, that is to say mayan and
batterit facouns and quarter fallcouns, slingis, pestelent
serpitantis,[3] and doubill doggis witht hagbut and cullvering,
corsebowis and handbowis. Scho had iij[c] marienaris to

---

[1] besides   [2] usually called ' basilisks '
[3] usually called ' serpentines '

saill hir,[1] sex scoir of gounnaris [2] to wse hir artaillye for this scho had ane thouwsand men of weir by hir captans skipiris and quarter maisteris. Quhene this scheip past to the sie and was lyand in the rade,[3] the king gart schot ane cannon at hir to say hir gif scho was wicht,[4] bot I hard say it deirit [5] hir nocht and did her lyttill skaith.[6]

Pitscottie, *Chronicles of Scotland* (Scot. Text Soc.), i, 251–2

[1] This is no exaggeration, for the names of 295 'mariners of the great ship' appear in the *Treasurer's Accounts* (iv, 502–5). The skipper was paid £7 a month ; Pernot the Frenchman received £8 2s a month ; and the average seaman's wage was 35s a month.

[2] But only 14 gunners and 4 'men' are named in the *Treasurer's Accounts*.

[3] roadstead   [4] strong   [5] injured

[6] It is possible that Pitscottie derived some of his information ('I hard say') from Sir Andrew Wood.

Chapter Seven

THE CHURCH

The Struggle against Papal Control of Appointments

The greater benefices—the bishoprics and abbacies which the Scots called ' the prelacies '—were nominally elective, but the effective voice might in practice lie with the crown or a local magnate, whose pressure a chapter was in no position to resist. Nomination to lesser, non-elective benefices was by the patron, who might be a bishop, a corporation such as a monastery, or a layman. From about 1300 there had been a steady development of papal control over appointments. In the elective benefices the popes turned their right to confirm—or to quash—an election into a right to ' provide,' while to the non-elective benefices they applied rules whereby benefices falling vacant in certain circumstances were ' reserved ' for disposal at the *curia* ; in either case lay influence could be ignored. This centralising process, which had been initiated in the interests of ecclesiastical independence, was fostered partly from motives of profit, and was accelerated by the Great Schism (1378–1417), during which rival papal courts had to exact financial support.

The healing of the Schism was accompanied and followed by the Conciliar Movement, which, as part of its policy of reforming the church ' in head and members,' proposed to reverse the centralising process, but without success. Martin V, whom the Scots ultimately accepted at the close of the Schism (vol. 1, pp. 198–9) succeeded in maintaining and developing rules of reservation, including the general reservation of bishoprics and monasteries of an annual value of more than 200 florins, gold of the *camera*.[1]

The papal court had thus become, and remained, the market where ecclesiastical promotion could be ' purchased ' ; to Rome, therefore, went all ambitious Scottish clerks, and much good Scottish money went with them. A clash was inevitable with the kings of Scots, who found themselves deprived of a voice in the

---

[1] In 1431 the florin was equated to 8s sterling, and in 1446 to 6s 8d.

selection of prelates who by their office had seats in parliament and were often councillors, while royal rights of patronage were undermined and bullion was drained from the country.

James I concentrated on the restriction of the export of money and the control of the movements of Scottish churchmen, in a series of acts which created the crime of 'barratry' or unauthorised dealings at Rome.

Legislation against recourse to Rome

Item it is statut be the haill parliament and the king forbiddis that na clerk pass nor sende procuratour for him over the see but special leif of our lorde the king askit and obtenyt.

Item in lykewys it is statut be the haill parliament and the king forbiddis that ony clerk of his realme in tyme to cum purches ony pensione out of ony benefice secular or religious under all payne that he may tyne aganis the kingis maiestie or rais ony pensioun grantit in tyme bygane in ony maner of wayis under the panis forsaide.

Item it is ordanit that na man haf out of the realme golde nor silver bot he pay xl d. of ilk punde of custum to the king under the payne of tynsal of all gold and silver at beis fundyn and x lb. to the king for the unlawe.

A.P.S., ii, 5, cc. 14, 15, 16

The king, with the consent of the whole parliament, statuted and ordained that all and sundry clerks of his realm sailing or crossing overseas for any reason whatsoever shall exchange their money for their expenses to be incurred outwith the realm with money-changers established within the realm or at least with merchants within the realm ; of which exchange and with what money-changer or merchant it be made, and of their passage outwith the realm, they shall certify the chancellor of our lord king for the time ; and any layman betaking himself to parts beyond the sea shall likewise be obliged to make his exchange within the realm as is aforesaid, upon which he shall certify the chamberlain of Scotland by sufficient documents, and of the reason for his crossing, on pain of twenty pounds to be applied to the uses of our lord king.

A.P.S., ii, 14, c. 2 (translated)

1428.   Item the thre estatis has statute and it is confirmyt be the king that na clerk religious na seculare pas oute of the realme bot gif he cum to his ordinare first or than to the chanceller of the realme and schaw to thame gude and honest cause of his passage and mak faith to thame that he do no baratry and haf his letteres of licence and witnessing therapone ; and gif ony dois the contrary or makis baratry, fra it be kende with sufficient and gude document, that he underly the statute made agayn thaim that has money oute of the realme.   And at this statute be nocht allanerly ex-tendit to thaim that dois baratry in tymis to cum bot als to thaim outewith the realme now that beis convict of baratry.   Ande als the king forbiddis that ony of his liegis sende ony expensis til ony baratoure that now is outewith the realme na gif thaim help na favore in quhat degre at ever thai atteigne to quhil thai cum hame to the realme, under the payne of breking of the act of the parliament.

A.P.S., ii, 16, c. 9

As a result of this legislation, James became involved in a dispute with the papacy which centred largely on the careers of Cameron, the king's secretary, who became bishop of Glasgow and chancellor and whom the pope blamed for the barratry acts, and of Croyser, archdeacon of Teviotdale, a papal *protégé* whom James summoned to trial for breach of those acts and who was ultimately convicted as a traitor.   Scotland adhered to the council of Basel, which represented the anti-centralising party in the church, but it appears that towards the end of James's reign the instability of his position in Scotland—and perhaps the divided state of opinion in the Scottish church—rendered him disposed to submit to the pope.

   In James II's minority, the strife of faction was aggravated by the activities of the adherents of the anti-pope set up by the council of Basel, who were not suppressed until 1443.   The able James Kennedy, bishop of St Andrews, was a papalist both by conviction and from the desirability of having papal support in a troubled political situation, and there was no renewal of anti-papal legislation until after his death in 1465. In 1450, however, the crown's right, during vacancies of sees, to present to benefices in episcopal patronage, was formally acknowledged by the bishops,[1] and it was later reaffirmed by the provincial council and by parliament [2]; this was bound to conflict with papal claims.

In the reign of James III controversy arose over the abbeys, in which there had hitherto been in the main what the Scots called ' free election,' which meant secular influence and no papal interference. In 1466, when the pope gave to Bishop Graham of St Andrews the abbey of Paisley, to be held *in commendam* with his bishopric, the Scottish parliament legislated against the purchase at Rome of benefices *in commendam*, and also on the export of money.[3] In 1469 and 1471 it was enacted that abbeys and other benefices which had not previously been provided for at Rome should not be purchased there but should continue to have ' free election.' [4] The further acts, of 1482 and 1484, printed below, show an intention to maintain James I's restrictions and to protect the crown rights of patronage.

Renewed legislation against barratry

1482. It is statute and ordanit that the actis of parliament made of before anent the purchesing of pensionis furth of beneficis secular or religious be put to execucioun and that na man use ony processis of ony pensioun impetrate contrare the saide actis under the panys contenit in the sammyn actis, that is to say rebellioun and proscripcioun of the realme.

A.P.S. ii, 144, c. 9

1483/4. Anent impetraciouns made in the court of Rome incontrare oure soverane lordis privilege the sege vacand

---

[1] As part of a compromise over crown rights *sede vacante*, the king on his side surrendering his claim to the moveables of deceased bishops (*A.P.S.*, ii, 37–8, 61–2).

[2] *A.P.S.*, ii, 133, c. 7 ; 141, c. 16 ; 172, c. 14 ; Patrick, *Statutes of the Scottish Church*, 82–3

[3] *A.P.S.*, ii, 85, c. 4 ; 86, c. 10   [4] Ibid., 98, c. 21 ; 99, c. 4

it is statut and ordanit be oure soverane lord and his thre
estatis that the actis made concerning his patronage the
sege vacand be put in execucioun apoun the brekaris of
the said actis, and that the chancellar . . . sal writ to oure
haly fader . . . for the defence of our soverane lordis
patronage. . . .

Alsa for the eschewing of the grete skaith and dammage
that the realme daily sustenis be having of mone furth of
the realme be prelatis and clerkis for promociouns and pleis
in the court of Rome, it is statut and ordanit . . . that in
tym tocum ilk prelait or clerk that passis or sendis to the
court of Rome for promociouns or pleis sall cum to the
kingis chekker and befor the auditouris of the samyn prufe
and mak knawin his finance made in merchandise of the
realme to the avale of the some that he spendis in the court
of Rome. . . .

A.P.S. ii, 166, cc. 9, 11

The last years of James III's reign were a period of recurrent
disturbance in civil affairs, and the dissensions were reflected in
the church, for the king's political opponents had their own
candidates for some benefices, and certain prelates appointed by
the pope were not acceptable to the king. The lesson was that
strife was apt to be intensified, and order harder to maintain,
if the king had no voice in appointments. This plea was advanced
in the following petition, which indicates the recurrent rivalry
between persons provided at Rome and those nominated by the
king in Scotland.

Petition that the pope await the supplications of the Scottish king

1485. Because thair is certane personis barratouris quhilkis
. . . has movit plede and questioun and vexit and trublit
certan personis promovit to benefices be presentacioun of
our soveran lord the tyme of the vacacioun of sege of
bischoprikis incontrare to our soveran lordis privilege, . . .
the said commissaris sal thairfor desire at our said haly
fader the paip to put silence to the said personis barraturis
and mak all pleys and debaitis now movit be thaim aganis

ony parti concerning our said soverane lordis privilege
and beying incontrare thairof to cess all sic pleys in tyme
tocum ; and als to desire that his halines wald consider the
grete distance of this realme fra the court of Rome that he
thairfor graunt to our soverane lord and his successouris
to supercede and delay the disposicioun apoun ony prelaciis
or digniteis elective for the space of sex monethis that our
soverane lordis writing and supplicacioun may be send
for the promocioun of sic personis as is thankfull to his
hienes sa that thair be na personis promovit to prelaciis
nor digniteis without avise of his hienes sen all the prelatis
of his realme has the first vote in his parlment and of his
secrete counsale.

A.P.S., ii, 171, c. 9

That the pope should accede to such a request represents a change
of policy, possibly due to the obvious need to bolster up James's
failing authority.   Already in 1483 Pope Sixtus IV had issued
bulls commanding the Scottish nobles and prelates to obey the
king ; now, in 1487, Innocent VIII sent a legate to present to
James the Golden Rose as a mark of papal favour and to apply
ecclesiastical censures in support of the crown,[1] and also granted
the following indult.
    The terms of the indult represent a compromise between royal
and papal claims.   The crown received the right to have its
recommendations heard, and was guaranteed the enjoyment of
its rights during vacancies for the better part of a year ; the
pope retained his general reservation system and his formal right
to provide to the prelacies, together with the promotion taxes—
though for these he was now liable to have to wait longer.

The Indult of Innocent VIII to James III

1487. [*The popes, our predecessors, have been accustomed to give
a hearing to the petitions of Catholic monarchs, and, in making
provisions (in consultation with the cardinals) to cathedral churches
and to monasteries worth more than 200 florins, gold of the camera,
yearly, have proceeded with great deliberation, and, out of regard*

[1] Herkless and Hannay, *Archbishops of St Andrews*, i, 122–5

to the estate of the princes of the dominions where the benefices lie, have sometimes postponed the provision to permit the secular power to indicate preference for a candidate.] [1] Following in the footsteps of our predecessors, we are content and grant (as we have stated by word of mouth to our venerable brothers William, archbishop of St. Andrews, and Robert, bishop of Glasgow, your envoys sent to us to offer your accustomed obedience to the holy see) that, on the occurrence of vacancies of churches and monasteries of this sort within your kingdom and dominions, we shall postpone the appointment for at least eight months, and meantime, during that period of eight months, await the letters and humble supplications thereon of you and your successors, kings of Scotland, remaining in the same faith and devotion, so that, on receiving intimation, we may the better be able to proceed to these provisions as we shall think expedient ; urging our successors that in such provisions they take equal care to observe our practice.

Herkless and Hannay, *Archbishops of St Andrews*, i, 157–8

The indult was not a perpetual privilege (though Innocent had advised his successors to follow his example), but the Scots insisted on treating it as such. Innocent died in July 1492, and in 1493 it was ordained, with reference to the indult, ' that oure soverane lord mak the samin privilege and bull be observit and kepit and suffer na promotionis to gang throw in the contrare,' and penalties were imposed on those who violated it.[2] Besides thus insisting on observance of the indult, the Scots appealed to the practice of earlier times, anterior to the late papal aggression in monastic appointments, providing that all benefices ' quhilkis passis now to the court of Rome,' but ' war disponit in the realme be electiounis and uther wais in the tyme of King James the first ' be disponed within the realm in future as they had been in James I's time.[3]

The following act, of 1496, suggests that both the acts of parlia-

[1] Innocent also granted to James and his successors permission to have mass publicly in places subject to interdict.

[2] *A.P.S.*, ii, 232, c. 4   [3] Ibid., c. 3

ment and the indult were being violated, and also that recourse
to Rome now had novel features, possibly the practice of *resignatio
in favorem*, whereby a beneficed person resigned at Rome in favour
of a successor, reserving a liferent—a practice which in effect
eliminated vacancies and precluded the normal operation of
patronage.

Act for the protection of crown control

1496.   For the eschewing of innumerable skaith and
dampnage that his hienes realme and liegis dalie incurris
and sustenis throw the exhorbitant coistis and expensis
dalie done be kirkmen upoun the impetratioun and purchessing at the court of Rome beneficis elective and diverse
utheris that mycht be gevin and providit within the realme,
contrair the actis of parliament maid thairupoun and
contrair diverse faculteis and privilegis that our soverane
lord and his progenitouris of gude mynde hes had and hes
of the court of Rome, and als in purchessing and inbringing
of novelteis and innovationis in the kirk without the avisement of our soverane lord, in uter heirschip and destituting
of the realme of all money . . . [*no spiritual persons are to
pass from the realm without intimation to their ordinaries, and
both spiritual and temporal persons must have licence from the
king or the chancellor*].

A.P.S., ii, 237–8, c. 2

In practice the indult continued in the main to be observed
throughout the reign of James IV.   In the period after Flodden
Pope Leo X attempted to make capital out of the difficulties
of the Scots, and treated the Scottish prelacies as at his disposal.
Only in January 1518/19 did Leo finally confirm the indult (by
a bull preserved in the Register House).[1]

Growing royal confidence is reflected in the terms of an act
of parliament of November 1526, which explicitly claimed that
' nomination ' pertained to the king.

[1] Papal bulls, No. 45

Assertion of royal right to nomination to prelacies

1526. *On the narrative that, although* ' quhen prelacyis sic as bischeprykis or abbacys hapnis to vaik the nominacioun thairof pertenis to our soverane lord and the provisioun of the sammyn to our haly fader the paip,' *yet this rule had been violated, the estates ordained that* ' quhatsumever persone or personis in ony tyme tocum takis ony bischeppis placis, castellis or strenthis or enteris be thare awn auctorite in abbais to hald thai placis but our soverane lordis command letteris or chargis or desyre of the conventis thairof at tymis quhen sic bischepryis or abbacyis vakis or ony uther tyme thai nocht vakand, but the kingis auctorite, thai sall incur the cryme of tresone and leise majestie.'

A.P.S., ii, 309–10

In 1535 the pope expressly admitted a crown right of nomination, and at the same time the period of delay to await supplication was extended to twelve months.[1]

The indult, operated by collusion between pope and king without regard to the welfare of the church, had produced sufficiently scandalous appointments even under James IV, who made his illegitimate son, Alexander, archbishop of St Andrews at the age of eleven. That papal control would have produced no better results is indicated by the attempt of Leo X, in the period after Flodden, to intrude Italians into Scottish prelacies. Even had the pope possessed the will to intervene on moral grounds, his power to do so vanished when, in the 1530s, the English Reformation came to strengthen the hands of the Scottish king, who could now exact his own terms for continued allegiance to Rome. In these circumstances, appointments to benefices became more scandalous still.

Petition of James V on behalf of his sons

1533. [*On 27 February 1532/3, James V wrote to Pope Clement VII as follows:*] As I have three illegitimate sons

---

[1] Keith, *History of Affairs of Church and State*, i, 461–4

(two of them being the children of an unmarried father and mother, the third of an unmarried father only), I am obliged to confess to your Holiness that the fault is my own (although it might indeed easily be attributed to youth), and I acknowledge the error of human weakness. Yet that natural fatherly affection, common to all creatures, which nature prompts, urges every man to have regard for the welfare of his offspring as of himself ; for to be a father and yet not be moved by concern for the care of his children would be at once ungrateful and unnatural. We therefore beg your Holiness, of your clemency and courtesy (which we have hitherto experienced in every matter) to dispense with those our sons, by the grace of your apostolic authority, that, notwithstanding their defect of birth, they may, when their age allows, be duly promoted (outwith the terms prescribed by law) to all holy orders, even that of priesthood, and that at present, notwithstanding their minority as well as their defect of birth, they may, after receiving the clerical character, hold any church dignities whatsoever (*quecunque, quotcunque et qualiacunque sacerdotia*), either secular or regular of any order, in title or commend, even two, three, four or more incompatible benefices, and greater dignities *post pontificales* in cathedral and metropolitan churches and the first dignities in collegiate churches, and also monasteries, abbeys and priories (deputing coadjutors therein until they reach mature years). Let your Holiness grant also that hereafter it be not necessary to narrate their defect of birth in apostolic impetrations for any of them, and that their letters seem not on that account to be surreptitious. Finally, let your Holiness grant that when they attain their twentieth year they may be able to be promoted to the dignities of archbishop, primate and bishop. . . .

Caprington Letter Book (Register House), fo. 6 ; printed, with some divergences, in Theiner, No. mxxx

The complete capitulation of the papacy and the ascendancy of a wholly secular view of the monastic property is reflected in the following act.

The diversion of monastic revenues to the state

1542/3. [*On a supplication by the comptroller relating that the governor*] haldis ane greit house and is at mair sumpteous expensis nor umquhile our said soverane lord held in his tyme [*and that*] he wantis mekle bayth of propritie and casualitie, [*the lords of parliament*] for the maist part thinkis expedient and necessar that the frutis of the abbacyis and prioryis pertening to the kingis gracis sonnis, thame selfis being honestlie furnissit and sustenit efferand to thair minoritie and estate and convent of the samyn and thair placis to be uphaldin in all necessaris deulie as efferis, that the superplus of the frutis be convertit and deliverit to the quenis grace comptrollar for the honorable sustentatioun of hir grace my lord governour hir tutour and affaris of this realme, considerand the urgent cause apperand instantly and siclik during thair minoritie quhill thai be of perfite aige, and that na compt nor reknyng be laid to the charge of my said lord governour nor nane utheris thairfore in tyme tocum nor sall incur ony danger thairthrow in thair landis nor gudis.

A.P.S., ii, 424

THE ERECTION OF THE ARCHBISHOPRICS

The tradition whereby the Scottish Church had bishops but no archbishops remained unbroken until 1472. The elevation, in that year, of the see of St Andrews to archiepiscopal and metropolitan rank came about in peculiar circumstances and certainly not in response to any national demand. Bishop Graham, through his reliance on Rome and his acceptance of the *commenda* of Paisley, found himself in opposition to the policy of the Scottish crown (*supra*, p. 84). In 1471 he went to Rome, obviously to seek papal support,[1] which was forthcoming in the erection of his see as an archbishopric.

---

[1] Herkless and Hannay, *Archbishops of St Andrews*, i, 42–3

The sees now subjected to St Andrews included not only those which had previously acknowledged no metropolitan, but also three others which had previously been subject to metropolitans outwith Scotland. (a) Orkney had hitherto been in the province of Nidaros (Trondheim), but was now territorially in Scottish possession. (b) The diocese of Sodor (Sudreys) and Man had also been in the province of Nidaros. The Scottish portion of this bishopric had become a separate entity—the see of The Isles—owing to the loss by the Scots of the Isle of Man and, subsequently, the Schism, when England and Scotland acknowledged different popes. (c) Galloway had passed from the effective control of York during the Schism and had become in practice one of the Scottish bishoprics by the reign of James I.

Bull erecting the archbishopric of St. Andrews

1472. Sixtus . . . Since in the famed realm of Scotland, in which a large number of notable cathedral churches are known, there is said to be no metropolitan church, and for that reason for every case which the inhabitants of that realm wish to plead against their ordinaries at the time, and for the appeals which they, oppressed in their courts, put forward, they must, not without very grave perils, inconveniences and expenses, have recourse to the Roman *curia* or abandon their rights untried, and it sometimes happens that these cases are drawn to a forbidden court and dealt with there, and the same ordinaries because of the lack of a Metropolitan and the distance of the Roman *curia* have a more free opportunity for overburdening and overstepping their power with impunity, thinking it is easier to do illicit things, and excesses and crimes which are wont to be punished by the metropolitans in their provinces in the aforesaid kingdom often remain unpunished : and since the venerable church of St. Andrew of the said kingdom is distinguished and famous among the other churches of the kingdom, for a celebrated city and ample diocese in which our dearest son in Christ, James, king of Scotland, and his predecessors, kings of Scotland for the time, were wont frequently to make residence with their court, and surrounded by a well-watered plain, adorned by the pleasantness of clergy and people and worthy to be of a deserved metropolitan prelacy :

We . . . erect the aforesaid church and episcopal seat of St. Andrews into a metropolitan and the archiepiscopal seat of the whole realm aforesaid, and we honour it in like manner and adorn it by the gift of special grace by the title of metropolitan dignity and archiepiscopal honour, and we assign to it Glasgow, Dunkeld, Aberdeen, Moray, Brechin, Dunblane, Ross, Caithness, Whithorn, Lismore, Sodor or the Isles and Orkney, the churches of the said realm, with their cities, dioceses, rights and all pertinents, and the whole aforesaid realm for its archiepiscopal province, and the prelates of the same churches for its suffragans and all the clergy of the cities and dioceses aforesaid for its provincials and we subject them to it in respect of archiepiscopal rights . . . so that the archbishop of St. Andrews shall claim for himself metropolitan and archiepiscopal right in the said kingdom and in each of the aforesaid cities and dioceses, and that the bishops of Glasgow, Dunkeld, Aberdeen, Moray, Brechin, Dunblane, Ross, Caithness, Whithorn, Lismore, Sodor or the Isles and Orkney shall be obliged to him in all and sundry as their metropolitan and archbishop and shall be bound in those things in which suffragans are held to their archbishop and shall be bound according to canonical sanctions :

And we decree that to our venerable brother Patrick, bishop of St. Andrews, and to his successors, bishops of St. Andrews for the time, shall be assigned the pall and cross in token of the plenitude of pontifical office and the archiepiscopal dignity, and the church of St. Andrews as Metropolitan ; and that the said present bishop and those who will be in their time bishops of St. Andrews ought to be esteemed and in all future times called and named archbishops of St. Andrews, ought to wear the archiepiscopal and metropolitan insignia, and be able to do, conduct, exercise, pursue and administer the rights, jurisdictions and all and sundry things which metropolitans can

of right do and exercise in their cities, dioceses and provinces. . . .

We ordain that the archbishop and church of St. Andrews
aforesaid and also the beloved sons the chapter of the same
church of St. Andrew shall hold and enjoy all and sundry
privileges, exemptions, immunities, apostolic graces and
indults and any other things which archbishops, metropolitan churches and their chapters can in any way use
and enjoy from custom or of right ; and that the aforesaid
suffragans, their clergy and people altogether shall show
reverence and honour to their said archbishop and metropolitan. . . .

Given at Rome at St. Peter's 13 August 1472, in the
first year of our pontificate.

Translated from Robertson, *Concilia Scotiae*, i, cx

St Andrews did not secure unchallenged supremacy over the
Scottish province. Aberdeen was exempted from its jurisdiction
from 1474 to 1480, Glasgow received exemption in 1488, Moray
was exempt from about 1509 until 1514, and there was a proposal
to renew Aberdeen's exemption in 1513. Jealousy of the new
rank of St Andrews was especially keen in Glasgow, but—just as
had happened with St Andrews itself—it was largely for personal
reasons that Glasgow was made an archbishopric. Archbishop
Schevez of St Andrews had been a supporter of James III, and
was not *persona grata* to the government which came into power
after Sauchieburn. Blackadder of Glasgow, on the other hand,
was then in favour.[1] That was the background to the following
act of parliament, which led to the elevation of Glasgow to
archiepiscopal status in 1492.

Decision of the estates that Glasgow should be an archbishopric

1489. Item it is concludit and ordanit be oure soverane
lord and his thre estatis that for the honour and gud public
of the realme the sege of Glasgw be erect in ane archi-

[1] The body of councillors appointed, in June 1489, to serve in constant attendance on the king included Blackadder but not Schevez
(*A.P.S.*, ii, 215, c. 8).

bischoprik with sic previlegiis as accordis of law and siclik as the archibischoprik of York has in al dignites emuniteis and previlegiis as use and consuetud is and as salbe compakkit and aggreit betuix the said bischop of Glasgow and the prelatis and baronis that oure soverane lord will tak with him to be avisit with. And that nane of the kingis leigis do in the contrar hereof under the kingis indignacioun and panis of brekin of his actis of Parliament.

A.P.S., ii, 213, c. 2

Bull erecting the archbishopric of Glasgow

1492. Innocent. . . . Noticing that in the whole realm of Scotland there is merely one metropolitan, namely the church of St. Andrews, to which Glasgow and all the other churches of the said realm are subjected by metropolitan right, and that if there were in the realm one other metropolitan church to which some part of the said realm were assigned for its archiepiscopal province, then, for a more beneficial and more diligent exercise of metropolitan jurisdiction and the convenience of the churches which would be subjected to its metropolitan right, it would be to the advantage of those, present and to come, of the presiding prelates and of the clergy and people of the cities and dioceses which could likewise more easily and conveniently have recourse in their occasions to the president of the church which would be erected into a metropolitan and it would be to the honour and adornment of the same church and the said kingdom whose kings and inhabitants have always been faithful and devoted to the apostolic see, and having due respect to the persistent requests which have been and are made to us by our very dear son in Christ, James IV, illustrious king of the said kingdom, and the three estates viz. the clergy, the nobles or magnates and the people of the said kingdom, after mature deliberation on these matters with our brothers the cardinals of the Holy Roman Church, on their advice, to the praise and glory of God, and the exaltation of the Catholic faith, by apostolic authority, by the tenor of the presents, we separate, divide and dismember the churches, cities and dioceses of Glasgow aforesaid, Dunkeld, Dunblane, Whithorn and Lismore, from the province of the aforesaid metropolitan church of St. Andrews, and we release and totally free our venerable brothers of the same churches thus separated, the bishops and beloved sons, clergy and lay, of the cities and dioceses from the lordship, superiority and jurisdiction of our venerable brother William recent and present archbishop of St. Andrews.

We wish that the churches so separated and their prelates, also the clergy and people of the same cities and dioceses be not in future subject to the metropolitan right of St. Andrews, and by the advice of the same brothers and by the said authority, we erect and create the aforesaid church of Glasgow, distinguished and notable among the other cathedral churches of that realm and adorned by the beauty and celebrity of its city, the size of its diocese, the number of the clergy and people of the diocese and the fertility of its land, into a metropolitan with the archiepiscopal dignity, jurisdiction and superiority, with the bearing of the cross and other metropolitan signs ; and with the same consent and authority we grant and assign to it the prelates of the churches of Dunkeld, Dunblane, Whithorn and Lismore as its suffragan bishops, and the aforesaid clergy and people of the same churches, cities and dioceses for its provincials, clergy and people, and we wish that they be subject in so far as all metropolitan and archiepiscopal superiority, jurisdiction and rights to the present archbishop of Glasgow and that they should be as members obedient to the head and should answer to all archiepiscopal rights, notwithstanding apostolic constitutions and ordinances and letters and privileges granted to the archbishop of St. Andrews. . . .

Translated from Registrum Episcopatus Glasguensis
(Maitland Club), ii, 470–2

GENERAL STATE OF THE CHURCH

The general state of the church is illustrated by two documents, one at the beginning, the other at the end, of this period. James I was not merely concerned to check papal aggression, but had a genuine regard for the welfare of the church ; this emerges in his letter to the prelates of the Benedictine and Augustinian orders, and is also indicated by his foundation, in 1429, of the Charterhouse at Perth—Scotland's only house of the strict Carthusian order. The act of 1541 ' for reforming of kirks and kirkmen,' came, much less fittingly, from a government which had itself done much to induce disregard for spiritual and moral considerations.

James I's letter to the prelates of the Benedictine and Augustinian Orders

1425. James, by the grace of God king of Scots, to the venerable fathers in Christ the abbots and priors of the orders and rules of St. Benedict and St. Augustine, greeting and an ascent to the highest reaches of perfection. The downhill condition and most threatening ruin of holy religion, now declining from day to day from the original establishment of its foundation, fill us with apprehension and impel us the more sharply to rouse your sluggish minds and the sloth of their torpor. Accordingly it is meet to bestir you and to recall to your hearts how in our realm the decline of monastic religion, everywhere defamed and reduced to contempt, particularly through the laxity of prelates, tends to destruction, even as of old Mother Jerusalem was despised by degenerate sons and repudiated by ignoble fathers, and herself truly—which we relate sadly, with repressed bitterness—thrown to earth, cast down and dishonoured : against whose pitiful or rather pitiable over-throw there cries aloud to the ears of the Lord the Daughter of Hosts, Holy Syon, the Church, [saying] that its regular discipline, of old shining with angelic countenance and drawn up like a terrible array of strongholds, [now] through the fathers of iniquity and undisciplined sons turns away from us its face, because it is left stricken and afflicted with disgrace, foul and fit for the deepest compassion, through your evil work and example. Wherefore, and by reason of the foregoing, wounded in the casket of our soul and heavy in our heart, deeply touched, desiring to the utmost that as soon as possible the foregoing be reformed, we require and warn your religious fatherhoods, exhorting you in the bowels of Jesus Christ that, laying aside excuses for all your faults and slackness, you apply yourselves, at convenient place and time, to the reformation of this your holy religion—too far, as we have said, decayed—and that with diligent consideration and ripe discussion you take care to find by convenient ways, according to God's will, especially in the holding of general chapters, in what manner the fervour of religion can most easily be revived to its pristine state, lest through your negligence and idleness the munificence of kings, who formerly for their preservation and the salvation of their subjects notably endowed your monasteries in olden days and nobly enriched them, may repent of having erected walls of marble when it considers that you have so shamelessly abandoned your religious character. So let there arise with vigour against this disgraceful plague a holy severity, and let a firm discipline, with spiritual fervour more fully conceived, take away all these occasions of decay. Observing that where the bond of discipline is despised the only result can be that religion is shipwrecked, we, therefore, desiring to quicken you, intend, while you apply yourselves to the foregoing, to make every effort and by royal protection to direct and defend you and your deeds according to God's will, constraining and repelling (so far as we are obliged) gainsayers if any be ; we shall rejoice also to have you as interceders who may pray for our royal estate, by whom surely the honour and profit of our realm shall prosper. May the Highest direct your fatherhoods to be successful and fortunate in the cultivation of your religion and in all godly issues. Given under the testimony of our privy seal in our parliament at Perth, 17 March in the 19th year of our reign.

A.P.S., ii, 25 (translated)

Act for ' reforming of kirks and kirkmen '

1541. . . . Becaus the negligence of divyne service, the grett unhoneste in the kirk throw nocht making of reparatioun to the honour of God Almychty and to the blissit sacrament of the altar, the Virgyne Mary and all the haly sanctis and als the unhonestie and misreule of kirkmen baith in witt, knawlege and maneris, is the mater and cause that the kirk and kirkmen are lychtlyit [1] and contempnit : for remeid hereof, the kingis grace exhortis and prayis oppinly all archibischopis, ordinaris and uthir prelatis and every kirk man in his awne degre to reforme thare selfis, thair obedienciaris and kirkmen under thame, in habit and maneris to God and man and that thai cause in every kirk within thair diocy under thare jurisdictioun, cure, reule, reparatioun and reparaling to be honestlie and substantiouslie maid and done to the honour of God Almychti, the blissit sacrament and divine service, every kirk eftir the qualite and quantite of the rentis, and giff ony persoun allegiand thame exemit and will nocht obey nor obtemper to thare superiour in that behalf the kingis grace sall find remeid tharfore at the papis halynes and siclik aganis the saidis prelatis giff thai be negligent.

A.P.S., ii, 370, c. 4

The ' abuse of cursing '

Before the Reformation it was an important function of the church and its courts to issue ' monitions ' or ' cursings.' Gradually, however, this ' diligence ' came to be used for offences so trivial that the threatened censures were mocked and despised and the whole system brought into disrepute. In the 1530s reformers attacked the ' abuse of cursing,' alleging that a bishop would sell

---

[1] despised

for a ' plack ' a letter of cursing against ' all that look over our dyke,' and a priest invoke solemn maledictions for the theft of a porridge-stick, a flail and a horn spoon.[1]

The monition proper was in Latin, issued in the name of a bishop, and it directed some cleric of lower rank to denounce those who had incurred its penalties of excommunication, aggravation, reaggravation and interdict. This denunciation was pronounced in the vulgar tongue, either at the altar when the parishioners were assembled for divine service, or in some other public place. The denunciation or ' cursing ' from which extracts are given below followed an excommunication of Border reivers by Archbishop Dunbar of Glasgow in 1525. It appears that, while the general tenor of the denunciation, and particularly its closing phrases, must have been stereotyped, the composer was at liberty to introduce elaboration and expansion of the curse, with suitable historical illustrations and local allusions.

[*The priest first relates that the archbishop's letters telling of his distress at the violent deeds of reivers in many parts of his diocese, have commanded*] me or ony uthir chaplane to denunce, declair and procleme thame oppinlie and generalye cursit at this merket croiss and al uthere public placis. [*Then, in the name of the Trinity, the Blessed Virgin, the angels, patriarchs and apostles and a variety of saints, he declares the criminals to be*] cursit, wareyt,[2] aggregit and reaggregit with the grete cursing.

I curse thare heid and all the haris of ther heid, I curse thare face, thare ene, thare mouth, thare neyse, thare tounge, thare teith, thare cragis, thare schulderis, thare breystis, thare hartis, thare stomokis, thare bakis, thare waymes, thare armys, thare leggis, thare handis, thare feyt, and everilk part of thare bodys fra the top of ther heides to the sole of ther feyt, before and behynde, within and without ; I curse thame gangand, I curse thaim rydand, I curse thame standand, I curse thame sittand, I curse thaim

---

[1] Knox, *History of the Reformation in Scotland* (ed. Dickinson), i, 15–16

[2] wareyt = curseth

eittand, I curse thaim drynkand, I curse thaim walkand, I curse thaim slepand, I curse thaim rysand, I curse thaim lyand, I curse thaim at hame, I curse thaim fra hayme, I curse thaim within the houssis, I curse tham without the houssis, I curse thare wyiffis, thare bayrnis and ther servandis participant with thame in thare evil and myscheiffus deidis ; I wayry thare cornis, thare catall, thare woll, thare scheip, thare horsis, thare swyne, thare geyse, thare hennis, thare cokkis and all ther quyk gudis, I wayry thare hallis, thare chalmeris, thare beddis, thare kechynis, thare stabillis, thare bernys, thare byris, thare berneyardis, thare cail-yardis, thare pleuchis, thare harrowis and all the gudis and houssis that ar necessar for thare sustentatioun and welefare.

All the malysonis and waryesonis that ever gatt warldly creature sen the beginnyng of the warld to this houre mot lycht apoun thame—the maledictioun of God that lychtit apoun Lucifere and al his fallowis that straik thame fra the hevin to the deip pott of hell mot lycht apoun thame . . . the watteris and riveris of Tuede Teviot Clyde Nyth Esk Euse and Annande and all utheris watteris quhare tha ryde gang or pass mot droun thaim as the Reid Sey drounit kyng Pharao and the peple of Egipt perseuande Goddis peple of Israel . . . the maledictioun that lychtit suddandlie apoun fayr Absalon rydand contrare his fadere kyng David, servand of God, throuch the wod quhen the branchis of ane tree fred him of his horse and hangit him be the hair mot lycht apoun tham, rydand aganis trew Scottismen, and hang thame siclike that all the warld ma see the vengiance of God cum apoun thame, . . . and als all the vengeancis that ever was takin sen the warld began for oppyn synnis and al the plagis and pestilence that ever fell on man or beist mot fall apoun thame for thare oppin reyffis saikles slauchteris and schedding of innocent blude.

I dissevir and partis thame fra the kirk of God and deliveris thame quyk to the devill of hell thare perpetualy to remane condampnit in body and saule quhill thai convert to God and mak amendis for thare cruell trespasses,

I interdyte all and syndry the kyrkis abbais collegis chapellis and oritouris citteis burghis tounis castellis villagis and houssis and all and quhatsumever placis that thai cum to or remanis in fra all messis sayng and celebration of divine service and ministratioun of the sacramentis of halykirk except the sacrament of baptisme alanerly ; and thare bodeys at happinnis to dee under this cursing and inter-dictioun to be cassyn furth to doggis and beistis and nothir to be erdit in kirk nor kirkyard bot in myddinis myris and uthire vile and foull places ; and attour I forbyd and inhibitis al preistis and kirkmen under the pane of the gret cursing to schryif or absolve thame of ther synnis quhil thai be first assoilyeit fra this cursing ; I forbid and inhibitis alsua al Cristin man and woman til have ony cumpany with thame eittand drynkand speikand prayand lyand gangand standand or ony uthir deid doand under the pane of deidlye syne. I discharge al bandis actis contractis aithis and obligationis maid to thame be ony personis othire of lautie kyndnes or manrent sa lang as thai sustene this cursing and interdictioun sua that na man be bundin to thame and that thai be bundin til all men. I tak fra thaim and cryis doune al the gude deidis that ever tha did or sal do quhill thai ryse fra this cursing. I declair thame part-less of al matynis messis evinsangis dirigis or uthire prayeris on buke or beid of al pilgramagis and almous deidis done or to be done in haly kirk or be Cristin peple induring this cursyng ; and fynaly I condampne thame perpetualy to the deip pott of hell to remane with Lucifere and Baelzebub and al ther fallowis devillis of hell and ther bodeys to the galloussis first to be hangit syne revyn and ruggit with doggis swyne and utheris vyle beistis abhominable to al the warld ; and as the sounde of this bell gais fra your eris and the lycht of this candle fra your sycht sa mot thare saulis gang fra the visaige of God almychty and ther gude fame fra the warld quhill tha forbeire ther oppin synnis reiffis thyftis slauchteris murthuris spulyeis and byrnyngis foresaidis and ryise fra this terrible cursing and interdic-tioun and mak satisfactioun for ther misdedis and cum to the boissum of haly kirk to ressave and do pennance for the remission of ther oppin synnis foresaidis.

St. Andrews Formulare (Stair Soc.), i, No. 229

' HERESY '

Information about the early history of ' heresy ' in Scotland is extremely scanty. From the cases of Resby and Crawar we may safely deduce that even at an early stage Scottish opinion was influenced by the development of reforming thought in England and Bohemia, arising out of the work of Wyclif (d. 1384) and Hus (d. 1415). The references in the University Statute of 1416 and the Act of Parliament of 1425 perhaps suggest that the dislocation in church life occasioned by the Schism had provided a fertile field for the sowing of the new teaching. Subsequently, a long period of silence is broken by the case of the ' Lollards of Kyle ' in 1494—in itself an isolated incident, but from its nature indicative of the continuance of a body of reforming opinions.

1406–7. *James Resby*

In the same year [1406 ; *day and month left blank*] James Resby, an English priest of the school of John Wycliffe, was burned, condemned as a heretic in a council of the clergy under Master Laurence of Lindores, inquisitor of heretical irregularity, a truly genuine clerk and famous theologian, of holy life and of the highest praise.

This James, although he was held in much renown through his preaching to simple folk, nevertheless included exceedingly dangerous tenets in his teaching. The first of these was that the Pope is not the vicar of Christ ; the second that no one is a pope or a vicar of Christ unless he is holy. And he held forty of suchlike or worse tenets.

Bower, *Scotichronicon*, xv, xx

Combustio Jacobi Henrici apud Perth. A.D. 1407.

Registrum Episcopatus Glasguensis, ii, 316

1416. *Act of the University of St Andrews against Lollardy*

At a Congregation of the University of St Andrews, held on the tenth day of June 1416, it was enacted that all who commenced masters of arts should swear, among other things, that they would resist all adherents of the sect of Lollards.

' Item jurabitis quod ecclesiam defendetis contra insultum lollardorum, et quibuscunque eorum secte adherentibus pro posse vestro resistetis.'

McCrie, *Life of Andrew Melville*, i, Note D
(quoting MS. Records of the University)

1425. *Act of Parliament against heresy*

Item anentis heretikis and lollardis that ilk bischop sall ger inquyr be the inquisicione of heresy quhar ony sik beis fundyne ande at thai be punyst as lawe of halykirk requiris Ande gif it misteris [1] that secular power be callyt therto in suppowale and helping of halykirk.

A.P.S., ii, 7, c. 3

1433. *Paul Crawar*

In the days of King James the First, about the year of God 1431,[2] was deprehended in the University of St Andrews one named Paul Craw,[3] a Bohemian, who was accused of heresy before such as then were called Doctors of Theology. His accusation consisted principally that he followed John Hus and Wycliffe in the opinion of the sacrament, who denied that the substance of bread and wine was changed by virtue of any words ; or that confession should be made to priests ; or yet prayers to saints departed. While that God gave unto him grace to resist them, and not to consent

[1] if need be

[2] cf. Bower's account, *Scotichronicon*, xvi, xx, where the date is given as 1433.

[3] For a note on Paul Craw, Crawar or Kravar, see J. H. Baxter, *Copiale Prioratus Sanctiandree*, 460.

to their impiety, he was committed to the secular judge (for our bishops follow Pilate, who both did condemn and also wash his hands), who condemned him to the fire ; in the which he was consumed in the said city of St Andrews about the time afore written. And to declare themselves to be the generation of Sathan who, from the beginning, hath been enemy to the truth, and he that desireth the same to be hid from the knowledge of men, they put a ball of brass in his mouth to the end that he should not give confession of his faith to the people, neither yet that they should understand the defence which he had against their unjust accusation and condemnation.

Knox, i, 7

1494. *Articles of the Lollards of Kyle*

In the year of God 1494,[1] were summoned before the King and his Great Council, by Robert Blacader, called Archbishop of Glasgow, the number of thirty persons, remaining some in Kyle-Stewart, some in King's-Kyle, and some in Cunningham ; amongst whom [were] George Campbell of Cessnock, Adam Reid of Barskimming, John Campbell of New Mylns, Andrew Shaw of Polkemmet, Helen Chalmers Lady Polkellie [and Marion] Chalmers Lady Stair. These were called the LOLLARDS OF KYLE. They were accused of the Articles following, as we have received them forth of the Register of Glasgow [2] :

I First, That images are not to be had, nor yet to be worshipped.

II That the relics of saints are not to be worshipped.

III That laws and ordinances of men vary from time to time, and that by [3] the Pope.

---

[1] The date can be fixed as falling between 17 March and 10 June 1494.

[2] This ' Register ' was probably the records of the Official—that is, the presiding officer or judge—of the ecclesiastical court of the Diocese of Glasgow. They are not now known to exist. (But see the criticism in *Juridical Review*, xlviii, 128.)

[3] without regard to, or despite

IV That it is not lawful to fight, or to defend the faith. (We translate according to the barbarousness of their Latin and dictament.[1])

V That Christ gave power to Peter only, and not to his successors, to bind and loose within the Kirk.

VI That Christ ordained no priests to consecrate.

VII That after the consecration in the Mass, there remains bread ; and that there is not the natural body of Christ.

VIII That tithes ought not to be given to ecclesiastical men (as they were then called).

IX That Christ at his coming has taken away power from kings to judge.[2] (This article we doubt not to be the venomous accusation of the enemies, whose practice has ever been to make the doctrine of Jesus Christ suspect to kings and rulers, as that God thereby would depose them of their royal seats where, by the contrary, nothing confirms the power of magistrates more than does God's word.—But to the Articles.)

X That every faithful man or woman is a priest.

XI That the unction of kings ceased at the coming of Christ.

XII That the Pope is not the successor of Peter, but where he said, " Go behind me, Sathan."

XIII That the Pope deceives the people by his Bulls and his Indulgences.

XIV That the Mass profiteth not the souls that are in purgatory.

XV That the Pope and the bishops deceive the people by their pardons.

XVI That Indulgences ought not to be granted to fight against the Saracens.

XVII That the Pope exalts himself against God, and above God.

---

[1] phraseology. The additions to Articles IV, VIII, IX, XIX and XXXI, included within parentheses, are evidently comments by Knox himself.

[2] That is, in matters of religion, though Knox seems to confuse the issue.

xviii That the Pope can not remit the pains of purgatory.

xix That the blessings of the bishops (of dumb dogs they should have been styled) are of no value.

xx That the excommunication of the Kirk is not to be feared.

xxi That in to no case is it lawful to swear.

xxii That priests might have wives, according to the constitution of the law.

xxiii That true Christians receive the body of Jesus Christ every day.

xxiv That after matrimony be contracted, the Kirk may make no divorcement.

xxv That excommunication binds not.

xxvi That the Pope forgives not sins, but only God.

xxvii That faith should not be given to miracles.

xxviii That we should not pray to the glorious Virgin Mary, but to God only.

xxix That we are no more bound to pray in the Kirk than in other places.

xxx That we are not bound to believe all that the doctors of the Kirk have written.

xxxi That such as worship the Sacrament of the Kirk (we suppose they meant the Sacrament of the altar) commit idolatry.

xxxii That the Pope is the head of the Kirk of Antichrist.

xxxiii That the Pope and his ministers are murderers.

xxxiv That they which are called principals in the Church, are thieves and robbers.

Knox, i, 8–9

The influence of the Lutheran Reformation, which began in 1517, did not take long to reach Scotland. The Act of Parliament of 1525, printed below, suggests that Scottish commercial contacts with continental ports provided a ready channel for the import of Lutheran literature. The significant addition to the Act, in September 1527, indicates the development of Lutheran teaching within the country, and has a direct bearing on the case of Patrick Hamilton.

Hamilton, born in 1503, was a grandson of James, first Lord Hamilton, and of royal descent on both the paternal and maternal sides. He became abbot, or commendator, of Fearn, about 1517, and subsequently studied at Paris, Louvain and St Andrews. After being accused of heresy in 1527 he fled to the continent, and at Marburg publicly offered for disputation his thesis on Faith and Good Works. Returning to Scotland, he was tried and sentenced, being liable to punishment not only under the established laws of the church but also under the 1527 ' additio ' to the statute of 1525.

1525. *Act anent heresy*

. . . Forsamekle as the dampnable opunyeounis of heresy are spred in diverse cuntreis be the heretik Luther and his discipillis and this realm and liegis has fermelie persistit in the halifaith sen the samin was first ressavit be thaim and never as yit admittit ony opunyeounis contrare the Cristin faith bot ever has bene clene of all sic filth and vice, there-fore that na maner of persoun strangeare that hapnis to arrife with thair schippis within ony part of this realm bring with thaim ony bukis or werkis of the said Lutheris, his discipillis or servandis, desputt or reherse his heresyis or opunyeounis bot geif it be to the confusioun thairof [and that be clerkis in the sculis alanerlie] [1] under the pane of escheting of thair schippis and gudis and putting of thair persounis in presoun, and that this act be publist and proclamit outthrow this realme at all portis and burrowis of the samin [2] sa that thai may allege na ignorance thairof [and all uther the kingis liegis assistaris to sic opunyeounis be punist in semeible wise and the effect of the said act to strik apon thaim etc.[3]].

A.P.S., ii, 295, c. 4

[1] A marginal addition
[2] For letters under the signet to Aberdeen for publication and enforce-ment of this Act, see *Extracts from Council Register of the Burgh of Aberdeen*, i, 110–11.
[3] Addition made by the chancellor and lords of council, 4 September 1527.

This act against heresy was repeated and ratified in 1535, with the marginal addition ' that nane of tham have, use, kepe or consele ony bukis of the sadis heretikis or contenand thair doctrine and opinionis bot that thai deliver the samin to thair ordinaris within xl days under the panis forsadis (*A.P.S.*, ii, 342).

1528. *Sentence on Patrick Hamilton*

Christi nomine invocato. We, James . . . archbishop of St Andrews, . . . with the counsel, decree and authority of the most reverend fathers in God and lords, abbots, doctors of theology, professors of the holy scripture and masters of the university, assisting us for the time, sitting in judgment within our metropolitan church of St Andrew, in the cause of heretical pravity against M. Patrick Hamilton, abbot or pensionary of Ferne . . . have found the same M. Patrick many ways infamed with heresy, disputing, holding, and maintaining divers heresies of Martin Luther and his followers, repugnant to our faith and which is already condemned by general councils and most famous universities. . . . And he being under the same infamy, we decerning before him to be summoned and accused upon the premises, he of evil mind (as may be presumed) passed to other parts, furth of the realm, suspected and noted of heresy. And being lately returned, not being admitted, but of his own head, without licence and privilege, hath presumed to preach wicked heresy. We have found also, that he hath affirmed, published and taught divers opinions of Luther, and wicked heresies, after that he was summoned to appear before us and our council. . . . We . . . do pronounce . . . the said M. Patrick Hamilton . . . to be an heretic . . . and therefore to be condemned and punished, like as we condemn and define him to be punished . . . and therefore do judge and pronounce him to be delivered over to the secular power, to be punished, and his goods to be confiscated. . . .

Foxe's *Acts and Monuments*, quoted by Laing,
Works of John Knox, i, 510–11

Among the prosecutions for heresy in the 1530s, interest attaches to the case of David Stratoun because it illustrates the difficulty which the church now found in collecting its dues—a feature of the period for which there is ample evidence elsewhere. Extracts from Knox's account of Stratoun are given below. Another trial, that of Sir John Borthwick, in 1541, is remarkable partly because the articles of accusation against him have been preserved and partly because Borthwick escaped to England and survived to have the sentence of the cardinal-archbishop formally revoked by the superintendent of Fife twenty years later.[1]

1534. *The case of David Stratoun*

In judgment were produced two, to wit, David Stratoun, a gentleman, and Master Norman Gourlay, a man of reasonable erudition, of whom we must shortly speak. In Master Norman appeared knowledge, albeit joined with weakness. But in David Stratoun could only be espied, from the first, a haterent against the pride and avariciousness of the priests ; for the cause of his delation was, he had made to himself a fish boat to go to the sea, [and] the bishop of Moray (then being prior of St Andrews) and his factors urged him for the teind thereof. His answer was, if they would have teind of that which his servants won in the sea, it were but reason that they should come and receive it where he got the stock ; and so, as was constantly affirmed, he caused his servants cast the tenth fish in the sea again. Process of cursing was led against him, for non-payment of such teinds, which, when he contemned, he was delated to answer for heresy. It troubled him vehemently ; and therefore he began to frequent the company of such as were godly. . . . When he, with the foresaid Master Norman, was produced in judgment . . . great labours were made that the said David Stratoun should have recanted. . . . But he ever standing at his defence, alleging that he had not offended, in the end was adjudged

---

[1] *Register of the Kirk Session of St. Andrews* (Scot. Hist. Soc.), i, 89–104; *St Andrews Formulare*, ii, No. 469.

unto the fire ; and then, when that he perceived the danger, asked grace of the king (which he would willingly have granted unto him), the bishops proudly answered, That the king's hands were bound in that case, and that he had no grace to give to such as by their law were condemned. And so was he, with the said Master Norman, after dinner, upon the twenty-seventh day of August, the year of God 1534 foresaid, led to a place beside the Rood of Greenside ; and there those two were both hanged and burnt, according to the mercy of the papistical kirk.

Knox, i, 24–5

CHAPTER EIGHT

EDUCATION AND LETTERS

THE UNIVERSITIES

By the end of the fifteenth century Scotland enjoyed three universities. Glasgow, founded at the instance of James II and Bishop Turnbull of Glasgow, was to be complementary to, rather than to compete with, the facilities provided at St Andrews,[1] and Aberdeen derived its existence from the initiative of Bishop Elphinstone half a century later. Behind the foundations of both Glasgow and Aberdeen there lies an interest in the encouragement of legal studies, reflecting an increasing concern in the late fifteenth and early sixteenth centuries with the failure of justice in the courts of the judges ordinary (and notably the sheriffs and the barons), and reflecting also new attempts to improve the administration of the law. The ' Education Act ' of 1496 was also part of the endeavour to secure better justice in the courts of the ordinaries, while, significantly, the licence granted to Chapman and Millar to set up ' ane prent ' laid stress upon the printing of the ' books of our laws ' and the ' acts of parliament.'

1451. *Foundation Bull of the University of Glasgow*

Nicholas, bishop, servant of the servants of God, for perpetual memory of the matter. Amongst other blessings which mortal man is able in this transient life by the gift of God to obtain, it is to be reckoned not among the least that by assiduous study he may win the pearl of knowledge, which shows him the way to live well and happily, and by the preciousness thereof makes the man of learning far to surpass the unlearned, and opens the door for him clearly to understand the mysteries of the universe, helps the ignorant, and raises to distinction those that were born in

[1] See R. K. Hannay, ' Early University Institutions at St Andrews and Glasgow : A Comparative Study,' in *Scot. Hist. Rev.*, xi, 266–83.

the lowest place. And therefore the Apostolic See, the prudent administrator of spiritual as well as of temporal things, and the steady and unfailing friend of every commendable undertaking—to the end that men may be moved the more readily to win so lofty a height of human condition, and having won it, may dispense it again to others, always with increase thereof—encourages some, prepares places for others, aids and fosters others, and loads them with gracious favours. Forasmuch, therefore, as it was lately shown to us on behalf of our dearest son in Christ, James, the illustrious king of Scots, that the said king, laudably intending not only the weal of the commonwealth, and indwellers and inhabitants of the country subject to him, but also of neighbouring lands, was very desirous that a university, with every lawful faculty, should be set up and ordained by the Apostolic See in his city of Glasgow, as being a place of renown and particularly well fitted therefor, where the air is mild, victuals are plentiful, and great store of other things pertaining to the use of man is found, to the end that there the Catholic faith may be spread, the simple instructed, equity in judgment upheld, reason flourish, the minds of men illuminated and their understandings enlightened. We, having carefully considered the premises, and also the uncommon sincerity of faith and devotion which the said king is known to bear towards us and the Roman church, are moved with fervent desire that the said city may be adorned with the gifts of the sciences, so that she may produce men distinguished for ripeness of judgment, crowned with the ornaments of virtue, and erudite with the dignities [? learnings] of the various faculties, and that there may be an overflowing fountain of the sciences, out of whose fullness all that desire to be imbued with the lessons of knowledge may drink. Having, therefore, with careful deliberation, deeply weighed all these things, and especially the suitableness of this city, which, as we have heard, is said to be particularly meet and well fitted for multiplying the seeds of learning, and bringing forth salutary fruits, not only for the advantage and profit of the said city, but also of the indwellers and inhabitants of the whole kingdom of Scotland and the regions lying round about, we, being moved with fatherly affection, and inclined by the supplications of the said king in that behalf, to the praise of God's name, and propagation of the orthodox faith, erect, by apostolic authority, a university in the said city, and decree and also ordain that henceforth such university may flourish in the said city in all times to come for ever, as well in theology and canon and civil law as in arts, and every other lawful faculty. And that the doctors, masters, readers and students there may brook and enjoy all and sundry privileges, liberties, honours, exemptions and immunities granted by the Apostolic See, or otherwise in any manner of way to the masters, doctors and students in the university of our city of Bologna : and that our reverend brother, William, bishop of Glasgow, and his successors for the time being, bishops of Glasgow, shall be rectors, called chancellors, of the foresaid university, and shall have the like power and authority over the doctors, masters, scholars and others of such university as the rectors of the schools of the said university of Bologna have. And that those who in process of time shall merit to obtain a diploma in the faculty in which they study, and licence to teach, may be able to instruct others ; and also that those who seek the honour of mastership or doctorate to be conferred on them shall be presented by the doctor or doctors and master or masters of the faculty in which the examination is to be held, to the bishop of Glasgow now and for the time being, and if the church of Glasgow lack the solace of a pastor, to the vicar or official in spiritual things of our beloved sons of the chapter of the said church. Which bishop, or vicar, or official, having called together the other doctors and masters then teaching there, shall diligently attend personally or by deputy to the examination of those that are to be promoted in those things which in any way are requisite for the degree of master or doctor, according to the wont and custom commonly observed in other universities, and shall bestow on them such licence, or confer such honour of mastership, if they shall be found fit and qualified for the same. And those who shall have been examined and approved in the said university of the city of Glasgow, and shall have got such licence to teach, and degree, as aforesaid, shall thenceforth, without any other examination and approval, have full liberty to be regents and to teach, as well in the said city as in each and all other universities in which they shall choose to rule and teach, notwithstanding any statutes and customs, even although strengthened by oath, apostolic confirmation, or any other guarantee, and whatsoever else there may be in the contrary. Let none therefore in any wise infringe this writing of our erection, constitution and appointment, or with foolhardy daring go in the contrary thereof; but if any one shall presume to attempt this, let him know that he shall incur the wrath of Almighty God, and of the blessed apostles Peter and Paul. Given at Rome, at St Peter's, the year of our Lord's incarnation, one thousand four hundred and fifty, the seventh of the Ides of January, and the fourth year of our pontificate.

See *Charters etc. of the City of Glasgow*, 1175–1649
(Burgh Rec. Soc.), pt. ii, pp. 31–5

1495. *Foundation of University of Aberdeen*

The foundation bull of the university of Aberdeen, 10 February 1494/5, is in similar form to that of Glasgow. The king's petition related that ' there are certain places separated from the rest of his kingdom by arms of the sea and very high mountains, in which dwell men rude and ignorant of letters, and almost barbarous, who, on account of the too great distance from the places in which universities flourish, and the dangerous passage to such places, cannot have leisure for the study of letters, nay, are so ignorant of these letters that, not only for preaching the word of God to the people of those parts but also for administering the sacraments of the church, proper men cannot be found ' ; and requested the foundation, in Old Aberdeen, ' in which a temperance of air prevails, and abundance of victuals, convenience of dwellings, and plenty of other things pertaining to the requirements of human life are found,' of a university of general study ' as well in theology and canon and civil law and medicine and the liberal arts as in every other lawful faculty.' The pope granted the petition, appointing the bishop of Aberdeen and his successors chancellors of the university. (See *Nat. MSS. Scot.*, iii, No. viii.)

' EDUCATION ACT '

1496.

This Act, popularly attributed to William Elphinstone, bishop of Aberdeen, is a statement of aims and of educational aspirations rather than a record of achievement. Its purpose was definite —to provide legal training for the sons of those who enjoyed local jurisdictions so that, in due course, local justice could be improved and thereby the pressure of appeals and complaints to the central courts could be relieved. There is no evidence that the Act was ever effective.

It is statute and ordanit throw all the realme that all barronis and frehaldaris that ar of substance put thair eldest sonnis and airis to the sculis fra thai be aucht or nine yeiris of age and till remane at the grammer sculis quhill thai be competentlie foundit and have perfite latyne and thereftir to remane thre yeris at the sculis of art and jure sua that thai may have knawlege and understanding of the lawis. Throw the quhilkis justice may reigne universalie throw all the realme sua that thai that ar schreffis or jugeis ordinaris under the kingis hienes may have knawlege to do justice that the pure pepill sulde have na neid to seik our soverane lordis principale auditouris for ilk small iniure. And quhat baroune or frehaldar of substance that haldis nocht his sone at the sculis as said is haifand na lauchfull essonye bot failyeis heirin fra knawlege may be gottin thairof he sall pay to the king the soum of xx pounds.

A.P.S., ii, 238, c. 3

THE PRINTING PRESS IN EDINBURGH

The chief purposes of the establishment of a printing press in Edinburgh were closely defined in the licence granting the monopoly of book production in Scotland to Chapman and Millar. Printing was seen as a solution to the problem of disseminating knowledge of the law and the statutes throughout the realm, but Chapman and Millar clearly found the printing of the laws too difficult, and no volume of printed Acts appeared until the first volume of the ' Black Acts,' containing the Acts of Parliament from 1424 to 1564, was published in 1566, to be followed later by Sir John Skene's collection covering the period 1424 to 1597. The first known production of the Scottish press was a miscellany which included works of Dunbar and Henryson ; but in 1509/10 the Aberdeen Breviary, Elphinstone's adaptation of prevailing forms for Scottish use, came from the press, and was intended to take the place of the Sarum Breviary which had hitherto been largely used in Scotland. Chapman and Millar tried to assert their right to prevent the import of books, and in January 1509 obtained a decree from the Lords of Council to enforce their monopoly.

1507.

[*King James makes it known to his subjects*] that forsamekill as oor lovittis servitouris Walter Chepman and Andro Millar burgess of our burgh of Edinburgh, has at our instance and request, for our plesour, the honour and proffit of our realme and liegis, takin on thame to furnis and bring hame ane prent with al stuf belangand tharto and expert men to use the samyne, for imprenting within our realme of the bukis of our lawis, actis of parliament, croniclis, mess bukis and portuus [1] efter the use of our realme with additiouns and legendis of Scottis sanctis now gaderit to be ekit thairto and al utheris bukis that sal be sene necessare and to sel the sammyn for competent pricis be our avis and discretioun, thair labouris and expens being considerit.

[1] breviaries

And becaus we understand that this can nocht be per-furnist without rycht greit cost, labour and expens, we have grantit and promittit to thame that thai sal nocht be hurt nor preventit thairin be ony utheris to tak copyis of any bukis furtht of our realme, to ger imprent the samyne in utheris cuntreis to be brocht and sauld agane within our realme to caus the said Walter and Androu tyne thare greit labour and expens.

And als it is divisit and thocht expedient be us and our counsall that in tyme cuming mess bukis, manualis, matyne bukis and portuus bukis eftir our awin Scottis use and with legendis of Scottis sanctis as is now gaderit and ekit be ane reverend fader in God and our traist counsalour Williame bischop of Abirdene and utheris be usit generaly within al our realme als sone as the sammyn may be imprentit and providit ; and that na maner of sic bukis of Salusbery use be brocht to be sauld within our realm in tyme cuming. . . .

R.S.S., i, No. 1546

CHAPTER NINE

THE REFORMATION

THE EVENTS OF 1543

After the death of James V (14 December 1542) it seemed for a time that pro-English and reforming opinions would triumph. Cardinal Betoun, head of the pro-French and papal party, was frustrated in an attempt to seize power, and was committed to ward ; the Earl of Arran, heir presumptive to the throne, was acknowledged as governor and, with the support of the Anglophil elements (reinforced by a number of prominent Scots who had been captured at Solway Moss and released on the understanding that they would further English interests in Scotland), proceeded to authorise the circulation of the Scriptures in the vernacular and to enter into negotiations with Henry VIII whereby Queen Mary should be betrothed to Prince Edward of England.

A series of events soon occurred which completely transformed the situation. By April (1543) Betoun was free and in association with John Hamilton, abbot of Paisley, the governor's half-brother. The churchmen reminded Arran that his own legitimacy depended on ecclesiastical authority, which had annulled his father's first marriage, and hinted that the same authority could therefore set him aside. The earl of Lennox, who was heir presumptive if Arran were declared to be illegitimate, came over from France in May. Further pressure was brought to bear on the governor by the prospect of a Hamilton marriage for Mary if the English match was abandoned. Patriotic resentment against the English alliance was meanwhile aroused by Henry's demands for the custody of the infant queen and for the succession in the event of her death. The treaties of Greenwich, as finally drawn up, contained safeguards for the Scots, but even so Arran was already wavering when he ratified them, and very shortly after he had done so he came to an understanding with Betoun (to whom his son was delivered as a hostage) and renounced the reforming policy. Henry's lack of confidence in Arran had led him, for his part, to decline to ratify the treaties, and he antagonised the

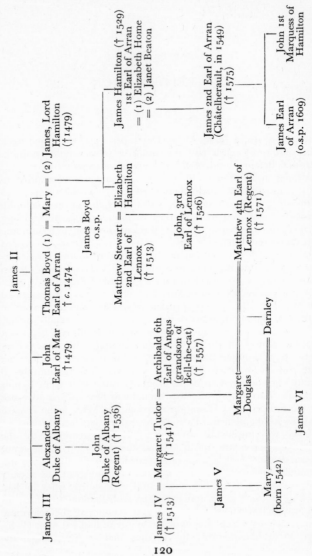

STEWARTS—HAMILTONS—(ANGUS) DOUGLASES

James II

James III

Alexander
Duke of Albany

John
Duke of Albany
(Regent) († 1536)

John
Earl of Mar
† 1479

Thomas Boyd (1) = Mary = (2) James, Lord
Earl of Arran   Hamilton
† c. 1474   († 1479)

James Boyd
o.s.p.

James Hamilton († 1529)
1st Earl of Arran
= (1) Elizabeth Home
= (2) Janet Beaton

Matthew Stewart = Elizabeth
2nd Earl of   Hamilton
Lennox
(† 1513)

James 2nd Earl of Arran
(Châtelherault, in 1549)
(† 1575)

John, 3rd
Earl of Lennox
(† 1526)

James Earl
of Arran
(o.s.p. 1609)

John 1st
Marquess of
Hamilton

James IV = Margaret Tudor = Archibald 6th
(† 1513)   († 1541)   Earl of Angus
                          (grandson of
                          Bell-the-cat)
                          († 1557)

Matthew 4th Earl of
Lennox (Regent)
(† 1571)

James V

Margaret
Douglas

Darnley

Mary
(born 1542)

James VI

120

James, 2nd Earl of Arran, was next in succession to the throne only if his father's divorce from Elizabeth Home was valid ; if that divorce was invalid, then Matthew, 4th Earl of Lennox, was next in succession to the throne.

Scots by the arrest of some Scottish merchants—an action which was made the ground for the formal denunciation of the treaties by the Scottish Estates in December. Laws against heresy were passed, and action was taken in Dundee and Perth, where there had been attacks on religious houses.

Act declaring the earl of Arran governor, 13 March 1542/3

All the lordis sperituale temporale and commissioneris of burrowis representand the thre estatis of parliament hes declarit and declaris James, erle of Arrane, Lord Hammiltoun, secund persoun of this realme and narrest to succede to the crone of the samin falyeing of our sovirane lady and the barnis lauchfullie to be gottin lauchfullie [*sic*] of hir body and nane utheris and be resoun thairof tutour lauchfull to the quenis grace and governour of this realme, and he to use the said office in all thingis unto the perfite aige of our said sovirane lady and all the lieges of this realm to answer and obey to the said erle as tutour lauchfull to hir grace and governour forsaid in all thingis concerning the said office conforme to the actis maid hereupoune of befor, quhilkis thai ratife and appreve in this present parliament.

A.P.S., ii, 411, c. 1

Act authorising the Scriptures in the vernacular, 15 March 1542/3

Anent the writting gevin in be Robert lord Maxwell in presens of my lord gouvernour and lordis of artiklis to be avisit be thaim gif the samin be resonable or nocht of the quhilk the tenour followis : It is statute and ordanit that it salbe lefull to all our souirane ladyis lieges to haif the haly write baith the new testament and the auld in the vulgar toung in Inglis or Scottis of ane gude and trew translatioun and that thai sall incur na crimes for the hefing or reding of the samin providing alvayis that na man despute or hald oppunyeonis under the panis contenit in the actis of parliament The lordis of artiklis beand avisit with the said writting findis the samin resonable and therfor thinkis that the samin may be usit amangis all the

lieges of this realme in our vulgar toung of ane gude trew
and just translatioun becaus thair was na law schewin nor
producit in the contrare And that nane of our said
souirane ladyis lieges incur ony crimes for haifing or reding
of the samyn in forme as said is nor salbe accusit thairfor
in tyme tocum And that na personis despute argoun or
hald oppunionis of the samin under the saidis panis contenit
in the forsaidis actis of parliament.

A.P.S., ii, 415, c. 12

Despite its unusual form this was undoubtedly an Act passed by
the Parliament of March 1543, as shown by the charge to the
Clerk Register for its proclamation. Also, immediately following
the Act, the register contains a protestation by the Archbishop
of Glasgow in his own name and on behalf of all the prelates
present, being one of the three Estates of parliament, opposing
the passing of the Act until the whole question had been considered by a provincial council. It is noticeable that the Act
does not bear to have been concluded by ' the three estates.'

Order for the proclamation of the Act authorising the Scriptures in the vernacular

Gubernator

Clerk of Registri. It is oure will and we charge you that
ye gar proclame this day at the marcat croce of Edinburgh
the actis maid in oure souirane Ladyis parliament that
suld be proclamit and gevin furth to hir liegis and in speciale
the act maid for having of the new testament [1] in ~~Inglis~~
wulgare toung with certane additionis, and thaireftir gif
furth the copyis thairof actentik as efferis to all thame that
will desyre the samyn and inserte this oure command and
charge in the bukis of parliament for youre warrant subscrivit with oure hand At Edinburgh the xix day of
marche the yeir of God J^m v^c and xlij yeris /

James G

A.P.S., ii, 425a

[1] It should be noted that this charge refers only to ' the new
testament,' whereas the Act referred to ' the haly write baith the new
testament and the auld.'

The Treaties of Greenwich, 1 July 1543

[*A treaty of peace, to endure for the lives of Henry and Mary and for a year after the death of the first to die, was accompanied by the marriage treaty, which follows.*]

We have agreed and in name of those by whose special mandate we have sufficient authority for the underwritten do promise that the illustrious and noble prince Edward, eldest son and nearest apparent and undoubted heir of the unconquered and most potent prince Henry VIII, by the grace of God king of England, France and Ireland, Defender of the Faith and Supreme Head on Earth of the Church of England and Ireland, as yet of less age and not six years old, shall marry and have to wife . . . Mary, Queen of Scotland, now also minor and not yet out of her first year.

[*As soon as the marriage takes effect and is consummated, if King Henry be still alive, Mary shall enjoy lands in England to the value of £2,000 sterling yearly ; on Henry's decease, the value is to be increased to £4,000. As the estates of Scotland have appointed certain barons to have the custody of Mary's person, they are to retain it as long as she be in Scotland. Henry is to send to Scotland an Englishman of noble or gentle birth, with his wife or another woman of noble or gentle birth, with their followers and family to the number of twenty persons or less, to live in Mary's household and have free access to her so that they may oversee her feeding and education. As soon as Mary completes her tenth year and reaches her eleventh, she shall be taken in the next month to the vicinity of Berwick to be shown to those whom Henry (if he survive) or Edward shall send there so that they may accompany her to the presence of the English king. Before her departure from Scotland, the contract of marriage shall be concluded by proxy. Within two months of the present treaty, there shall be delivered six Scots nobles as hostages for the observance of the foregoing terms.*]

It is agreed, treated and concluded that, notwithstanding any other effect hoped herefrom through the marriage to follow, the kingdom of Scotland shall nevertheless retain the name of kingdom and be called the kingdom of

Scotland, with all its laws and lawful liberties of the same kingdom, as they have always been, from the beginning, rightly and continuously used and observed and approved in the same kingdom of Scotland.

[And] that if, after the arrival of the most illustrious lady Mary in England and the consummation of her marriage with the most illustrious prince Edward, it happen (which God forbid) the said illustrious prince to die without issue by Mary, in that case the said most illustrious princess Mary is to have free faculty and power to return to the kingdom of Scotland . . . without any impediment or obstacle.

[And] that, at the time when the illustrious princess Mary is brought to the kingdom of England by the present convention, a noble man James, earl of Arran, governor of the kingdom of Scotland, who by that name shall meantime both uplift the fruits of the kingdom and intromit with the goods of the said queen, shall—both himself and his heirs and successors—be at that time freed and discharged by the most illustrious king of England and illustrious prince Edward, and be rendered quit of the fruits received and all the moveable goods with which the said governor has intromitted, reserving only from these moveable goods which then remain a convenient part and portion which is required to direct the person of the said most illustrious princess Mary into England. . . .

[And] that within two months from the date of these presents the present treaty shall be sworn, confirmed and ratified [*by Henry under his great seal and subscription and on the part of the kingdom of Scotland by authority of the three estates and with the consent of the governor, under the seal of Mary.*]

Foedera, xiv, 786–96

Arran's recantation

[*On 25 August Arran solemnly ratified the treaties of marriage and peace with England. Between 4 and 8 September following there took place the* volte-face *described by Knox in these words :*]

The unhappy man . . . quietly stole away from the Lords that were with him in the Palace of Holyroodhouse, passed to Stirling, subjected himself to the Cardinal and to his counsel, received absolution, renounced the profession of Christ Jesus his holy Evangel, and violated his oath that before he had made for observation of the contract and league with England.

[*Knox himself adds the marginal note :*] The governor violated his faith, refused God, and took absolution of [the] devil. [*Arran did penance for his apostasy on 8 September.*]

Knox, i, 50

Denunciation of the treaties of Greenwich, 11th December 1543

The quhilk day anentis the artikle proponit tuiching the pece and contractis of mariage laitlie tane and maid betuix the ambassatoris of our soverane lady the quenis grace and the commissaris of the king of Ingland betuix our said soverane lady and Edward prince of Ingland sone and apperand air to the king of Ingland gif the samyn suld be observit and keipit or nocht. My lord governour and thre estatis of parliament fyndis that the said peice was takin concludit and endit in the begynnyng of the moneth of Julii last bypast betuix the saidis ambassatoris and commissaris of bayth the realmes and the selis to have bene interchengit betuix that and the first day of September nixt therefter exclusive, and thane the said peace was proclamit bayth in Ingland and Scotland and throw pretence tharof the merchandis of Scotland put thair schippis and guidis to the see, and lang befor the said first day of Semptember thai war takin be Inglismen and haldin thame selfis, thair schippis and guidis as yit unrestorit bot demanit as inimeis notwithstanding the said pece and divers message send for delivering of thame. Quhar throw the said king of Ingland hes violate and brokin the said pece and tharfor and becaus the said contract of mariage was grantit for the said peice to have bene had observit and keipit betuix the twa realmes, quhilk was nocht keipit bot brokin and violet be the said

125

king of Ingland as said is, and als becaus my lord governour send bayth the contractis of pece and mariage ratifiit apprevit and sworn be him and selit with our soverane ladeis gret sele according to the indentis befor the said first day of Semptember and causit the samyn to be deliverit to the said king of Ingland quha was requirit be the ambassatoris send be my lord governour to have deliverit the saidis contractis in siclik maneir ratifyit apprevit and sworn be him, and he refusit to do the samyn. My lord governour and thre estatis in parliament forsaid has declarit and declaris the saidis contractis to be expirit in thame selfis and nocht to be keipit in tyme cuming for the part of Scotland be law, equite and just resoun.

A.P.S., ii, 431, c. 2

The ' Rough Wooing '

In his fury at his failure to secure the Scottish marriage by peaceful negotiation, Henry VIII now launched on Scotland, in 1544 and 1545, the cruel invasions of the earl of Hertford, known as the ' Rough Wooing.' As the invaders came from a land which had now cast off the papal authority and had dissolved the monasteries, they were especially destructive of religious houses, and the ruinous condition of the Border abbeys and of Holyrood dates substantially from this period. The devastation caused throughout Lowland Scotland is indicated in the following English documents.

1544. *Instructions of the Privy Council to Hertford*

. . . Put all to fyre and swoorde, burne Edinborough towne, so rased and defaced when you have sacked and gotten what ye can of it, as there may remayn forever a perpetuel memory of the vengeaunce of God lightened upon [them] for their faulsehode and disloyailtye. Do what ye can out of hande, and without long tarying, to beate down and over throwe the castle, sack Holyrod house, and as many townes and villaiges about Edinborough as ye may conveniently, sack Lythe and burne and subverte it and all the rest, putting man, woman and childe to fyre and swoorde without exception where any resistence shalbe made agaynst you, and this done, passe over to the Fyfelande and extende like extremityes and destructions in all townes and villaiges wherunto ye may reche convenyently, not forgetting among all the rest so to spoyle and turne upset downe the Cardinalles town of St Andrews, as thupper stone may be the nether, and not one stick stande by an other, sparing no creature alyve within the same, specially such as either in frendeship or blood be alyed to the Cardinall.

Hamilton Papers, ii, No. 207 (10 April 1544)

Destruction by Hertford's Expeditions

1544.

Exployts don upon the Scotts from the Beginning of July [to 17th November]

Sum Total

Towns, Towers, Stedes, Barnekyns, Paryshe Churches, Bastell-Houses [cast down or burnt]   .   192
Scotts slain   403
Prisoners taken   816
Nolt   10386
Shepe   12492
Nags and Geldings   1296
Gayt   200
Bolls of Corn   850
Insight Geare etc.

Haynes, *State Papers* (1740), 43-51

1545.

Fortresses, Abbeys, Frere-houses, Market Townes, Villages, Towres & Places brent, raced, and cast downe by

commandment of Therll of Hertforde . . . Betwene the
8th of Sept and the 23d of the same

Sum Total 287

    Whereof are

In Monasteries and Frearhouses 7
In Castells, Towres and Piles 16
In Market Townes 5
In Villagies 243
In Mylnes 13
In Spytells and Hospitalls 3

Haynes, *State Papers* (1740), 52–4

WISHART AND BETOUN

George Wishart represents a new element in the Scottish Reformation, for he had been in touch with the Swiss reformers at Zurich.
In his teaching [1] we find that emphatic rejection of all beliefs
and practices for which express scriptural warrant could not be
adduced which was to characterise the pronouncements of John
Knox and was to be prominent in the formal statements of the
Scottish reformers in 1560. After spending some time at Cam-
bridge, Wishart returned to Scotland, probably in the company
of English commissioners engaged in the negotiations of 1543,
a fact which may suggest that his mission should not be dissociated
from a political background. But the fair prospects of 1543 proved
illusory, and it was under changed and difficult conditions that
Wishart proceeded to teach in Montrose, Dundee, Ayrshire and
finally East Lothian, where he was apprehended, at the order
of Cardinal Betoun, early in January 1546. An account of
Wishart's trial, condemnation and death (on 1 March 1545/6),
reproduced by John Knox, who had begun to associate with
Wishart shortly before his arrest, dwells with care and admiration
on the end of a man who was evidently conspicuous for his mild
and lovable nature.

The evidence is insufficient to identify the reforming preacher

[1] So far as it is reflected in the account we have of his examination
(Knox, ii, 236–43).

with the ' Scottish man called Wysshert ' who had been involved in English plots for the murder of Betoun—and what is known of the reformer's character is inconsistent with such an identification ; but such plots there had been, and the desire to avenge Wishart's death now became a further motive for the removal of the cardinal, whose Francophil policy had already been blamed for the suffering caused by the English invasions, and who had also his private enemies among Scottish lairds.

Betoun's murder (29 May 1546) and the seizure of his castle produced a singularly unstable situation. That there was some slight chance of a general protestant revolt is perhaps indicated by the acts of council of 11 June, inveighing against assistance to the rebels and expressing concern about the safety of church properties ; but if there was such a chance it soon vanished, and there was no change of government or of policy. Yet Governor Arran could not press the ' Castilians ' [1] too hard, for his son was in their hands, and might be transferred to English or French custody if those powers intervened in Scotland. The death of Henry VIII (28 January 1546/7) made Hertford (Somerset) protector of England, and Somerset, who continued Henry VIII's policy, had no reason to trust, or to favour, Arran ; when, on 31 March, Francis I of France died, it seemed likely that English intervention would precede French, and at this point Knox decided to enter the castle. In fact, French action anticipated any action by England, and the castle surrendered on 31 July 1547.

1546. *The Burning of George Wishart*

The sons of darkness pronounced their sentence definitive, not having respect to the judgment of God. When all this was done and said, my Lord Cardinal caused his tormentors to pass again with the meek lamb unto the Castle, until such time [as] the fire was made ready. When he was come into the castle, then there came two grey fiends,[2] Friar Scott and his mate, saying, ' Sir, ye must make your confession unto us.' He answered, and said, ' I will make no confession unto you. Go fetch me yonder man that

---

[1] i.e. those, reformers and others, who now held the castle of St. Andrews

[2] Knox's usual term for friars

preached this day, and I will make my confession unto him.' Then they sent for the subprior of the abbey,[1] who came to him with all diligence ; but what he said in this confession, I cannot show. . . .

When that he came to the fire, he sat down upon his knees, and rose again ; and thrice he said these words, ' O Thou Saviour of the world, have mercy upon me : Father of Heaven, I commend my spirit into Thy holy hands.' When he had made this prayer, he turned him to the people, and said these words : ' I beseech you, Christian brethren and sisters, that ye be not offended at the word of God for the affliction and torments which ye see already prepared for me. But I exhort you, that ye love the word of God, your salvation, and suffer patiently, and with a comfortable heart, for the word's sake, which is your undoubted salvation and everlasting comfort. Moreover, I pray you, show my brethren and sisters, which have heard me oft before, that they cease not nor leave off to learn the word of God, which I taught unto them, after the grace given unto me, for no persecutions nor troubles in this world, which lasteth not. And show unto them that my doctrine was no wives' fables, after the con-stitutions made by men ; and if I had taught men's doctrine, I had got greater thanks by men. But for the word's sake, and true Evangel, which was given to me by the grace of God, I suffer this day by men, not sorrowfully, but with a glad heart and mind. For this cause I was sent, that I should suffer this fire for Christ's sake. Consider and behold my visage, ye shall not see me change my colour. This grim fire I fear not ; and so I pray you for to do, if that any persecution come unto you for the word's sake ; and not to fear them that slay the body, and afterward have no power to slay the soul. Some have said of me, that I

---

[1] i.e. John Winram, whose very temperate sermon had been in marked contrast to the brutality attributed to John Lauder, Wishart's principal accuser (Knox, ii, 233–4). Winram seems even at this time to have been a moderate reformer rather than a rigid conservative, and he later became superintendent of Fife in the reformed church.

taught that the soul of man should sleep until the last day ; but I know surely, and my faith is such, that my soul shall sup with my Saviour this night, or it be six hours, for whom I suffer this.' . . .

Then, last of all, the hangman, that was his tormentor, sat down upon his knees and said, ' Sir, I pray you, forgive me, for I am not guilty of your death.' To whom he answered, ' Come hither to me.' When he was come to him he kissed his cheek and said, ' Lo ! Here is a token that I forgive thee. My heart, do thine office.' And then, by and by, he was put upon the gibbet, and hanged, and there burnt to powder. When that the people beheld the great tormenting of that innocent, they might not withhold from piteous mourning and complaining of the innocent lamb's slaughter.

Knox, ii, 244–5

1546. *Acts of Council following the murder of Cardinal Betoun*

The quhilk day, the Quenis Grace, my Lord Governour, and Lordis of Counsel, understandand that the personis that committit the cruel slauchter of umquhile ane maist reverend fader in God, David Archbischop of Sanctandrois, Cardinal Legate Apostolik and Chancellar of Scotland, with utheris that ar cumin to thame sensyne and takis the said slauchter planelie upoun thame, hes takin and withholdis the castel of Sanctandrois, and ar planelie fortifiit, menteinyt, helpit, and suppleit with otheris our Soverane Ladyis liegis, quilk is prejudiciale to hir Graces autoritie. Tharefor ordanis letteres to be direct to heraldis, pursevantis, masseris, and utheris officiaris of armes, chargeing thame that tha pas to the mercat croces of the burrowis of Dunde, Perth, Forfar, Cowper, Sanctandrois, Edinburgh, pere of Leith, Kirkcaldy, Disart, Kingorne, Crale, Hadington, Northberwik, Dunbar, and all utheris places neidful, and thair, be oppin proclamatioun, command and charge all and sindry our said Soverane Ladyis liegis, of quhat degree that evir tha be of, that nane of thame tak upoun hand to pas, commoun, talk, nor speik with any of the saidis personis being within the said castel of Sanctandrois, within the samin or outwith, be thair selffis, messengeris or ony uther immediate personis ; nor yit tak upoun hand to sell, or furnes thame with ony mete, drynk, quhete, bere, malt, mele, flour, nor salt, fish, flesh, fyre, or ony maner of gunneris munitioun, or wappynnis, awther be sey or land, under the pane of tinsel of lyff, landis, and gudis, with certificatioun to tham and tha falye, that tha salbe callit to particular diettis and scharplie punist thairfor as accordis with all rigour.

Register of the Privy Council, i, 26 (11 June 1546)

The quhilk day, my Lord Governour, with avise of the Quenis Grace and Lordis of Counsal, understandand that throw the occasioun of this troublous tyme, and grete inobedience maid baith to God and man in the committing of diverse enorme and exhorbitant crymes, it is dred and ferit, that evill disponit personis will invaid, distroy, cast doun, and withhald abbays, abbay places, kirkis, alswele paroche kirkis as utheris religious places, freris of all ordouris, nunreis, chapellis and utheris spirituale mennis houssis, aganis the lawis of God and man, and incontrair the liberte and fredome of halikirk and actis of parliament maid thairupoun observit and kepit in all tymes bigane ; and for eschewing and stopping of all sik inconvenientis it is divisit, statute, and ordanit that lettres be direct our all partis of this realme, and all Shereffis, Stewartis, Ballies, and thair Deputis, and to the Provostis, Aldermen, and Ballies of burrowis, and to utheris officiaris of the Quenis, Shereffs in that part, chargeing tham to pas to the mercat croces of all burrowis within this realme, and thare, be oppin proclamatioun, command and charge all and sindry our Soverane Ladyis liegis, that nane of thame tak upon hand [to invaid] ony of the saidis kirkis, religious places, or utheris kirkis and kirkmennis houssis forsaidis, or to withhald, intromitt, or tak the samin at thair awine hand be way of deid in ony tymes cuming, or to spulye the jowellis or ornamentis of the kirk ordanit for Goddis service and dedicat to the samyn, under the pane of tinsell of lyff, landis, and gudis. And giff ony sik kirkmennis houssis or places be ellis takin be quhatsumevir personis, ordanis the takaris and withhaldaris of the samin to restor and deliver the samin again to the awneris thairof and thair factoris, under the said pane, and ordanis this Act to be ratiffyt in Parliament.

Reg. Privy Council, i, 28–9 (11 June 1546)

PINKIE AND THE TREATY OF HADDINGTON, 1547–8

Somerset had been too late to relieve the defenders of St Andrews Castle, but he invaded Scotland later in the year and won an easy victory at Pinkie. On the eve of the battle there was an act of council on the lines of those for Harlaw and Flodden,[1] but including an assurance that church livings would remain with the kin of the holders. English troops were soon in occupation of large tracts of Lowland Scotland, and in the spring of 1548 established themselves firmly at Haddington, as headquarters from which they could dominate the south-east. The Scots had little hope of regaining this strategic centre without external aid. They appealed to France for help, and when it came a combined Franco-Scottish force laid siege to the town. But French assistance was given only on conditions, and the Scottish Estates, meeting at the nunnery of Haddington on 7 July 1548, had to agree that their young queen should be sent to France to become the bride of the heir to the French throne, thereby ' putting everything into the hands of the French king.' But there was no immediate interference in Scottish domestic affairs, and, moreover, the Franco-Scottish agreement necessitated an understanding between the French crown and the earl of Arran, whose son, having no longer the prospect of marrying Mary, was taken to France as a hostage (though with the promise of a notable French bride).[2] On the other hand, Arran was guaranteed the governorship during Mary's minority, with no inquiry into his financial

---

[1] See *supra*, p. 60   [2] *Balcarres Papers* (Scot. Hist. Soc.), i, 197–8

dealings [1] ; the bulls appointing his brother, John, as Betoun's successor, were at last released ; and a few months later he himself received the rich French duchy of Châtelherault.

Act on the eve of the battle of Pinkie, 8 September 1547

The quhilk day my lord governour and all the nobill men baronis frehaldaris and gentilmen, being convenit and assemblit togidder to pas fordwart for defens of this realm and resisting of our auld ynemeis of Ingland now instantlie approchand to my lord governour and his army, hes divisit, statute and ordanit alsweill be my lord governouris awin consent as be consent of the nobill men baith spirituale and temporall, that, gif it sal happin, as God forbid, ony erle, lord, baron, frehaldar, vassal, subvassale, fewaris, malaris, takkismen, rentalaris and possessouris or commonis to be slane or tak seiknes quhairthrow thai happin to deceis at this present army, that thar airis, executoris or assignis sall frelie haif thar awin wardis, relevis and mariages in thar awin handis to be disponit tharupoun as thai sall think expedient, and siclik thar wyffis barnis executoris or assignis sall brouk and jois thar takkis stedingis rowmes [2] and possessionis alsweill of kirklandis as of temporall mennis landis and enter tharto and remane tharwith frelie for the space of five yeris without ony gressum or entres silver payand allanerlie maill and dewiteis usit and wont.

And the said acte alsweill to extend upoun kirkmennis vasallis and temporall mennis as the quenis and forther ordanis the Clerk of Register to extend the samyn acte in the maist ample and largest forme to the effect forsaid and to register the samin in the bukis of consale.

The quhilk day my lord governour with avise and consent of all the prelattis, kirkmen, erles, lordis, baronis and all utheris patronis of benefices baith spirituall and temporall understandand that the haill body of the realm is passand fordward at this tyme to resist our auld inemeis of Ingland

---

[1] Ibid., ii, xxxvi–viin   [2] portions of land

now cuming in this realme to invaid the samyn, ordanis that quhatsumever kirkman that happynnis to be slane in this present army hurt to the deid or takkis seiknes in the samyn and deis in the said seikness gangand remanand or cumand tharfra that the nerrest of the said kirkmennis kin salhaif the presentatioun provisioun and collatioun of his benefice for that tyme allanerlie, and the samyn to be disponit to the narrest of his kin that happynnis to be slane or deceiss in maner forsaid maist abill therfor, and the proffittis of thir beneficis with the fruttis speciall on the ground with the annett therefter to pertene to thaim and thair executouris alsweill abbottis, prioris and all utheris religious men and all uther kirkmen.

A.P.S., ii, 599–600, cc. 2, 3

1548. *The Treaty of Haddington*

In the Parliament . . . haldin at the
Abbay of Hadingtoun [7 July 1548].

The quhilk day Monsiour Dessy [1] Lieutennent generall of the navy and armie send be the maist Christin king of France for support of this Realme at this present tyme schew . . . how that the said maist Christin king hes set his haill hart & minde for defence of this Realme, desyrit in his said maisters name for the mair perfyte union and indissolubill band of perpetuall amitie lig & confederatioun the mariage of our soverane Lady, to the effect that the said maist Christin kingis eldest sone and Dolphin of France may be conjunit in matrimonie with hir grace to the perpetuall honour plesour and proffeit of baith the Realmes, observand and keipand this Realme and liegis thairof in the samin fredome liberteis & lawis as hes bene in all kingis of Scotlandis tymes bypast ; and sall mantene & defend this Realme and liegis of the samin as he dois the Realme of France and liegis thairof . . . . And thairfoir

[1] André de Montalembert, sieur d'Essé

desyrit my Lord Governour and thre Estatis of Parliament
to avise heirwith and gif thair determinatioun thairintill
gif the desyre foirsaid be ressonabill & acceptabill or not.
The Quenis grace our soverane Ladyis maist derrest mother
being present, my Lord Governour and thre Estatis of
Parliament foirsaid all in ane voice hes fundin and decernit
and be censement of Parliament concludit the desyre of the
said Monsiour Dessy Lieutennent in name of the said maist
Christin king his maister (Monsiour Dosell [1] his Ambassa-
dour present in the said Parliament confirmand the samin)
verray ressonabill, and hes grantit that our said Soverane
Lady be maryit with the said Dolphin at hir perfyte age,
and presentlie gevis thair consent thairto swa that the said
king of France keip manteine and defend this Realme liegis
of the samin liberteis & lawis thairof as he does his awin
realme of France and liegis of the samin. . . .

My Lord Governour in our soverane ladyis name ratifeis
and apprevis in this present Parliament the determinatioun
and consent of the thre Estatis of the samin being present
concerning the mariage of our Soverane Lady with the
Dolphin of France conforme to the act of Parliament maid
thairupone, provyding alwayis that the king of France, the
said Dolphinnis derrest fader, keip and defend this realme,
lawis and liberteis thairof, as his awin realme, liegis and
lawis of the samin and as hes bene keipit in all kingis tymes
of Scotland bypast, and to mary hir upone na uther persoun
bot upon the said Dolphin allanerlie.

A.P.S., ii, 481–2

ARCHBISHOP HAMILTON'S POLICY OF REFORM FROM WITHIN

The provincial council of the Scottish church, meeting in 1549,
1552 and 1559, freely admitted the prevalence of grave abuses,
and passed statutes designed to reform them. To remedy clerical
immorality, churchmen of all ranks were urged to amend their

---

[1] Henri Cleutin, sieur D'Oysel et de Villeparisis et Saint-Aignan

lives and to confine themselves to their ecclesiastical functions, discipline was to be restored to the monastic houses and greater care was to be taken in admitting men to orders. To combat clerical ignorance, provision was made for the teaching of grammar, divinity and canon law in cathedrals and for sending one or more monks from each monastery to a university. As a practical contribution towards the better education of the clergy, the archbishop in 1554 completed the organisation and endowment of St Mary's college at St Andrews. So that enlightenment should be spread to the people, the councils laid down certain regulations for preaching.

A further step towards the instruction of the laity, pending the training of sufficient preachers, was the issue, in accordance with a decision of the council of 1552, of Archbishop Hamilton's *Catechism*, a statement of doctrine which suggests that the archbishop, though conservative, was not wholly intransigent. It shows signs of the influence of German and English productions of the moderate reforming school, and is quite free from invective against the reformers and their teaching. At some points, for instance in its guarded statement on the sacrificial character of the Eucharist, it is at variance with the *formulae* in which the council of Trent defined the faith for the churches which adhered to the Roman see, and it has been said that in its emphasis on the place of faith in justification it is actually heretical by Tridentine standards. Certainly on this latter issue, and also in its complete silence about papal authority, it represents views not unlike those for which Patrick Hamilton and Sir John Borthwick had been condemned. On the whole the *Catechism* strongly suggests that had political circumstances in Scotland been favourable to a reformation along the lines of Henry VIII's proceedings, clerical support would not have been lacking. Hamilton's production was a substantial book, of 207 leaves. Later, in accordance with a canon of the council of 1559, there was issued a ' Godlie Exhortation ' on the Eucharist, a leaflet of two leaves known to the people as the ' Twapenny Faith.'

But the statutes of the councils are important rather because they are eloquent of the abuses condemned than because they produced results. No scheme of reform could hope to be effective unless it provided for, and secured, a large measure of redistribution of the ecclesiastical revenues. As it was, the wealth and resources of the church were concentrated in the bishoprics, cathedrals, abbeys and collegiate churches, which were maintained at the expense of the parishes, and there was no possibility of an educated clergy and an instructed laity until the balance was redressed. This truth, to which the councils did not allude, is hinted at in a remarkable petition presented to the pope by Cardinal Sermoneta, on behalf of the Scottish Crown, in 1556, which draws a picture of the Scottish church as lurid as that by any protestant pamphleteer. Among other matters, the cardinal mentioned the ruinous condition of church buildings, a subject which was exercising Archbishop Hamilton, whose account of the churches in the Merse is printed below. Complementary to Sermoneta's petition is the report of the Jesuit de Gouda in 1562, which castigates the Scottish bishops. It emerges beyond any doubt that among contemporaries, whatever their theological views, there was no attempt to deny the corruption of the Scottish church ; we can go further, and say that there was no divergence as to the necessity for reform —the only argument was as to the method to be adopted for that end.

Acts of the Provincial Councils

1549.

. . . The present convention of the ordinaries, prelates, and other ecclesiastics and clergy of this realm has been assembled in the Holy Ghost . . . to restore tranquillity and preserve complete unity in the ecclesiastical estate : intently observing how many heresies cruelly assail the Lord's flocks committed to their pastoral care ; and wishing utterly to extirpate these same . . . . And whereas there appear to have been mainly two causes and roots of evils which have stirred up among us so great dissensions and occasions of heresies, to wit, the corruption of morals and profane lewdness of life in churchmen of almost all ranks, together with crass ignorance of literature and of all the liberal arts . . .

Patrick, *Statutes of the Scottish Church*, 84

Item this synod exhorts that neither prelates nor their subordinate clergy keep their offspring born of concubinage in their company, nor suffer them directly or indirectly to be promoted in their churches, nor under colour of any pretext to marry their daughters to barons or make their sons barons out of the patrimony of Christ.

Patrick, *Statutes*, 92

[Repeated, and in much fuller terms, in 1559—Patrick, *Statutes*, 164-5]

Likewise it is statute that no cleric having the means of an honourable livelihood according to his own calling engage in secular pursuits, especially by trading, either for the sake of gain buying that he may sell over again at a profit what he has purchased, or by leasing farms from others allow himself to be withdrawn by farm work from spiritual exercises to the neglect of his proper cure of souls.

Patrick, *Statutes*, 92

[Repeated, and in much fuller terms, in 1559—Patrick, *Statutes*, 166]

1549.

The present convention beseeches in the bowels of Jesus Christ, and for the stirring-up of piety exhorts the ordinaries, all of them and each of them, as well as the rest of the prelates and the incumbents of benefices in the realm, to reform their life and morals to better purpose . . . that by this means all occasions of heresy in this realm may be more easily obviated . . . lest the very persons rashly proceed to the rigorous correction of the morals of others, who are themselves implicated in notorious offences, since from this cause arises the greatest scandal to the laity, and the largest proportion of the heresy.

Patrick, *Statutes*, 124

1552. *Regulations for the use of Hamilton's* Catechism

Considering, moreover, that the inferior clergy of this realm and the prelates have not, for the most part, attained such proficiency in the knowledge of the holy Scriptures as to be able, by their own efforts, rightly to instruct the people in the Catholic faith and other things necessary to salvation, or to convert the erring . . . this present convention decrees and ordains that a certain book, written in our vulgar Scottish tongue, and, after the most elaborate revision, approved by the opinions and votes of the most prudent prelates in the whole realm, and of the most learned theologians and other churchmen . . . shall be put into the hands of rectors, vicars, and curates, as much for the instruction of themselves as of the Christian people committed to their care : which book it orders to be called a catechism, that is to say, a plain and easy statement and explanation of the rudiments of the faith . . . to be published and reproduced in many copies . . . . And of this catechism the several chapters and the sundry sections . . . shall be read, with the greatest possible reverence, by the rectors in person, or by their vicars or curates who take charge of the parish, standing in the pulpit, vested in surplice and stole, on all Sundays and holydays . . . in a loud and audible voice, distinctly, clearly, articulately, and with attention to the stops . . . . The said rectors, vicars, or curates must not go up into the pulpit without due preparation, but they must prepare themselves with all zeal and assiduity for the task of reading by constant, frequent, and daily rehearsal of the lesson to be read, lest they expose themselves to the ridicule of their hearers when, through want of preparation, they stammer and stumble in midcourse of reading.

Patrick, Statutes, 143–6

Hamilton's Catechism *on the Eucharist*

First it is callit the Eucharist, that is to say, gud grace, because it contenis him really and essentially, quhilk is the well and giffar of grace, of quhais aboundance we all ressave. It is callit the Communioun, for be worthi ressaving of this sacrament al trew Christin men and wemen are joynit al togidder amang thame self as spiritual memberis of ane body, and also ar joynit all togidder to our salviour Christ, heid of the same mistik bodye. It is callit the sacrifice of the altar, because it is ane quick and special remembrance of the passioun of Christ, as it is said in the evangil of S. Luke. *Hoc facite in meam commemorationem.* Do this in my remembrance. Now the passioun of Christ wes the trew sacrifice quhilk wes offerit for our redemptioun. . . . This blissit sacrifice of the altar is ane quick memorial, ordanit to reduce to our mynd the passioun of our salviour Christ. . . . Quhen we ressave this sacrament in remembrance of his passioun, in deid we confess and grant that he deit for us, that be his dede we mycht get remissioun of our syns and eternal lyfe.

Extract from Hamilton's Catechism—' The Sacrament
of the Altar ' (folio cxl)

Hamilton's Catechism on Justification by Faith

Brevely, to commit ourself hailely to God, to put our hail traist and confidence in his help, defence, gudness & gracious provisioun in all our necessiteis, perellis, dangeris, mistaris, infirmiteis, in all forsakand our awin will, and with obediens commit all to the gracious will of God. Siclyk faith had Daniel, quhen he was put in the cave amang the lyonis. Siclyk faith had Susanna, quhen sche was unjustly condamnit to the deade. Siclyk faith had Jonas, quhen he was thre dais and thre nychtis in the wame of the quhail. Siclyk faith had the thre children, callit Ananias, Azarias and Misael, quhen thai wer cassin into the byrnand fornace. This is the special faith of ane trew christin man, quhilk standis in the general faith afore rehersit and in sure confidence and hoip of Goddis mercy. This faith obtenis to us the abundant grace of the haly spret, quhilk pouris into our hartis the trew lufe of God and of our nychtbour. This is the faith special, leiffand and wyrkand, that is sa mekil commendit of our salviour in the evangil, and of sanct Paule in his epistillis. This is the faith that justifeis a christin man according as sanct Paule sais to the Romanis : *Justificati ergo ex fide pacem habemus ad deum.* We being justifyit be faith, hais peace in our conscience with God. This is the faith that makis us the barnis of God, according as sanct Paul sais to the Galathianis : *Omnes enim filii dei estis per fidem, que est in Christo Jesu.* Ye ar all the sonnis of God be faith, quhilk is in Christ Jesu. . . .

Extract from Hamilton's *Catechism*—' An Introduction
to the Creed ' (folio xciii)

1556.   *Cardinal Sermoneta to Pope Paul IV*

All nunneries of every kind of religious women, and especially those of the Cistercian order . . . have come to such a pass of boldness that they utterly contemn the safeguards of chastity. [For] not only do they wander outside the monastic enclosures in shameless fashion through the houses of seculars, but they even admit all sorts of worthless and wicked men within their convents and hold with them un-chaste intercourse. [Thus] they defile the sacred precincts with the birth of children, and bring up their progeny about them, go forth abroad surrounded by their numerous sons, and give their daughters in marriage dowered with the ample revenues of the Church. . . . Moreover, seeing that the over-great revenues of the monks seem to be the cause of this unbridled licence, an account of their incomes should be taken, and, when a portion suitable for them has been set aside, the surplus should be applied to the restora-tion of churches and other buildings, which are falling to decay. . . . For about forty years various prelates and other ecclesiastical persons have alienated (usually in favour of the more powerful nobles) a great quantity of immove-able goods of notable value belonging to churches, monas-teries and ecclesiastical benefices . . . without any reckoning of the loss or gain to the said churches. . . . Very many churches and monasteries had been established of old in stately buildings, but within the last ten years or thereabouts had been reduced to ruins by hostile inroads, or, through the avarice and neglect of those placed in charge, were crumbling to decay. . . . Wherefore her most serene Majesty [Queen of Scots] made earnest suit to your Holiness to appoint prelates of those regions, who, by sanction of censure and penalty, might compel the aforesaid rulers, abbots and heads of churches to restore such places as are in need, and to spend a fourth part of all and sundry fruits coming from such benefices as are held by them on the restoration and repair of the said churches, monasteries and benefices.

J. H. Pollen, *Papal Negotiations with Queen Mary*
(Scot. Hist. Soc.), 528–30

1556. *The state of the churches in the Merse*

[*Archbishop Hamilton addresses the dean of Christianity of the Merse on 9 April 1556 :*] In the last general visitation of our diocese of St Andrews, made by us in person, we visited, among our other deaneries, that of the Merse. We discovered, and saw with our own eyes, that a great many of the parish churches—their choirs as well as their naves —were wholly thrown down and as it were levelled to the ground ; others were partly ruinous or threatening collapse in respect of their walls and roofs ; they were without glazed windows and without a baptismal font and had no vestments for the high altars and no missals or manuals, so that their parishioners could not hear the divine services or masses therein as befits good Christians, neither could masses be celebrated nor the church's sacraments administered ; the fault and shortcoming belonging to the parishioners as well as to the parsons. [*Special mention is made of the churches of Langton, Simpreme, Fogo, Hume, Greenlaw and Nenthorn (pertaining to Kelso) ; Stichell, Earlston, Ayton, Lamberton, Edrem, Ednam, Swinton, Auldcambus and Fishwick (pertaining to Coldingham) ; Merton and Smailholm (pertaining to Dryburgh) ; Duns, Ellem, Whitsome, Foulden and Mordington.]*

Reg. Ho. Ecclesiastical Documents, No. 8 (translated)

1562. *Report of the Jesuit de Gouda*

Benefices are constantly bestowed on children, and on absolutely unworthy persons, who care for nothing so little as for God's honour and the service of the church. One and the same person holds many benefices, sometimes even in the same church. For instance, the son of one prelate has been appointed to the archdeaconry and two canonries in his father's church. The second cause [of decay] is the lives of priests and clerics, which are extremely licentious and scandalous ; and a third cause is the absolutely supine negligence of the bishops. . . . I will not describe the way in which these prelates live, the example they set, or the sort of men they choose as their successors. It is no wonder that, with such shepherds, the wolves invade the flock of the Lord, and ruin all.

Pollen, *Papal Negotiations*, 138

THE ADMINISTRATION OF MARY OF GUISE, 1554–9

Châtelherault had remained governor, though now committed to the French alliance and to the maintenance of the authority of the church,[1] and it might be that any attempt to unseat him in favour of Mary of Guise, the Queen-Mother, would arouse patriotic resentment,[2] besides antagonising the whole Hamilton interest. The risk diminished when, with Mary Tudor's accession (1553), England ceased to be a potential ally of Scottish protestants, but even so it was considered more prudent to buy out the duke than to remove him by force or fraud. Consequently,

[1] cf. *A.P.S.*, ii, 482, c. 1

[2] In 1552 parliament ratified the rescinding of the action which Mary of Guise had taken for Arran's deposition in 1544, at the time of Hertford's invasion (*A.P.S.*, ii, 489, c. 29).

Archbishop Hamilton, who had been Treasurer, was guaranteed the arrears due to his office [1]; the dowager pledged herself to secure the duke a complete discharge for all his intromissions since 1542 [2]; and John Hamilton, one of the duke's sons, at last received the long-awaited bulls admitting him to the rich abbey of Arbroath. Thus the duke was brought to a 'voluntary' resignation, and, although Henry II of France, in December 1553, had obtained a judgment of the *parlement* of Paris that Mary was of age to dispose of the regency when she entered (and not when she completed) her twelfth year, yet the Scottish estates were explicit that Arran's resignation, in April 1554, was ' or [before] the queen's perfect age.'

With Arran's resignation, Mary of Guise was appointed regent ; and now Scotland was to be used, in the French interest, against England, which was by this time linked to Spain through the marriage of Mary Tudor to Philip (July 1554). Frenchmen were appointed to Scottish offices of state, fortresses were garrisoned by French soldiers ; money had to be found for payment of troops and for the erection of a fort at Kelso, as well as for the young queen's establishment in France ; and there were soon complaints against the evidence of French domination. John Knox and other reforming preachers were active in 1555–6, and, while patriotic resentment against the French must have favoured the protestant cause, the new regent, influenced by the international situation, had to treat the reformers with leniency, while Archbishop Hamilton, in the interests of his house (next in succession to the throne) could not afford to do otherwise. The year 1556 brought fresh proposals for taxation and for military action against England, but renewed opposition to them, and although hostilities opened in 1557 little was accomplished. In 1558 Mary's marriage to Francis was finally celebrated, and in November the Scots— Châtelherault protesting for his interest as heir presumptive— even consented that Francis should have the crown matrimonial. By this time Mary Tudor was dead, but it was not yet clear that Elizabeth's accession would lead to a complete reversal of the political situation.

[1] No less than eleven gifts to Archbishop Hamilton passed the privy seal on one day (15 March 1553/4), and a number of others followed shortly afterwards (*Reg. Sec. Sig.*, iv, Nos. 2570 et seq.).

[2] *Acts of the Lords of Council in Public Affairs*, 630

The change of Governor, 1554

[*On 12 April 1554 the Dowager and the three estates entered into a bond to Châtelherault narrating the latter's disbursements, in the national interest, not only of the crown revenues but of his private patrimony, and his readiness to demit the administration*] now or the pupillar aige of oure said soverane lady be perfytit and completit, nochtwithstanding that the said tutorie and admynistratioun with the haill rentis [*etc.*] of the said realme and domynionis pertenis and suld pertein to the said noble prince during oure said soveranis pupillar aige foirsaid ; [*and undertaking*] to warrand, freith, relefe and keip skaithles [*the said duke and his agents at the hands of the queen and her successors*] off all soumes of money, poise, gold, silver cunyeit and uncunyeit, jowellis, precious stanis, bannatis, ringis, targattis, abilyementis with all the apparralling thairof, horse, meris, nolt, scheip, cattell, plennischeingis of houssis, plait and uthair werk alsweill gold as silver or uther mettall quhatsumever . . . with all uther guidis, geir, jowellis and thingis quhatsumever alsweill nocht nemmit as nemmit pertenyng or that ony wyis mycht pertene to oure said soverane be deceise of hir said umquhile maist noble fader, intromettit with be the said noble and mychtie prince, his officiaris, mynisteris or factouris in his name in ony tyme bygane sen the deceise of our said soveranis umquhile maist noble fader foirsaid and siclike of all rentis, revennewis, males, fermis, proffittis and dewiteis quhatsumever baith of propirtie and casualitie off all oure said soveranis realme and domyniounis and all uther thingis pertenyng thairto. . . .

A.P.S., ii, 604

The Dowager had to practise somewhat with her brethren, the Duke of Guise and the Cardinal of Lorraine, the weight whereof the Governor after felt : for shortly after her returning, was the Governor deposed of the government, (justly by God, but most unjustly by men), and she made Regent in the year of God 1554 ; and a crown put upon her head, as seemly a sight (if men had eyes) as to put a saddle upon the back of an unruly cow. And so began she to practise practice upon practice how France might be advanced, her friends made rich, and she brought to immortal glory. . . . And in very deed, in deep dissimulation, to bring her own purpose to effect, she passed the common sort of women, as we will after hear.

Knox, i, 116–17

1555. *Act against those speaking evil of the Queen's Grace and of the French*

Forsamekill as divers seditious persounis hes in tymes bypast rasit amangis the commoun pepill murmuris and sclanders, speiking aganis the Quenis grace and sawing evill brute anent the maist Christin king of Frances subjectis send in this realme for the commoun weill and suppressing of the auld inimeis furth of the samin, tending throw rasing of sic rumoris to steir the hartis of the subjectis to hatrent aganis the prince and seditioun betuix the liegis of this realme and the maist Christin kingis liegis foirsaidis and for eschewing of sic inconvenientis as mycht follow thairupone, it is devisit, statute and ordanit that gif ony persounis in tymes cumming be hard speikand sic unressonabill commoning quhairthrow the pepill may tak occasioun of sic privie conspiracie aganis the prince or seditioun aganis the maist Christin kingis subjectis foirsaidis the samin being provin salbe punist according to the qualitie of the fault in thair bodyis and gudis at the Quenis grace plesoure. And in caice the heirar thairof report not the samin unto the Quenis grace or hir officiaris to the effect that the samin may be punist as accordis, that he sall incur the saidis panis quhilkis the principall speikar or rasar of sic murmuris deservis.

A.P.S., ii, 499–500, c. 39

1558. *The Marriage of Mary and Francis*

' Mary was publicly married to the Dauphin on Sabbath, the 24th of April 1558, in the Cathedral of Notre Dame.[1] . . . The marriage was marked by a transaction of deep duplicity. The Commissioners sent by the Scottish Parliament to France, " for completing of the mariage of our Soverane Lady with my Lord Dolphin," were charged with Instructions intended to protect Mary's interests on the one hand, and to safeguard the liberties of her country on the other. Accordingly, for the latter purpose, on the 15th of April—nine days before the marriage—she acknowledged, over her own seal and signature, and over those of her curator, the Duke of Guise, that the Scottish Acts, Articles and Instructions were for the evident advantage of herself and her kingdom ; and she bound herself and her successors, by her " royal word," faithfully to observe and keep the laws, liberties and privileges of Scotland, to all the subjects of that kingdom, as they had been kept by their most illustrious kings.[2] On the 30th of April—six days after the marriage—a similar document was signed by Francis and Mary as " King and Queen of Scots, Dauphin and Dauphiness of France." [3] On the 26th of June, Francis, as King of the Scots, declared that he not only wished to preserve their prerogatives, immunities and ancient liberties intact and inviolate; but also to increase, amplify and strengthen them.[4] Over and above these documents, Henry and Francis promised, in their letters-patent of 19th April 1558, that they would maintain the liberties of Scotland ; and that, should Mary die without issue, the nearest heir should succeed to the Scots crown without hindrance.[5]

' Nevertheless, Mary had been induced, on the 4th of April, to sign secretly three documents of a very different kind.' [6]

I

Mary, queen of Scotland . . . has said and declared that, in the event of her decease without heirs begotten of her

---

[1] See *S.H.R.*, xxxi, 41 et seq.   [2] *A.P.S.*, ii, 518

[3] Ibid., 518–19   [4] Ibid., 519

[5] *A.P.S.*, ii, 508–11   [6] Hay Fleming, *Mary, Queen of Scots*, 22–3

body—which God forbid—she has given and by these presents gives, by pure and free gift, to take effect on her death, to the king of France who is or shall be, the kingdom of Scotland according to what it consists of and comprises, besides all such rights to the kingdom of England as can or shall belong and pertain to her now and in time to come. . . .

II

The same Lady has said and declared that she wills and ordains that, in the event of her decease without heirs of her body, the king of France who is or shall be shall have and enjoy the kingdom of Scotland, the fruits, revenues and emoluments thereof, and retain the full possession thereof until he be paid and fully reimbursed in a million of gold or such other sums which shall be found due for the complete satisfaction and recompense of those outlays and expenses in law and in fact incurred in the maintenance, defence and protection of the estate of that kingdom.

III

' In the third document, [Mary] referred to the Scottish intention of assigning her kingdom—in default of heirs of her body—to certain lords of the country, as a depriving her of her liberty of disposing of it ; and protested that, whatever assent or consent she had given or might give to the Articles and Instructions sent by the Estates of her kingdom, she willed that the dispositions made by her in favour of the kings of France should be valid, and have full effect.'

Labanoff, *Lettres*, i, 50–6 ; Hay Fleming, op. cit., 24

THE PROTESTANT REVOLUTION

In 1557 there had evidently been hopes of a revolutionary outbreak, for some of the Scots lords invited Knox to return from Geneva. They later changed their minds, and stopped him at Dieppe, but in December the first Band or Covenant was drawn up and signed. Next year certain articles were presented to the dowager, at whose instance a summons went out from the primate, on 31 January 1558/9, for a meeting of the provincial council, which assembled in March. It offered a certain amount of satisfaction to the reformers, and in its proposals for the better payment of parish priests, the alleviation of vexatious exactions from the laity, and the more efficient supervision of the lower clergy, it anticipated the Book of Discipline ; but it refused to authorise services in the vernacular. These steps represented the moderate policy of reformation by consent ; but on 1 January 1558/9 had appeared ' The Beggars' Summons,' containing a threat of violent dispossession of the friars.

Meantime, Elizabeth's policy was becoming clearer, and a European peace was being negotiated (Treaty of Câteau-Cambrésis, concluded in April) which would involve the cessation of the state of war between Scotland and England and perhaps a combination of the papalist powers, France and Spain. It seems that the conclusion of Anglo-Scottish hostilities, in the first days of March, was regarded in Scotland as marking the beginning of the revolution. Yet little appears to have happened until May ; then Knox finally returned, Mary of Guise outlawed the protestant preachers and, the Beggars' Summons becoming operative, some friaries were attacked. Military operations commenced, but, although the reformers enjoyed some initial successes, their outlook was far from favourable, for the dowager had professional soldiers and the assurance of French help, while on the other hand it was hard to move Elizabeth, and the duke of Châtelherault, although he had been in touch with England since January, could not leave the dowager's side as long as his son was in France. When young Arran did at length escape and reached Scotland (with English assistance), his father at once joined the Lords of the Congregation.

The insurgents now felt strong enough formally to ' depose ' Mary of Guise (21 October 1559) and to transfer power to a

'Great Council of the Realm.' But money sent to them by Elizabeth was intercepted, an unsuccessful engagement compelled the abandonment of Edinburgh, and their forces, diminished by desertion, withdrew part to Glasgow and part to St Andrews. The French forces, based on Leith, were admirably placed for operations in Fife, until Elizabeth's fleet appeared in the Firth of Forth (23 January 1559/60). The formal agreement with England, in the treaty of Berwick (27 February), was followed by the entry of an English army into Scotland at the beginning of April, and the siege of Leith went on until the death of Mary of Guise on the night of 10–11 June.

English and French commissioners arrived in Scotland in June, and on 6 July concluded the treaty of Edinburgh, which provided for the withdrawal of foreign forces from Scotland and for the abandonment by Francis and Mary of the arms and style of sovereigns of England. The treaty was accompanied by certain concessions from the Scottish sovereigns to their subjects, *inter alia* authorising the meeting of a parliament, which, however, was not to deal with the religious question but to submit it to the king and queen.

While the outcome of the revolt was still in doubt, the reformers had submitted to the 'Great Council' their programme for polity and endowment, the first Book of Discipline, the proposals in which, if they could take effect at all, could do so only through the action of a government enthusiastic for the protestant cause and strong enough to ignore many of the claimants to a share in the ecclesiastical revenues. When the parliament met, it accepted the reformed Confession of Faith and passed statutes forbidding the saying of mass and the exercise of authority derived from Rome. While these measures gave the reformed church recognition *quoad sacra*, nothing was accomplished for its endowment, the Book of Discipline was passed by, and the entire structure of the old *régime* remained intact. Financial questions were in fact disrupting the unity of the reforming party, and the lords who finally agreed to subscribe the Book of Discipline (in January 1560/1) did so only with the qualification that beneficed men supporting the reformation should enjoy their livings for life, provided that they contributed to the maintenance of ministers.

1557. *The first Band or Covenant*

We persaving how Sathan In his membris the Antechristes
of oure tyme, crewellie dois Raige seiking to downetring
and to destroye the Evangell of Christ, and his Congregatioune : awght according to our bownden dewtye, to
stryve in oure maisteres Cawss, even unto the deth : Being
certane of the victorye, in HIM : The quhilk our dewtie
being weill consyderit : WE do promis before the Maiestie
of God, and his Congregatioune : that we (be his grace)
sall with all diligence continewallie applie oure hoill power,
substaunce, and oure very lyves to mentene sett forwarde
and establische the MAIST BLISSED WORDE OF GOD, and his
Congregatioune : And sall lawboure, at oure possibilitie,
to haif faithfull ministeres purelie and trewlie to minister
Christes Evangell and Sacramentes to his Peopill : We sall
mentene thame, nwrys thame, and defende thame, the haill
Congregatioune of CHRIST, and everye member thereof, at
oure haill poweres, and waring of oure lyves aganis Sathan
and all wicked power that dois intend tyrannye or troubill
aganis the forsaid Congregatioune · Onto the quhilk holie
worde and Congregatioune we do joyne ws : and also
dois forsaik and Renunce the Congregatioune of Sathan
with all the superstitioune, abhominatioune, and Idolatrie
thereof : And mareattour sall declare oure selfues mani-
festlie Innemies tharto : Be this oure faithfull promis,
before God, testefyit to his Congregatioune, be oure Sub-
scriptiones at thir presentes · At Edinburgh the   day
of December The yere of God ane thowsaunde fyve hundreth
fiftie sevin yeres : God callit to wytnes.·/·(*Signed :*) A. ERLE
OF ERGYL, GLENCARNE, MORTOUN, AR. LORD OF LORN,
JHONE ERSKYNE.

Nat. MSS. Scot., iii, No. xl

1559. *Articles presented to the Queen Regent*

Articles proponit to the Quene Regent of Scotland be
sum temporall Lordis and Barronis, and sent be hir

Grace to the haill Prelatis and principallis of the clargie convenit in thair Provincial Counsall in Edinburgh.

In the first, rememberand that our Sovirane Lord of gud memorie that last decest, in his lait Actis of Parliament for the common wele of this realme, thocht necessair to mak ane publict exhortatioun unto my Lordis the Prelatis and rest of the Spirituale Estate for reforming of ther lyvis and for avoyding of the opin sclander that is gevin to the haill Estates throucht the said Spirituale mens ungodly and dissolut lyves : And siclyk remembring in diverss of the lait Provinciale Counsales haldin within this realm, that poynt has bene treittet of, and sindrie statutis Synodale maid therupon, of the quhilkis nevertheless thar hes folowit nan or litill fruict as yitt, bot rathare the said Estate is deteriorate, nor emends be ony sic persuasion as hes bene hidertills usit : And sin the said Estate is mirror and lantern to the rest, it is maist expedient therefore that thai presentlie condescend to seik reformation of thair lyvis, and for executing deuly of thair offices, evry ane of them effeiring to thair awin vocation and cure committit unto thaim to do, and naymlie that oppin and manifest sins and notour offencis be forborn and abstenit fra in tym to cum, etc.

Item, that thai provid for prechings and declarings of Goddis Word sinceirly and treuly to be made in every paroch kirk of this realm upon all Sondays and utheris Holie Dayis, at the lest on Yule, Pasche, Witsondie, and every thrid or feird Sonday ; and quhair that the peple ar maist ungodlie and ignorant of thar deuty to God and man, that in thai placis preachingis of Goddis Word and gud manners may be sa aft maid that be Goddis grace thai may be brocht frae thar ungodlie leving to the dew obedience of God and man, and sua that in all placis quhair maist neid is, oftest and maist ernist preching to be maid and hed, and effeiring to the quantitie of the perochin, etc.

Item, that all prechers of the Word of God, or thai be admittit to prech the samen publicklie to the peple, that thai be first examinit deuly gif thair doctrin and profession be conform to Goddis Word and Christen fath, and sicklyke if thai be of gud manners and of fitt knawlege and condition as thai may be hable to prech the Word of God decently to the peple.

Item, that thar be na curatis nor vicares of peroch kirks maid in tymes to cum bot sic as are sufficiantly qualifeit to ministar the sacramentis of Halie Kirk in sic form and order as after folowes ; and that thai can distinctly and plainly reid the Catechisme and utheris directions that sal be directit unto thaim be thar Ordinaris unto the peple, sua that every man and woman, hering and seing thaim execute the premissis sa decently, may the rather convert thaimselves fra ther inordinate leving, and tharby baith knaw how thai suld liefe and in deid and word use thaim-selvis accordingly, etc.

Item, forsameikle as thar is nathing that can move men mair to worship God, nor to knaw the effect, cause, and strenth of the sacraments of Halie Kirk, nor nathing that can move men to dishonor the saids sacraments mair then the ignorance and misknawladge tharof ; therefore, seeing that all Christin men and women, or thai be admittit to the using and ressaving of the saids sacraments, suld knaw the vigor and strenth of the samen, for quhat causes the samen was institute be God Almighting, quhow profitable and necessar thai ar for every Christin man and woman that deuly and reverendlie ar participants tharof ; there-fore, that thar be an godlie and fruitfull declaration set forth in Inglis toung to be first shewin to the people at all times, quhen the sacrament of the blessit Body and Blud of Jesus Christ is exhibit and distribut, and sicklyke when Baptism and Marriage are solemnizit in face of Halie Kirk ; and that it be declarit to thaim that assist at the sacraments quhat is the effect tharof, and that it be speirit at tham be the preist ministrant, gif thai be reddy to ressave the samen, with sick utheris interrogatories as ar necessar for instructing of the poynts of mens salvation, and requires to be answerit unto be all thai that wald be participant, etc. And thir things to be don before the using of the ceremony of Haly Kirk, etc.

Item, that the Common Prayers with Litanies in our vulgar toung be said in evry peroch kirk upon Sondays and uther Haly Dayis efter the Devin service of the Mess, and that the Evening Prayers be said efternein in likwyse.

Item, because that the corps presentes, kow, and umest claith, and the silvir commonlie callit the Kirk richts, and Pasch offrands quhilk is takin at Pasch fra men and women for distribution of the sacrament of the blessit Body and Blud of Jesus Christ, were at the beginning but as offrands and gifts at the discretion and benevolence of the givar only, and now be distance of tym the kirkmen usis to compell men to the paying tharof be authority and jurisdiction, sua that thai will not only fulminat thar sentence of cursing, but als stop and debar men and women to cum to the reddy using of the sacraments of Haly Kirk, quhile thai be satisfiet tharof with all rigor ; quhilk thing has na ground of the law of God nor Halie Kirk, and als is veray sclandrous and givis occasion to the puir to murmur gretymly aganes the State Ecclesiastick for the doing of the premissis : And tharfore it is thocht expedient that ane reformation be maid of the premissis, and that sick things be na mair usit in tymes to cum within this realm, at the lest that na man be compellit be authority of Haly Kirk to pay the premissis, but that it shall only remane in the free will of the giver to gif and offir sic things be way of almous and for uphalding of the preists and ministers of the Halie Kirk as his conscience and charitie moves him to : And quhair the curatis and ministers forsaids hes not eneuch of thar sustentation by the saids Kirk richts, that the Ordinares, every man within his awin diocesie, take order that the persons and uplifters of the uther deutys perteining to the kirk contributs to thar sustentation effeirindlie, etc.

Item, because the leigis of this realme ar havely hurt be

the lang process of the Consistorial jugement, as hes bene at mair length declarit and shewin unto my Lordis of the Spiritualitie, and that puir men havand just cause oft tymes are constrenit to fall fra thar rightuous action through lengthning of the saids process and exhorbitant expences that thai ar drawin unto as wele in the first instant as be appellation fra place to place, fra juge to juge, and last of all to the Court of Rome, albeit the matter were never sa small, and albeit men obtein sentences never sa mony be the Ordinar juges of this realme, yitt all in vain, and na execution sall folow therupon quhill the appellation be discussit in Rome, etc. : Therefore it is necessar that provision be maid for shortning of the process Consistorial for releiving of partyes fra exorbitant expenses, and that it be considerit quhat matters sall pass to Rome be appellation, of quhat avale worth and quantity thai suld be of, and that the appellation unto Rome suld not suspend the execution of sentences gevin heir within this realme.

Item, it is havelie murmurit and complenit unto the Quenis Grace be the fewars of kirkland, that thai ar compellit to pass to Rome to pley the reduction of thar infeftments, etc.

Item that the Actis of Parliament halden at Edinbrugh the twenty sexth day of June M.CCCC.XCI [II] be our Sovirane Lord King James the Fourd of gud memorie, anent the priveleges grantit be the Paps to the Kirk of Scotland, and benefices that passis to the Court of Rome, that hurts the priveleges of the Crown or the common wele of this realme, be put to dew execution, and it be decernit that the Lordis of the Session be juges competent to the braikers tharof, notwithstanding ony exemption or immunitie or privelege spirituale or temporale.

Item, that na manner of person within this realme pretend to usurp sic hardiment as to dishonor or speik irreverently of the sacrament of the blissit Body and Blude of our Saviour Jesus Christ, bot that the samin be haldin in sic reverence, honour, and worship as efferis Christin men to do, and is commandit be the law of God and Haly Kirk, and that

156

nane dishonour the Divine service of the Mess nor speik injuriouslie nor irreverentlie tharof.

Item, that na man pretend to use the sacraments and ceremonies of Marriage, Baptism, and blessit Body and Blud forsaid, nor suffer the samin to be ministrat, bot in sic manner as is aforesaid, and be sic persons as that ar admittit deulie, and ordanit to the administration tharof.

Item, that na manner of persons be sa bald as to burn, spulie, or destroy kirks, chappels, or religious places, and ornaments tharof, nor attempt ony thing be way of deid to the hurt and injuring tharof, or for deforming or innovating the lovable ceremonies and rites tharof usit in Haly Kirk, bot that thai be usit as afore, ay and quhile forder order be takin be the Prince and ministers of Haly Kirk having power, and the samin dewlie insinuet to tham, etc.

Patrick, *Statutes of the Scottish Church*, 156–60

1559. *The Beggars' Summons*

The Blynd, Cruked, Beddrelles,[1] Wedowis, Orphelingis,[2] and all uther Pure, sa viseit be the hand of God, as may not worke,

To the Flockes of all Freires within this Realme, we wische Restitutioun of Wranges bypast, and Reformatioun in tyme cuming, for Salutatioun.

Ye your selfes ar not ignorant (and thocht ye wald be) it is now (thankes to God) knawen to the haill warlde, be his maist infallible worde, that the benignitie or almes of all Christian people perteynis to us allanerly ; quhilk ye, being hale of bodye, stark, sturdye, and abill to wyrk, quhat under pretence of poverty (and neverles possessing maist easelie all abundance), quhat throw cloiket and huded simplicitie (thoght your proudnes is knawen) and quhat be feynyeit halynes, quhilk now is declared superstitioun and

---

[1] Bed-ridden   [2] Orphans

157

idolatrie, hes thire many yeiris, exprese aganis Godis word, and the practeis of his holie Apostles, to our great torment (allace !) maist falslie stowin [1] fra us. And als ye have, be your fals doctryne and wresting of Godis worde (lerned of your father Sathan), induced the hale people, hie and law, in seure hoip and beleif, that to cleith, feid [   ] [2] and nurreis yow, is the onlie maist acceptable almouss allowit before God ; and to gif ane penny, or ane peice of breade anis in the oulk [3] is aneuch for us. Even swa ye have perswaded thame to bigge [4] yow great Hospitalis, and manteyne yow thairin [   ] [2] force, quhilk onlye pertenis now to us be all law, as biggit and dotat to the pure of whois number ye are not, nor can be repute, nether be the law of God, nor yit be na uther law proceding of nature, reasoun, or civile policie. Quhairfore seing our number is sa greate, sa indigent, and sa heavelie oppressed be your false meanes, that nane takes cair of owre miserie ; and that it is better for us to provyde thire our impotent members, quhilkis God hes geven us, to oppone to yow in plaine controversie, than to see yow heirefter (as ye have done afore) steill fra us our lodgeings, and our selfis, in the meanetyme, to perreis and die for want of the same. We have thocht gude therfore, or we enter with yow in conflict, to warne yow, in the name of the grit God, be this publick wryting, affixt on your yettis quhair ye now dwell, that ye remove fourth of oure saidis Hospitales, betuix this and the Feist of Witsunday next,[5] sua that we the onlie lauchfull proprietares thairof may enter thairto, and efterward injoye thai commodities of the Kyrk, quhilkis ye haif heirunto wranguslie halden fra us. Certefying yow, gif ye failye,

[1] stolen

[2] This page at the end of the manuscript is badly torn down the **right**-hand side.

[3] once a week   [4] build

[5] Whitsunday was the term of entry and removing of tenants, the act of 1555 having laid down that no removing could be made unless forty days of warning had been given before the term of Whitsunday (*A.P.S.*, ii, 494, c. 12).

we will at the said terme, in hale nummer (with the help of God, and assistance of his sanctis in erthe, of quhais reddie support we dout not), enter and tak posessioun of our saide patrimony, and eject yow utterlie fourth of the same.

Lat hym therfore that before hes stollin, steill na mare ; but rather lat him wyrk wyth his handes, that he may be helpefull to the pure.

Fra the hale Citeis, Townes, and Villages of Scotland, the Fyrst Day of Januare 1558.[1]

Knox, ii, 255–6

1560. *Treaty of Berwick*

[*At Berwick on 27th February 1559/60 it is agreed between the representatives of Elizabeth of England and the representatives of James, Duke of Châtelherault*] secund personn of the realme of Scotland, and the remanent of the rest of the lordes of his parte joyned with him in this caus for mayteinance and defence of the auncient ryghteis and liberteis of their cuntree. . . .

That the Quenis Majestye having sufficientlie understanded alsweall by information sent from the nobilite of Scotland, as by the manifest proceadingis of the Frenche that thei intend to conquer the realme of Scotland, supprese the liberties thairof and unyte the same unto the Crown of France perpetualie, contrarie to the laws of the said realme and to the pacts, othes, and promessis of France ;

---

[1] That is, 1 January 1559. The ' Historie of the Estate of Scotland ' says that ' in the end of October preceeding [i.e. 1558], there wes ticketts of warning, at the instance of the whole poore people of this realme, affixt upon the doores of everie place of Friers within this countrey ' (*Wodrow Miscellany*, i, 57–8 ; and see *Extracts from the Council Register of Aberdeen*, Spalding Club, i, 315–16). As part of the background to this ' summonds,' it should be noted that, in the first half of the sixteenth century, many endowments of hospitals and almshouses had been transferred to the friars.

and being thairto most humilie and earnestlie required by the said nobilite for and in the name of the hole realme:

Shall accept the said realme of Scotland, the said Duck Chasteaulerault being declared by Acte of Parliament to be heyre apperand to the Crowne theirof, and the nobilite and subjectes of the same into hir Majesties protection and mayteinaunce onelie for the preservation of theym in their old fredomes and liberteis, and from conquest, during the tyme the mariage shall continew betuix the Queyn of Scottis and the Frenche King, and one yeir after: and for expelling owte of the same realme of such as presentlie goeth abowte to practise the said conquest.

Hir Majestie shall with all speyd send into Scotland a convenient ayd of men of warre on horse and foot to joyne with the power of the Scotishmen with artailye munition and all uthers instrumentis of warre mete for the purpose, alsweall by sea as by land not onelie to expel the present power of Frenche within that realme oppressing the same but also to stop as far as convenientlie may be all grytare forces of Frenche to enter thairin for the like purpose, and shall continew hir Majesteis ayde to the said realme, nobilite and subjectes of the same until the French being enenmis to the said realme be utterlie expelled thence. . . .

And yf in caise any fortes or strenthes within the said realme be wonne out of the handes of the Frenche at this present or any time hereafter, by Her Majesties ayde the same shal be immediatelie demolished by the Scottishmen, or delivered to the Duck and his partye at their optionn and choise. Neyther shall the power of England fortifye within the grownde of Scotland being owt of the bowndes of England, but by the advyse of the said Duck, nobilite and estates of Scotland. . . .

[*In return the Scots promise to support the English arms, to resist conquest or annexation by France and if England is invaded by France to send 2,000 cavalry and 2,000 infantry to England's aid.*]

Foedera, xv, 569–70

1560. *The First Book of Discipline*

The Book of Discipline consists of the report and recommendations on ecclesiastical polity and endowment which the ministers present in Edinburgh drew up at the request of the Lords of the Congregation. The Lords' commission was dated 29 April and the book was completed by 20 May 1560. Extracts from the book follow. (References are to Dickinson's edition of Knox's *History*.)

[The Kalendar]

Keeping of holy days of certain Saints commanded by man, such as be all those that the Papists have invented, as the Feasts (as they term them) of Apostles, Martyrs, Virgins, of Christmas, Circumcision, Epiphany, Purification, and other fond feasts of our Lady . . . we judge them utterly to be abolished from this Realm (281).

[Church Buildings]

As we require Christ Jesus to be truly preached, and his holy Sacraments to be rightly ministered ; so can we not cease to require idolatry, with all monuments and places of the same, as abbeys, monasteries, friaries, nunneries, chapels, chantries, cathedral kirks, canonries, colleges, other than presently are parish Kirks or Schools, to be utterly suppressed . . . (283).

Lest that the word of God, and ministration of the Sacraments, by unseemliness of the place come in contempt, of necessity it is that the churches and places where the people ought publicly to convene be with expedition repaired in doors, windows, thatch, and with such preparations within, as appertaineth as well to the majesty of the word of God as unto the ease and commodity of the people.[1] And because we know the slothfulness of men in this behalf, and in all other which may not redound to their private commodity, strait charge and commandment must be given

[1] ' Agreed on [by the Lords] ' in margin

that within a certain day the reparations must be begun, and within another day, to be affixed by your Honours, that they be finished. . . . Every Church must have doors, close windows of glass, thatch or slate able to withhold rain, a bell to convocate the people together, a pulpit, a basin for baptism, and tables for the ministration of the Lord's Supper . . . (320–1).

[Admission of Ministers]

It appertaineth to the people, and to every several congregation, to elect their Minister. . . . For altogether this is to be avoided, that any man be violently intruded or thrust in upon any congregation. But this liberty with all care must be reserved to every several kirk, to have their votes and suffrages in election of their Ministers (284–5).

The admission of Ministers to their offices must consist in consent of the people and Kirk whereto they shall be appointed, and in approbation of the learned Ministers appointed for their examination. . . . Other ceremony than the public approbation of the people, and declaration of the chief minister, that the person there presented is appointed to serve that Kirk, we cannot approve ; for albeit the Apostles used the imposition of hands, yet seeing the miracle is ceased, the using of the ceremony we judge not necessary (286).

[Readers and Exhorters]

To the kirks where no ministers can be had presently, must be appointed the most apt men that distinctly can read the Common Prayers and the Scriptures, to exercise both themselves and the kirk, till they grow to greater perfection ; and in process of time he that is but a Reader may attain to the further degree, and by consent of the kirk and discreet ministers, may be permitted to minister the sacraments ; but not before that he be able somewhat to persuade by wholesome doctrine, besides his reading, and be admitted to the ministry as before is said. Some we know that of long time have professed Christ Jesus, whose honest conversation deserved praise of all godly men, and whose knowledge also might greatly help the simple, and yet they only content themselves with reading. These must be animated, and by gentle admonition encouraged, by some exhortation to comfort their brethren, and so they may be admitted to administration of the sacraments. . . . If from Reading he begin to Exhort, and explain the Scriptures, then ought his stipend to be augmented ; till finally he come to the honour of a Minister. [*Later there is a reference to* the other sort of Readers, who have long continued in godliness, and have some gift of exhortation, who are in hope to attain to the degree of a minister.] (287–8, 290.)

[Family Allowances]

Difficult it is to appoint a several stipend to every Minister, by reason that the charges and necessity of all will not be like ; for some will be continuers in one place, [and] some will be compelled to travel, and oft to change dwelling place (if they shall have charge of divers kirks). Amongst these, some will be burdened with wife and children, and one with more than another ; and some perchance will be single men. If equal stipends should be appointed to all those that in charge are so unequal, either should the one suffer penury, or else should the other have superfluity and too much (288).

[The Care of the Poor]

Every several kirk must provide for the poor within the self. . . . We are not patrons for stubborn and idle beggars who, running from place to place, make a craft of their begging, whom the Civil Magistrate ought to punish ; but for the widow and fatherless, the aged, impotent, or lamed, who neither can nor may travail for their sustentation, we say that God commandeth his people to be careful. And therefore, for such, as also for persons of honesty fallen in[to] decay and penury, ought such provision be made that [of] our abundance should their indigence be relieved. How this most conveniently and most easily may be done in every city and other parts of this Realm, God shall show you wisdom and the means, so that your minds be godly thereto inclined. All must not be suffered to beg that gladly so would do ; neither yet must beggars remain where they choose ; but the stout and strong beggar must be compelled to work, and every person that may not work, must be compelled to repair to the place where he or she was born (unless of long continuance they have remained in one place), and there reasonable provision must be made for their sustentation, as the church shall appoint (290–1).

[Superintendents]

To him that travelleth from place to place, whom we call Superintendents, who remain, as it were, a month or less in one place, for the establishing of the kirk, and for the same purpose changing to another place, must further consideration be had. And, therefore, to such we think six chalders [of] bear, nine chalders [of] meal, three chalders [of] oats for his horse, 500 merks [of] money . . . be payed . . . yearly[1] (289).

Because we have appointed a larger stipend to those that shall be Superintendents than to the rest of the Ministers, we have thought good to signify unto your Honours such reasons as moved us to make difference betwix preachers at this time. . . .[2] We consider that if the Ministers whom God hath endued with his [singular] graces amongst us should be appointed to several and certain places, there to make their continual residence, that then the greatest part of this Realm should be destitute of all doctrine. . . .

[1] Equivalent in purchasing power to perhaps £3,000 sterling at the present day.

[2] i.e., when, in view of the shortage of ministers, it might have seemed preferable to appoint each to a parochial charge.

And therefore we have thought it a thing most expedient for this time that, from the whole number of godly and learned [men], now presently in this Realm, be selected twelve or ten (for in so many Provinces have we divided the whole),[1] to whom charge and commandment shall be given to plant and erect churches, to set order and appoint ministers . . . to the countries that shall be appointed to their care where none are now. . . . Nothing desire we more earnestly, than that Christ Jesus be universally once preached throughout this Realm ; which shall not suddenly be unless that, by you, men be appointed and compelled faithfully to travail in such Provinces as to them shall be assigned . . . (291).

These men must not be suffered to live as your idle Bishops have done heretofore ; neither must they remain where gladly they would. But they must be preachers themselves, and such as may make no long residence in any one place till their churches be planted and provided of Ministers, or at the least of Readers. . . . In visitation . . . they shall not only preach, but also examine the life, diligence, and behaviour of the Ministers ; as also the order of their churches, [and] the manners of the people. They must further consider how the poor be provided ; how the youth be instructed . . . (292–3).

[*The Book of Discipline, in its anxiety to show why the office of Superintendent was ' most expedient ' under existing circumstances, had relatively little to say about the permanent functions of the Superintendents—although it does allude to conditions ' after that the Church be established, and three years be passed ' (295). There is a very significant passage in the edict for the election of John Winram as Superintendent of Fife :* ' Wythowt the cayr [of] superintendentis, neyther can the kyrk[is] be suddenlie erected, neyther can th[ei] be retened in disciplin and unite of doctrin ; . . . o[f] Crist Jesus and of his apostolis we have command and exempill to appoynt me[n] to sic chergis ' (*Reg. of the Kirk Session of St. Andrews, i, 75*).]

---

[1] The ' provinces ' or dioceses actually numbered ten.

[Education]

Seeing that God hath determined that his Church here in earth shall be taught not by angels but by men . . . of necessity it is that your Honours be most careful for the virtuous education and godly upbringing of the youth of this Realm. . . . Of necessity therefore we judge it, that every several church have a Schoolmaster appointed, such a one as is able, at least, to teach Grammar, and the Latin tongue, if the town be of any reputation. If it be upland [i.e. rural] where the people convene to doctrine but once in the week, then must either the Reader or the Minister there appointed, take care over the children and youth of the parish, to instruct them in their first rudiments, and especially in the Catechism, as we have it now translated in the Book of our Common Order, called the Order of Geneva. And further, we think it expedient that in every notable town, and especially in the town of the Superintendent, [there] be erected a College, in which the Arts, at least Logic and Rhetoric, together with the Tongues, be read by sufficient Masters . . . (295-6).

The Grammar Schools and of the Tongues being erected as we have said, next we think it necessary there be three Universities in this whole Realm, established in the towns accustomed. The first in Saint Andrews, the second in Glasgow, and the third in Aberdeen.

And in the first University and principal, which is Saint Andrews, there be three Colleges. And in the first College, which is the entry of the University, there be four classes or seiges [i.e. chairs] : the first, to the new Supposts,[1] shall be only Dialectics ; the next, only Mathematics ; the third, of Physics only ; the fourth of Medicine. And in the second College, two classes or seiges : the first, in Moral Philosophy ; the second in the Laws. And in the third College, two classes or seiges : the first, in the Tongues, to wit, Greek and Hebrew ; the second, in Divinity (297-8).

[1] Here used in the sense of non-graduate scholars

[*At Glasgow and Aberdeen, one college is to comprehend Dialectics, Mathematics and Physics, a second Moral Philosophy (with Ethics, Economics and Politics), Municipal and Roman Laws, Hebrew and Divinity* (299).]

[Bursaries—on a means test]

We think it expedient that . . . there be . . . in Saint Andrews, seventy-two bursars ; in Glasgow, forty-eight bursars ; in Aberdeen, forty-eight ; to be sustained only in meat upon the charges of the College ; and [to] be admitted at the examination of the Ministry and chapter of Principals in the University, as well in docility [i.e., aptitude to learning] of the persons offered, as of the ability of their parents to sustain them their selves, and not to burden the Commonwealth with them (300).

[The Rents and Patrimony of the Kirk]

These two sorts of men, that is to say, the Ministers and the Poor, together with the Schools, when order shall be taken thereanent, must be sustained upon the charges of the Church. And therefore provision must be made, how and of whom such sums must be lifted. But before we enter in this head, we must crave of your Honours, in the name of the Eternal God and of his Son Christ Jesus, that ye have respect to your poor brethren, the labourers and manurers of the ground ; who by these cruel beasts, the Papists, have been so oppressed that their life to them has been dolorous and bitter. . . . Ye must have compassion upon your brethren, appointing them to pay so reasonable teinds, that they may feel some benefit of Christ Jesus now preached unto them (302–3).

Some Gentlemen are now as cruel over their tenants as ever were the Papists, requiring of them whatsoever before they paid to the Church ; so that the Papistical tyranny shall only be changed in the tyranny of the lord or of the laird . . . (303)

[*The decision of the Lords is given in this* additio : That these teinds and other exactions, to be clean discharged, and never to be taken in time coming : as, the Uppermost Cloth, the Corpse-present, the Clerk-mail, the Pasche Offerings, Teind Ale, and all handlings Upland, can neither be required nor received of godly conscience (303).]

Neither do we judge it to proceed from justice that one man shall possess the teinds of another ; but we think it a thing most reasonable, that every man have the use of his own teinds, provided that he answer to the Deacons and Treasurers of the Church of that which justly shall be appointed unto him. We require Deacons and Treasurers rather to receive the rents, nor the Ministers themselves ; because that of the teinds must not only the Ministers be sustained, but also the Poor and Schools. And therefore we think it most expedient that common Treasurers, to wit, the Deacons, be appointed from year to year, to receive the whole rents appertaining to the Church . . . (303).

The sums able to sustain these forenamed persons [i.e., ministers, teachers and the poor] and to furnish all things appertaining to the preservation of good order and policy within the Church, must be lifted off the teinds. . . . We think that all things doted to hospitality, all annual rents, both in burgh and [to] land, pertaining to Priests, Chantries, Colleges, Chaplainries, and to Friars of all Orders, to the Sisters of the Seans,[1] and to all others of that Order, and such others within this Realm, be received still to the use of the Church or Churches within the towns or parishes where they were doted. Furthermore to the upholding of the Universities and sustentation of the Superintendents, the whole revenue of the temporality of the Bishops', Deans', and Archdeans' lands, and all rents of lands pertaining to the Cathedral Churches whatsoever. And further, mer-

---

[1] i.e., the Convent of St Katharine of Sienna, which gave its name to the district of Sciennes in Edinburgh

168

chants and rich craftsmen in free burghs, who have nothing to do with the manuring of the ground, must make some provision in their cities, towns, or dwelling places, for to support the need of the Church (304).

[The Kirk Session]

Men of best knowledge in God's word, of cleanest life, men faithful, and of most honest conversation that can be found in the Church, must be nominated to be in election. . . . The election of Elders and Deacons ought to be used every year once . . . lest that by long continuance of such officers, men presume upon the liberty of the Church. It hurts not that one man be retained in office more years than one, so that he be appointed yearly, by common and free election ; provided always, that the Deacons, treasurers, be not compelled to receive the office again for the space of three years . . . (309-10).

The Elders being elected, must be admonished of their office, which is to assist the Minister in all public affairs of the Church ; to wit, in judging and decerning causes ; in giving of admonition to the licentious liver ; [and] in having respect to the manners and conversation of all men within their charge. . . .

Yea, the Seniors ought to take heed to the life, manners, diligence and study of their Ministers. If he be worthy of admonition, they must admonish him ; of correction, they must correct him. And if he be worthy of deposition, they with consent of the Church and Superintendent, may depose him . . . (310).

[Public and Family Worship]

Baptism may be ministered whensoever the Word is preached ; but we think it more expedient, that it be ministered upon the Sunday, or upon the day of prayers, only after the sermon. . . . Four times in the year we think sufficient to the administration of the Lord's Table . . . the first Sunday of March . . . the first Sunday of June . . . the first Sunday of September . . . and the first Sunday of December . . . ; we study to suppress superstition. . . . We think that none are apt to be admitted to that Mystery who cannot formally say the Lord's Prayer, the Articles of the Belief, and declare the Sum of the Law.

Further, we think it a thing most expedient and necessary, that every Church have a Bible in English, and that the people be commanded to convene to hear the plain reading or interpretation of the Scripture. . . . We think it most expedient that the Scriptures be read in order. . . . For this skipping and divagation from place to place of the Scripture, be it in reading, or be it in preaching, we judge not so profitable to edify the Church, as the continual following of one text.

Every Master of household must be commanded either to instruct, or else cause [to] be instructed, his children, servants, and family, in the principles of the Christian religion. . . . Men, women and children would be exhorted to exercise themselves in the Psalms, that when the Church conveneth, and does sing, they may be the more able together with common heart and voice to praise God.

In private houses we think it expedient, that the most grave and discreet person use the Common Prayers at morn and at night, for the comfort and instruction of others (313–4).

[*The Book of Discipline was ultimately subscribed, on* 27 *January* 1560/61, *by a number of the Lords, who promised* ' to set the same forward at the uttermost of our powers ' : *with, however, the following reservation*—' Providing that the Bishops, Abbots, Priors, and other prelates and beneficed men, which else have adjoined them to us, bruik the revenues of their benefices during their lifetimes, they sustaining and upholding the Ministry and Ministers, as is herein specified, for preaching of the Word, and ministering of the Sacraments of God ' (324).]

1560. *Treaty of Edinburgh*

[*It is agreed between France and England*] . . . that all military forces, land and naval, of each party shall withdraw from the realm of Scotland . . . that all warlike operations viz. in England and Ireland against the French or Scots, and in Wales against the English, Irish or Scots shall entirely cease. . . .

Since the realms of England and Ireland belong by right to the serene lady and princess Elizabeth and no other is therefore allowed to call, write, name or entitle himself or have himself called, written, named or entitled King or Queen of England or Ireland nor to use or arrogate to himself the signs and arms (vulgarly called armories) of the kingdoms of England or Ireland, it is therefore statute, pacted and agreed that the most Christian King [Francis] and Queen Mary . . . shall henceforth abstain from using or carrying the said title or arms of the kingdom of England or Ireland, they shall also prohibit and forbid their subjects lest any in the kingdom of France and Scotland and their provinces or any part of them shall use the said title and arms in any way, they shall also forbid, as much as they can, anyone from in any manner conjoining the said arms with the arms of the said realms of France and Scotland. . . .

Since it seems good to Almighty God in whose hands are the hearts of kings to incline the hearts of the said most Christian King [Francis] and Queen Mary to show mercy and kindness to their nobility and people of their realm of Scotland, and in turn the said nobility and people have spontaneously and freely professed and acknowledged their obedience and loyalty towards their said most Christian king and queen and promised that they will work to nourish preserve and perpetuate it, the said most Christian king and queen by their representatives have given assent to the prayers of the said nobility and the supplications of the people shown to them tending to the honour of the said king and queen, the common weal of the said kingdom and the preservation of their obedience . . . that the said most Christian King and Queen Mary will fulfil all those things which were granted by their representatives to the said nobility and people of Scotland at Edinburgh 6th July 1560 provided that the said nobility and people of Scotland fulfil and observe what was contained in the conventions and articles. . . .

These agreements were acted at Edinburgh in the said kingdom of Scotland 6th July 1560.

Foedera, xv, 593–7

Concessions to the Scots

i. Upon the complaint made by the nobility and people of this country against the number of soldiers kept here in time of peace, supplicating the lords deputies of the King and Queen to afford some remedy therein for the relief of the country ; the said deputies having considered the said request to be just and reasonable, have consented, agreed and appointed in the name of the King and Queen, that hereafter their Majesties shall not introduce into this kingdom any soldiers out of France, nor any other nation whatsoever, unless in the event of a foreign army's attempting to invade and possess this kingdom, in which case the king and queen shall make provision by and with the counsel and advice of the three estates of this nation. And as for the French soldiers that are just now in the town of Leith, they shall be sent back into France at the same time that the English naval and land armies together with the Scottish army shall remove in such form as shall be more amply devised. . . .

iv. Concerning the petition relating to the assembling of the States, the Lords Deputies have agreed, consented and appointed that the States of the kingdom may assemble in order to hold a Parliament on the 10th day of July now running ; and that on the said day the Parliament shall be adjourned and continued according to custom from the said 10th day of July until the 1st day of August next. . . .

And this assembly shall be as valid in all respects as if it had been called and appointed by the express commandment of the king and queen. . . .

v. Concerning the article relating to peace and war, the lords deputies have consented, granted and appointed that neither the king nor the queen shall order peace or war within Scotland but by the advice and consent of the three estates, conformable to the laws, ordinances and customs of the country, and as has formerly been done by their predecessors, kings of Scotland.

vi. Touching the petition presented to the lords deputies relative to the political government and the affairs of state within this kingdom, the said lords have consented, accorded and agreed that the three estates shall make choice of twenty-four able and sufficient persons of note of this realm ; out of which number the queen shall select seven, and the states five, for to serve as an ordinary council of state during her majesty's absence, for administration of the government. And it shall not be allowed for any person of what rank soever to meddle in any thing that concerns the civil government without the intervention, authority and consent of this council. And the said counsellors shall be obliged to convene as oft as they can conveniently, and not under six at a time. And when any matter of importance shall occur, they shall all be called to consult and give their orders therein ; at least, the greatest part must be present. . . . It is specially declared that the concession of this article shall in nowise prejudge the king and queen's rights for hereafter, nor the rights of this crown. . . .

vii. Concerning the petition presented to the lords deputies, respecting the offices of the crown, they have consented, agreed and appointed that hereafter the king and queen shall not employ any stranger in the management of justice, civil or criminal, nor yet in the offices of chancellor, keeper of the seals, treasurer, comptroller, and such like offices ; but shall employ therein the native subjects of the kingdom. *Item*, that their majesties shall not put the offices of treasurer and comptroller into the

hands of any clergyman, or other person who is not capable
to enjoy a state office.

VIII. The lords deputies have agreed that in the ensuing
parliament the states shall form, make and establish an act
of oblivion, which shall be confirmed by their majesties the
king and queen, for sopiting and burying the memory of
all bearing of arms, and such things of that nature as have
happened since the 6th day of March 1558[/9]. . . .

IX. It is agreed and concluded that the estates shall be
summoned to the ensuing Parliament according to custom :
and it shall be lawful for all those to be present at that
meeting who are in use to be present, without being fright-
ened or constrained by any person. . . .

X. It is agreed and concluded that there shall be a general
peace and reconciliation among all the nobility and other
subjects of Scotland, and it shall not be lawful for those
persons who have been called the Congregation nor for
those who were not of the Congregation to reproach each
other with anything that has been done since the . . . 6th
day of March.

XI. The Lords Deputies have offered, agreed and concluded
that neither the King nor Queen shall prosecute nor take
revenge for anything that is now past and gone ; nor shall
not allow their French subjects to prosecute nor revenge
the same, but shall forget the same as if it had never been
done . . . neither shall they denude or deprive any of their
subjects of their offices, benefices or estates which they held
formerly within this kingdom upon account of their having
had any meddling in the things which have fallen out since
the 6th day of March foresaid, nor yet assume a pretext
or colour from anything else to deal so by their subjects
but esteem and treat them in all time coming as good and
obedient subjects ; provided also that the saids nobles and
the rest of the subjects render unto their Majesties such an
entire obedience as is due from faithful and natural subjects
to their proper Sovereigns. . . .

XIII. It is agreed and concluded that if any bishops,
abbots or other ecclesiastical persons shall make complaint

that they have received any harm either in their persons or goods, these complaints shall be taken into consideration by the Estates in Parliament, and such reparation shall be appointed as to the saids estates shall appear to be reasonable. And in the meantime it shall not be lawful for any person to give them any disturbance in the enjoyment of their goods nor to do them any wrong, injury or violence. And whosoever shall act in contravention to this article shall be pursued by the nobility as a disturber of the publick weal and tranquillity. . . .

XVII. Whereas on the part of the nobles and people of Scotland there have been presented certain articles concerning religion and certain other points in which the Lords Deputies would by no means meddle, as being of such importance that they judged them proper to be remitted to the King and Queen ; Therefore the saids nobles of Scotland have engaged that in the ensuing Convention of Estates some persons of quality shall be chosen for to repair to their Majesties and remonstrate to them the state of their affairs, particularly those last mentioned, and such others as could not be decided by the Lords Deputies and to understand their intention and pleasure concerning what remonstrances shall be made to them on the part of this kingdom of Scotland.

Keith, *History of Affairs of Church and State in Scotland* (Spottiswoode Soc.), i, 298–306

The Acts of Parliament of August 1560 [1]

The thre estaitis then being present understanding that the jurisdictioun and autoritie of the bischope of Rome callit the paip usit within this realme in tymes bipast has bene verray hurtful and prejudiciall to our soveranis

---

[1] These acts passed by the ' Reformation Parliament ' contravened the terms of the ' Concessions ' granted to the Scots at the time of the Treaty of Edinburgh, in which it was expressly stipulated that the religious question should be submitted to the ' intention and pleasure ' of the king and queen.

autoritie and commone weill of this realme Thairfoir hes
statute and ordanit that the bischope of Rome haif na
jurisdictioun nor autoritie within this realme in tymes
cuming And that nane of oure saidis soveranis subjectis
of this realme sute or desire in ony tyme heireftir title or
rycht be the said bischope of Rome or his sait to ony thing
within this realme under the panis of barratrye that is to
say proscriptioun banischement and nevir to bruke honour
office nor dignitie within this realme. And the contro-
venaris heirof tobe callit befoir the Justice or his deputis
or befoir the lordis of sessioun and punist thairfoir conforme
to the lawis of this realme And the furnissaris of thame
with fynance of money and purchessaris of thair title of
rycht or manteanaris or defendaris of thame sall incur
the same panis And that na bischop nor uther prelat
of this realme use ony jurisdictioun in tymes to cum be
the said bischop of Romeis autoritie under the pane
foirsaid

Forsamekle as thair hes bene divers and sindrie actis of
parliament maid in King James the first secund thrid ferd
and fyftis tymes kingis of Scotland for the tyme and als in
our soverane Ladeis tyme not aggreing with Goddis holie
word And be thame divers personis tuke occasioun of
mantenance of idolatrie and superstitioun in the kirk of
God and repressing of sic personis as wer professouris of the
said word quhairthrow divers innocentis did suffir for
eschewing of sic in tyme cuming The thre estaitis of
parliament hes annullit and declarit all sik actis maid in
tymes bipast not aggreing with Goddis word and now
contrair to the confessioun of oure fayth according to the
said word publist in this parliament tobe of nane avale
force nor effect And decernis the saidis actis and every
ane of thame to have na effect nor strenth in tyme tocum
Bot the samyn to be abolishit and extinct for evir insafer
as ony of the saidis actis ar repugnant and contrarie to the
confessioun and word of God foirsaidis ratifiit and apprevit
be the saidis estaitis in this present parliament

Forsamekle as almichtie God be his maist trew and blissit word hes declarit the reverence and honour quhilk suld be gevin to him and be his sone Jesus Christ hes declarit the trew use of the sacramentis willing the same tobe usit according to his will and word Be the quhilk it is notoure and perfitlie knawin that the sacramentis of baptisme and of the body and blude of Jesus Chryst hes bene in all tymes bipast corruptit be the papistical kirk and be thair usurpit ministeris And presentlie notwithstanding the reformatioun already maid according to Goddis word yit nottheless thair is sum of the same papis kirk that stubburnlie perseveris in thair wickit idolatrie sayand mess and baptizand conforme to the papis kirk prophanand thairthrow the sacramentis foirsaidis in quiet and secreit places regardand thairthrow nather God nor his holie word Thairfoir it is statute and ordanit in this present parliament that na maner of persone or personis in ony tymes cuming administrat ony of the sacramentis foirsaidis secreitlie or in ony uther maner of way bot thai that are admittit and havand power to that effect and that na maner of person nor personis say messe nor yit heir messe nor be present thairat under the pane of confiscatioun of all thair gudis movable and unmovable and puneissing of thair bodeis at the discretioun of the magistrat within quhais jurisdictioun sik personis happynnis to be apprehendit for the first falt Banissing of the realme for the secund falt And justifying to the deid for the third falt And ordanis all sereffis stewartis baillies and thair deputis provestis and baillies of burrowis and utheris jugeis quhatsumever within this realme to tak diligent sute and inquisitioun within thair boundis quhair ony sik usurpit ministerie is usit messe saying or thai that beis present at the doing thairof ratifyand and apprevand the samyn and tak and apprehend thame to the effect that the panis abovewrittin may be execute upoun thame.

A.P.S., ii, 534–5, c. 2

But, according to the terms of the Treaty of Edinburgh, this parliament had exceeded its commission ; and Mary consistently

refused to ratify either the treaty or the legislation of the ' Reformation Parliament.' The accession of James VI in 1567, however, put the reformers once more in power, when at once they
asked for the re-enactment of these three acts (*Book of the Universal
Kirk of Scotland*, i, 107–8). This was done at a parliament held
in the ensuing December (*see* vol. iii), when also the Confession
of Faith was once more engrossed in the records of parliament.

MARY'S REIGN IN SCOTLAND, 1561–7

The revolution of 1560 had been carried through while Mary,
queen of France since July 1559, seemed likely to remain in
France and might even be displaced in Scotland by a nominee
of the reforming party. On 5 December 1560, however, Francis II
died, and it was soon evident that his widow would return to
Scotland to rule in person. Divisive tendencies between moderate
and extreme reformers, hitherto revealed in discussions on endowment, arose afresh over the attitude to be adopted towards Mary.
There were those, including Knox and the Hamiltons, to whom an
' idolatrous ' princess could not be acceptable, while a more politic
faction, headed by Lord James Stewart and Maitland of Lething-
ton, believed that if Mary were allowed the private exercise of her
own religion she might be shepherded into acknowledgment of the
reformed church and the English alliance. When Mary came to
Scotland, in August 1561, her prudence or good fortune put her
into the hands of the latter group.

Her first public act was a proclamation to reassure the protestants, and a few months later came financial provision for their
church, in the ' assumption of thirds,' which in conception was
a not unstatesmanlike attempt to satisfy the conflicting claimants
to shares in the ecclesiastical revenues. To the horror of protestant
extremists the queen had been allowed mass in her own chapel,
but the trend of her policy was disappointing to the more zealous
of her own co-religionists. In 1562 she led a campaign in the
North-East which crushed the Romanist party there ; in 1563
a large number of priests were punished for violating the statute
against the mass, and the parliament, while it refused the reformers'
demands for fuller establishment and endowment, did pass acts
in their favour.

Yet it had been apparent from the outset that Mary did not lack the ability to form a party of her own if she chose to follow an independent line ; and attempts to consolidate the moderate policy by engineering an understanding between Mary and Elizabeth were frustrated by the latter's refusal to acknowledge the Scottish queen as her heir. (Mary was either next in succession to Elizabeth or the rightful queen of England—if, as all true Roman Catholics held, the divorce of Henry VIII and Katharine of Aragon was invalid. Naturally, Elizabeth refused to name Mary as her successor, for that might simply be to encourage her own assassination by some religious extremist.) Mary looked for a time to a Spanish alliance and a marriage with the son of Philip II, a match plainly in the interest of international Roman Catholic policy. After this scheme had proved abortive, she fell in love with her cousin, Lord Darnley, who was next heir to England after Mary herself and was acceptable to English Roman Catholics ; this match combined two Roman Catholic claims to the English throne. With the marriage to Darnley (29 July 1565), Lord James (now earl of Moray) and other nobles raised a rebellion which Mary energetically suppressed ; and the reformed church now received less favourable treatment. In a few months Mary was estranged from her husband, to whom she refused the crown matrimonial. She was, besides, now neglecting her natural counsellors, and her attachment to her secretary, Rizzio, who seemed to supplant at once Darnley and the disaffected lords, provided a basis for a coalition between them. The favourite was murdered (March 1566), but Darnley abandoned his allies, who retaliated by exposing Darnley's part in the plot, and yet did not regain the dominating position which they had sought. Three months later Prince James was born.

In the latter part of 1566 Mary's renewed disgust at her husband was accompanied by a growing partiality for the earl of Bothwell. Before the end of the year there was talk of divorce (which, however, would make the prince illegitimate) or of dissolving the marriage by more violent means ; the archbishop of St Andrews was restored to jurisdiction which would enable him to annul Bothwell's marriage ; and substantial financial concessions were made to the reformed church. Darnley was murdered on 9 February 1567. Bothwell, universally regarded as the murderer, obtained his divorce on 7 May, and on the 15th married Mary, to the scandal of even her warmest supporters (including the

SUCCESSION TO THE ENGLISH THRONE

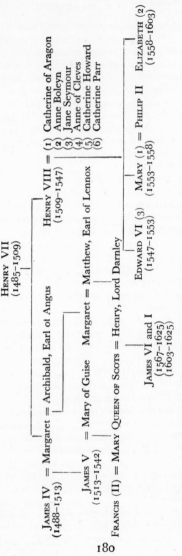

HENRY VII
(1485–1509)

JAMES IV = Margaret = Archibald, Earl of Angus
(1488–1513)

HENRY VIII = (1) Catherine of Aragon
(1509–1547) (2) Anne Boleyn
             (3) Jane Seymour
             (4) Anne of Cleves
             (5) Catherine Howard
             (6) Catherine Parr

JAMES V = Mary of Guise   Margaret = Matthew, Earl of Lennox
(1513–1542)

EDWARD VI (3)   MARY (1) = PHILIP II   ELIZABETH (2)
(1547–1553)   (1553–1558)   (1558–1603)

FRANCIS (II) = MARY QUEEN OF SCOTS = Henry, Lord Darnley

JAMES VI and I
(1567–1625)
(1603–1625)

Elizabeth succeeded to the English throne by virtue of an Act of Parliament.
Mary Queen of Scots was the rightful Queen of England if the divorce of Henry VIII and Catherine of
Aragon was invalid.
James VI (Mary's son) succeeded to the throne of England in 1603 on the death of Elizabeth.

pope). The queen had formally taken the reformed church under her protection in April, and the marriage ceremony was protestant, yet she was almost at once faced with a confederacy of nobles in arms. To them she surrendered at Carberry (15 June) and, imprisoned in Loch Leven Castle, was constrained to abdicate on 24 July.

1561.

The return of Mary

The nineteenth day of August, the year of God 1561, betwixt seven and eight hours before noon, arrived Marie Queen of Scotland, then widow, with two galleys forth of France. . . . The very face of heaven, the time of her arrival, did manifestly speak what comfort was brought unto this country with her, to wit, sorrow, dolour, darkness, and all impiety. For, in the memory of man, that day of the year was never seen a more dolorous face of the heaven than was at her arrival, which two days after did so continue ; for, besides the surface wet, and corruption of the air, the mist was so thick and so dark that scarce might any man espy another the length of two pair of boots. The sun was not seen to shine two days before, nor two days after. That fore-warning gave God unto us ; but alas, the most part were blind.

Knox, ii, 7

Proclamation against Alteration of the State of Religion, 25 August 1561

Forsamekle as the Quenis Majestie hes understand the grete inconventis that [may] cum throwch the division presently standing in this realme for the differens in materis of religioun, that hir Majestie is maist desirous to see pacifiit be any gude ordour to the honour of God and tranquillite of hir realme, and menys to tak the samyn be the avyse of hir Estatis sa sone as convenientlie may be ; and that hir Majesteis godly resolution thairin may be greitlie hinderit in cais ony tumult or seditioun be rasit amangis the liegis, gif ony suddane alteratioun or novatioun be preissit or attemptit befoir that the ordour may be establissed. Thairfore, for eschewing of the saidis inconvenientis, hir Majestie ordanis lettres to be direct to charge all and sindrie liegis, be oppin proclamatioun at the mercat croce of Edinburgh, and utheris places neidfull that they, and every ane of thame, contene thame selffis in quietnes, keip peax and civile societie amangis thame selffis ; and in the meyntyme, quhill the States of hir realme may be assemblit, and that hir Majestie have takin a finall ordour be thair avise and publict consent,—quhilk hir Majestie hopis salbe to the contentment of the haill,—that nane of thame tak upoun hand, privatlie or oppinlie, to mak ony alteratioun or innovatioun of the state of religioun, or attempt ony thing aganis the forme quhilk hir Majestie fand publict and universalie standing at hir Majesteis arrivall in this hir realme, under the pane of deid : with certificatioun that gif ony subject of the realme sall cum in the contrair heirof, he salbe estemit and haldin a seditious persoun and raser of tumult ; and the said payne sal be execute upoun him with all rigour, to the exemple of utheris. Attour, hir Majestie, be the avyse of the Lordis of hir Secrete Counsell, commandis and chargeis all hir liegis, that nane of thame tak upoun hand to molest or trouble ony of hir domestic servandis or personis quhatsumevir cumit furth of France, in hir Graces cumpany, at this tyme, in word, ded, or countenance, for ony caus quhatsumevir, other within hir palice or outwith, or mak ony [devisioun or ?] invasioun upoun ony of thame, under quhatsumevir cullour or pretence, under the said pane of deid ; albeit hir Majestie be sufficientlie persuadit that hir gude and loving subjectis wald do the samyn for the reverence thay beir to hir persoun and authorite, nochtwithstanding that na sic commandment war publist.

Register of the Privy Council, i, 266–7

The Assumption of Thirds of Benefices

On 22 December 1561 the archbishop of St Andrews and three bishops offered a quarter of their revenues for one year, to be

employed as the queen thought fitting, but the council, in view
of the uncertainty of the amount required for the maintenance
of the reformed clergy and for the 'support of the queen's
majesty, above her own proper rents, for the common affairs
of the country,' decided that if necessary a third or more of the
fruits of every benefice should be uplifted yearly ' until a general
order be taken.' On 15 February 1561/2 came the act of council
following.

1562.

The which day, forsamekle as the Queen's Majesty, by
the advice of the Lords of her Secret Council and others
divers of the Nobility, had of before, upon the xxii day
of December last bypast, ordained that if the fourth part
of the fruits and rents of all the benefices within this Realm
were not sufficient for the support of her Majesty and other
particular charges underwritten necessary to be borne for
the tranquillity of the country ; then the third part of the
said fruits, more or less, should be taken up to the effects
foresaid. And attour ordained letters to be directed
charging all and sundry beneficed men, on this side of the
Mounth, to produce their rentals upon the xxiv day of
January last bypast ; and the tenth day of February instant
was prefixed by the said letters for inbringing of all rentals
of the benefices beyond the Mounth ; with certification
that who produced not the said rentals at the days foresaid
respective, the Queen's Majesty and her Council would provide remedy. According to the which certification, her
Highness, with advice of her Council foresaid, has ordained
that those who have not produced their rentals, whole and
full intromission shall be had of their fruits, by them whom
her Majesty shall direct thereto ; and who have not given
in their just rentals, whatsomever part omitted in their said
rentals shall be intrometted with in like manner. And
further, having consulted ryply, and diligently advised
upon the common affairs and necessities concerning the
Queen's Majesty, and charges to be borne, for the common
weal of the Realm, and sustentation of the Preachers and

Readers, conform to the said Ordinance made thereupon of before, has found and declared the whole third parts of all benefices within this Realm, of which the rentals are produced, to be taken up by the person or persons to be nominated by her Majesty, and to begin upon this last crop of the year of God 1561, the same to be employed to the effect aforesaid : together with the whole fruits of the benefices whereof the rentals are not produced ; and also of samekle as is omitted in the rentals produced : And that order be directed by the Queen's Majesty to the Lords of Session that the old possessors may be answered of the remaining fruits of the said benefices ; providing that the third part foresaid be fully and wholly taken up by the persons to be deputed to the uptaking thereof : And this order to continue and stand ay and whill further order be taken by the Queen's Majesty with advice of her Estates. Moreover her Highness by the advice of her Council foresaid, has statute and ordained that all annuals, mailles, and duties within free burghs, or other towns of this Realm, as well pertaining to Chaplainries, Prebendaries, as to Friars, together with the rents of the Friars' lands, wherever they be, [and the] setting and disponing thereupon, be intrometted with, and taken up by such as her Grace shall depute thereto ; for employing of the same by her Highness, to Hospitals, Schools, and other godly uses, as shall seem best to her Highness, by the advice of her Council : And knowing that nothing is more commodious for the said Hospitals, nor the places of Friars as [are] yet standing undemolished, as also to the entertaining of Schools, Colleges, and other uses foresaid : Ordains the Provost and Bailies of Aberdeen, Elgin in Moray, Inverness, Glasgow, and other burghs of this Realm, where the same are not demolished, to entertain and uphold the said Friars' places standing in the said towns, upon the common good thereof, and to use the same to the common-weal and service of the said towns, ay and quhill the Queen's Majesty be further advised and take final order in such things, notwithstanding any other gift, title, or interest given to whatsomever persons of the said

places, with their yards, orchards, and pertinents, by our
Sovereign Lady of before.[1]

Knox, ii, 331–2

An analysis of the account of the collector general of thirds for
the year 1562 shows the system in operation :

Charge		Discharge	
Brought forward	£8,000	Expenses of collection etc.	£7,600
Arrears	6,000	Reformed church (stipends	
Money thirds	36,000	and allowed thirds)	26,250
Victual thirds sold	22,500	The crown (including	
(Unsold victual was		£11,500 for the guard)	12,700
worth nearly £20,000)		Remissions £8,500	
		Friars etc. 1,700	
		Pensions etc. 3,800	
			14,000
		Arrears	7,000
		Carried forward	5,000

Deducting expenses, arrears and balance unexpended, there
remained £53,000 available for distribution. Of this the reformed
church received a half, the crown less than a quarter, others
more than a quarter. See *Thirds of Benefices* (Scot. Hist. Soc.),
xxiii–xxiv.

Warrant for proclaiming the Queen's marriage with Darnley
1565.

MARIE be the grace of god Quene of Scottis To our Louittis
Lyoun King of armes and his brethir herauldis and to our
Louittis
Messingeris our shereffis in that part coniunclie and seueralie
specialie constitute greting fforsamekle as we intend at the
plesour and will of god to solemnizat and complete the

---

[1] For a final Act of the Privy Council in relation to the ingathering
of the Thirds of the Benefices, passed to prevent a fraudulent prior-
ingathering of fruits and rents, see *Register of the Privy Council of Scotland*,
i, 204–6.

band of matrimony in face of haly kirk with the Richt noble and Illustir prince Henry duke of albany etc. In Respect of the quhilk mariage and during the tyme thairof we will ordane and consentis that he be namyt and stilit king of this our kingdome and that all oure letres to be direct efter oure said mareage sua to be completit Be in the names of the said Illustir prince our future husband and ws as king and quene of Scotland Coniunclie OURE WILL IS heirfore and we charge you straitlie and commandis That incontinent thir our Letres sene ye pas to the mercat croce of our burgh of edinbugh and all vtheris places neidfull and thair be oppin proclamatiounmak publicatioun and intimatioun heirof to all and sindrie our Liegs and subditis as appertenis and therefter we ordane thir our letres to be registrat and insert in the buikis of our counsall ad perpetuam rei memoriam · quhairvnto thir presentis sall serue our clerk of Registre for a sufficient warrand · As ye will ansuer to ws thairupoun Deliuering thir our Letres be yow dewlie execute and indorsate agane to the berair Subscriuit with our hand and gevin vnder our signet at halirudhous the xxviij day of Januare of our Regnne the xxiii yere 1565

MARIE R.

National MSS. of Scotland, iii, No. xlviii

Mary's concessions to the Reformed Church, 1566

Towards the end of 1566 Mary suddenly began to show conspicuous tenderness towards the reformed kirk. The first of the two acts of council following secured to the ministers the right of succession to all benefices worth 300 merks or less ; and the second attempted to alleviate the distress caused by the crown's inroads on the thirds, by assigning a specified sum therefrom to the ministers, who were to have the right of collection.

1566.

Apud Edinburgh, tertio die mensis Octobris, anno Domini millesimo quingentesimo lxvi⁰.

The quhilk day, forsamekill as the King and Quenis Majesteis hes undirstand and considderit that the ministeris stipendis quhilkis necessarlie mon be payit furth of the thridis of the beneficies, extendis to sic a sowme that the saidis thridis is nocht abill, bayth to sustene the chargeis of thair Majesteis hous—attour the rent of thair propirtie, as alswa to sustene the saidis ministeris ; and eftir gude deliberatioun takin how thai may be sustenit with leist chargeis and expenssis, thair Hienessis hes fund it maist convenient, and als with avyise of the Lordis of thair Secreit Counsall statutis and ordanis ; that in tymes cuming all small beneficies, parsonages, vicarages, and utheris, extending in yeirlie rentall to the soum of thre hundrith markis, or within, as thai sal happin to vaik, sall alwayis be disponit to sic personages as the superintendentis and assemblie of the kirk, eftir dew examinatioun, sall find abill, qualifiit, and sufficient, and thaireftir nominat and present to thair Majesteis ; quhilkis being sa nominat and presentit, thair Hienessis sall admit thame, and be thair autoritie caus thame be answerit of the frutis and dewiteis of the saidis beneficies. Attour, quhensoevir ony Bischoprik, Abbacie, Pryorie, or uther Prelacie that hes the patronage of sic small beneficies sal happin to vaik and fall to thair Majesteis dispositioun and presentatioun, as lykewyise of all thame that ar presentlie vacand, thair Hienessis promittis in verbo principum, that thai sall alwayis retene in thair awin handis the power and titill of the dispositioun of the saidis small beneficies, to the effect abonewrittin ; and sall caus the personis to quhome thair Majesteis disponis the saidis pre-laciis and greit beneficies consent thairto, befoir thair Majesteis mak ony rycht of the principall to thame. And in caise it sall happin thair Majesteis ignorantlie or uther-wayis to gif or dispone ony of the saidis small beneficies be gift, presentatioun, or utherwayis, contrair this present act and ordinance, and ony wayis prejudiciall to the samyn ; their Majesteis expressitlie commandis thair Comptrollar present and to cum, his clerkis and collectouris, the keparis of the signet, previe seill and greit seill, and all utheris thair Hienessis officiaris, liegis, and subdittis, that thai on na wayis admit, allow, obtempir, or obey ony sic gift or presentatioun, or to pas the samyn throw the seillis, or grant lettres in the four formes thairupoun, bot to hald, repute, and esteme thame as previe writtingis purchest in defraud and prejudice of this present lovabill act and publict ordinance, nochtwithstanding ony charge or command gevin or to be gevin in the contrair, quhairunto thir presentis sall serve thame for a sufficient warrand. And siclike thair Majesteis ordanis and requiris the Lordis of Counsall and Sessioun, on na wayis to admit, allow, or attend to ony gift, provisioun, or presentatioun of quhatsumevir small benefice of the valu abonewrittin disponit be thair Majesteis, or utherwayis quhair the samyn is repugnant or contrarious to this present act and ordinance, and nocht disponit to qualifiit personis apt for the ministerie, examinat and admittit be the superintendentis and kirk in maner foirsaid ; and that lettres be direct for publicatioun heirof in dew forme as efferis.

Reg. Privy Council, i, 487–8

Forsamekill as the Ministeris within our realme this haill yeir bigane hes wantit thair stipendis in respect of sindry occasionis that hes intervenit, yit becaus we ar myndit and weill willit that the said ministerie be sustenit and inter-teneit in tyme cuming as efferis ; thairfoir, with avyise of oure Secreit Counsall, hes tane sic ordour as we mycht best for the present, and hes assignit for sustentatioun of the said Ministerie certane victuales and money in sindry places and cuntreis to be tane up and disponit be the said Ministerie and thair Collectouris or Chalmerlanis as thai sall think maist expedient, extending to the soum of ten thousand pundis money, and four hundrith chalderis victuale, as the particular assignationis maid thairupoun mair fullelie proportis. We, thairfoir, be avyise of our Counsall foirsaidis, ordanis and decernis that the said Ministerie and thair Collectouris and Chalmerlanis quhat-sumevir be thankfullie answerit and obeyit of the haill payment, alsweill of money as victuale foirsaid, throuchout oure haill realme quhairsoevir the samyn or ony part thairof is assignit ; and lettres thairupoun to be decernit and gevin furth, owther of horning or poinding respective, as the said ministerie sall think expedient and require, commanding expreslie oure Clerk of Register and Comptrollar, and all utheris quhome it efferis or salbe requirit thairto, to deliver the attentik copyis and extract of the said assignatioun to the ministerie, with expres inhibitioun to oure Comptrollar, or ony uther Chalmerlanis to intromet or mell ony maner of way with the saidis assignationis, or ony part thairof, under all heich panis that may follow thairupoun. Subscrivit with our hand at [Stirling, 20 December 1566].

Reg. Privy Council, i, 494

The marriage of Mary and Bothwell

1567.

Upoun the aucht day of the said moneth [*May 1567*] befoir none Marie, be the grace of God, quene of Scottis, wes proclamit in the palice of Halyrudhous, to be maryt with the said James, erle Bothwell. . . .

Upoun the nynt day of the said moneth of May, our soverane ladie and the said erle Bothwell wes proclamit in the college kirk of Sanct Geill to be mariyt togidder.

Upoun the ellevint day of the said moneth, our soverane ladie and the said erle Bothwell come furth of the castell of Edinburgh and wes lugeit in the abbay.

Upoun the tuelf day thairof betuix sevin and aucht houris at evin, James erle Bothwell wes maid duk of Orkney and Zetland, with greit magnificence, and four knychtis wes maid thairat ; viz. James Cokburne of Langtoun, Patrik Quhitlaw of that Ilk, James Ormestoun of that Ilk and Alexander Hepburne of Beinstoun ; and thair wes few or nane of the nobilitie thairat.

Upoun the fyftene day of May 1567 Marie, be the grace of God, quene of Scottis, wes maryt on James Duke of

Orknay, erle Bothwell, Lord Haillis Crichtoun and Liddis-
dail, great Admiral of Scotland, in the palice of Halyrudhous
within the auld chappell, be Adame Bischope of Orkney,
not with the mess bot with preitching, at ten houris afoir
none. Thair wes not many of the nobilitie of this realme
thairat, except the erle Crawfurd, the erle Huntly, the erle
Sutherland, my lordis Abirbrothok, Olyphant, Flemynge,
Glamis and Boyd, Johne Archbischope of Sanctandrois, the
bischope of Denblane, the bischope of Ross, Orknay, with
certane utheris small gentilmene quha awatit upone the
said Duke of Orkney. At this marriage thair wes nathir
plesour nor pastyme usit as use wes wont to be usit quhen
princes wes maryt.

Diurnal of Occurrents, 111–12

Act in favour of the Reformed Church

1567.

The quhilk day [*19 April 1567*] the quenis Maiestie having
considerit the estait of hir Maiestie's realme that it stude
at the tyme of hir arryvale furth of France and yit presentlie
standis at, ffoireseing alssua the commone weill of hir
cuntre gretumlie to be incressit and estabillishit be the
keiping of the commone peax and quietnes amangis all hir
gud subiectes. And like as hir hienes sen hir foirsaid
arryvall hes attemptit na thing contrar the estait of religioun
quhilk hir maiestie fand publictlie and universallie standing
at hir arryvale foirsaid Quhairby hir Maiestie is maist
worthy to be servit honorit and obeyit, richtswa hir hienes
intendis to continew in the samyne gudnes and government
in all tyme cuming quhairby all hir gud subjectes professouris of the Religioun foirsaid sall haif occasioun to praise
god for his gud happye and gratius government. . . .

Our said soverane with the awyse of the haill thre estaitis
of this parliament hes thocht neidfull and convenient to
dispense, cass, abrogat and annull like as hir Maiestie
presentlie dispensis, cassis, abrogattis and annullis all and
quhatsumevir lawis, actis and constitutionis, Canone, civile

or municipale with all uther constitutionis and practik penale Introducit contrar to the foirsaid religioun and professouris of the samyn And ordanis thame and thair posteritie in all tymes to cum to be fre and exemit from all pane corporall, infame, reproche, depryving from benefices dignitie or offices or uther cryme or pane quhatsumevir that may be Incurrit or impute to thame be vertew of the saidis actis, lawis, ordinances, canon, civil or municipal and practik for contravening of the samyne, renunceand the samyne and strenth thairof in favouris of oure saidis subiectis to the effect foirsaid.

And siclike the quenis Maiestie of hir auctorite Royall granttit to hir be God with the awyse of the thre estaitis foirsaidis takis to hir self and hir posteritie all hir gude subiectes thair beneficies, landis, officis, gudis and honoris to be under hir sure salfgard mantenance protectioun and defence perpetuallie aganis quhatsumevir foirane auctoritie, pouer, jurisdictioun and persute, be it ecclesiasticall or temporall, exemand hir foirsaidis subiectes from all compeirance summonding or obedience pretendit or to be pretendit heirefter aganis thame for the caussis foirsaidis be quhatsumevir foirane persoun or uther pretendand jurisdictioun or auctoritie throw thame, willing hir subiectes to duell in perpetuall securitie and quietnes within this realme be making of thair maist humbill and faithfull obedience to hir hienes and hir posteritie in all tymes cuming heirefter allanerlie. . . .

A.P.S., ii, 548, c. 2

1567. *The Abdication of Queen Mary*

Apud Edinburgh, xxv Julii anno Domini j^{m}v^{c}lxvii^{o}.

The quhilk day, in presens of the Lordis of Secreit Counsall and utheris of the Nobilitie, Prelattis, Baronis, and Commissaris of Burrowis convenit within the Tolbuyth of Edinburgh, comperit Patrik Lord Lindesay of the Byris and presentit the commissioun underwrittin subscrivit be the Quenis Majestie, oure Soverane Ladie, under hir Previe

Seill, desyrand the same to be opinlie red, of the quhilk the tennour follows :—

Marie, be the grace of God, Quene of Scottis, to all and sindry our Jugeis and Ministeris of Law, Liegis, and Sub-dittis quhome it efferis quhais knawlege thir oure lettres sal to cum greting : Forsamekill as sen our arryvall and returning within oure realme, We—willing the commoun commoditie, welth, proffeit, and quietnes thairof, liegis and subjectis of the samyn—haif employit oure body, haill sences, and forceis to governe the same in sic sort that oure royall and honorabill estait mycht stand continew with us and our posteritie, and our loving and kynd liegis mycht enjoy the quietnes of trew subjectis ; in travelling quhairin, nocht onelie is oure body spreit and sences sa vexit, brokin, and unquietit, that langar we are nocht of habilitie be ony maner to induir sa greit and tollerabill panis and travellis quhairwith we are altogidder weryit ; bot als greit com-motionis and troublis be sindry occasionis in the menetyme hes insewit thairin to oure greit grief. And seing it hes bene the plesour of the eternall God, of his kyndlie luf mercie and gudnes to grant unto us of our awin persoun ane sone quha in caise be the hand of God we be veseit, will, and rycht and of equitie man and aucht, to succeid to us and to the governament of oure realme ; and knawing that all creaturis ar subject to that immutabill decreit of the Eternall, and to randir and gif up this lyff temporall, the hour and tyme quhairof is maist uncertane. And in caise be deceis we be takin fra this lyff during the tyme of his minoritie, it may be doubtit greitlie that resistence and troubill may be maid to oure said sone, now native Prince of this oure realme, in his tendir yeris, being swa destitute of us, to succeid to that rowme and kingdome quhilk maist justlie of all lawis appertenis to him. Quhilk inconvenient be Goddis help and gude providence we meane to prevent in sic maner that it sall nocht ly in the power of ony unnaturall subjectis to resist Goddis ordinance in that behalf ; and understanding that na thing erthlie is mair joyus and happie to us nor to se oure said derast sone in oure awin lyftyme peciabillie placeit in that rowme and honorabill estait quhairto he justlie aucht and man succeid to ; We, of the moderlie affectioun we beir towart oure said onelie sone, have renunceit and dimittit, and be thir our lettres frelie of oure awin motive will, renunceis, and dimittis the governament, gyding, and governing, of this our realme of Scotland, liegis and subdittis thairof, and all intro-missioun and dispositioun of ony casualiteis, propirtie, benefices, offices, and all thingis appertening, or heirtofoir is knawin or heireftir sal happin to appertene thairto in favouris of oure said dearest sone, to that effect that he may be plantit, placeit, and possessit thairin ; use and exerce all thingis belanging thairto as native King and Prince of the samyn ; and siclike as we or ony of our pre-decessouris, Kingis of Scotland, hes done in ony tyme bipast. Attour, that this our dimissioun may tak the mair solempne effect, and that nane pretend ignorance thairof, we have gevin, grantit, and committit, and be thir oure lettres gevis, grantis, and committis oure commissioun, full fre and plane power, generall and speciall command, to oure traist cousingis Patrik Lord Lindesay of the Byris and Williame Lord Ruthven, and to ilk ane of thame, conjunctlie and severalie, to compeir befoir sa mony of the Nobilitie, Clergy, Burgessis, and uther peopill of oure realme as sal happin to be assemblit to that effect in our burgh of Strivi-ling, or ony uther place or places quhair it salbe thocht maist convenient, at ony day or dayis ; and thair publictlie in thair presence for us, in our name, and upoun oure behalf, dimit and renunce the governament, gyding, and rewling of this oure realme, liegis, and subjectis thairof, all intro-missioun with the propirtie, casualitie, or utheris thingis appertening to us thairby, and all rycht and titill that we had, hes, or may have be ony maner of way thairto, in favouris of oure said sone, to that effect that he may be inaugurat, placeit, and rowmit thairin, and the Croun Royall deliverit to him, and he obeyit in all thingis con-cerning the samyn, as we or oure predecessouris hes bene in tymes bipast ; and likewyise, be thir presentis, gevis, grantis, and committis full, fre, and plane power—to our rycht traist cousingis, James Erll of Mortoun Lord of Dalkeyth, Johnne Erll of Atholl, etc., Johnne Erll of Mar, Alexander Erll of Glencarne, Williame Erll of Menteith, Johnne Maister of Grahame, Alexander Lord Hume, Adame Bischope of Orknay, the Provestis of Dunde, Montroise—or ony of thame, to ressave the said renunciatioun and dismissioun in favouris of oure said sone ; and eftir the ressaving thairof, to plant, place, and inaugurat him in the kingdome ; and with all ceremoneis requisit to put the Croun Royall upoun his heid in signe and takin of the establissing of him thairin ; and in his name to mak and gif to the saidis Nobilitie, Clergy, Burgessis, and utheris oure liegis, his princelie and kinglie ayth, detfullie and lauchfullie as efferis ; and to ressave thair aythis for dew and lauchfull homage and obedience to be maid be thame to him in all tymes cuming as becummis subjectis to thair native King and Prince ; and generallie all and sindry uther thingis to do, exerce, and use that for suir performance and accomplisement heirof may or can be done, ferme and stabill haldand and for to hald all and quhatsumevir thingis in our name in the premissis ledis to be done in the word and faythfull promeis of ane Prince ; and ordanis thir our lettres, gif neid beis, to be publeist at all places neidfull. Subscrivit with oure hand, and gevin under oure Previe Seill, at Lochlevin, the xxiiii day of July, and of oure regnne the twenty fyve yeir, 1567.

Reg. Privy Council, i, 531–3

Appointment of Moray as Regent

Marie, be the grace of God, Quene of Scottis, to all and sindrie our Jugeis and Ministeris of oure lawis, liegis, and subdittis quhome it efferis to quhais knawlege thir oure lettres sal to cum, greting : Forsamekill as eftir lang greit and intollerabill panis and laubouris, takin be us sen oure arryval within oure Realme, for government thairof, and keping of the liegis of the samyn in quietnes, we have nocht onelie bene vexit in oure spreit, body, and sences thairby, bot als at lenth ar altogidder sa weryit thairof that oure habilitie and strenth of body is nocht habill langar to induir the samyn. Thairfoir and becaus na thing erdlie can be mair confortabill and happie to us in this erth, nor in our liftyme to se our maist deare sone, the native Prince of this our realme, placeit in the kingdome thairof, and the croun royall set on his head ; We, of oure awin fre will and speciall motive, haif dimittit and renunceit the governament, gyding, and governing of this our realme of Scotland, liegis and subjectis thairof, in favouris of oure said sone ; to that effect that in all tymes heireftir he may peciabillie and quietlie enjoy the samyn without troubill, and be obeyit as native King and Prince of the samyn be the liegis thairof. And undirstanding be ressoun of his tendir youth he is nocht of habilitie in his awin persoun to administrat in his kinglie rowme and governament as equitie requiris quhill that heireftir he cum to the yeris of discretioun ; and als knawing the proximitie of blude standing betuix oure said sone and oure dearest brother James Erll of Murray lord Abirnethie, etc., and havand experience of the naturall affectioun and kyndlie luff he hes in all tymes borne and presentlie beris towartis us, honour, and estait of our said sone, of quhais lufe and favour towartis him we can nocht bot assure oure self to quhome na grittar honour, joy, nor felicitie in erth can cum nor to se oure said sone inaugurat in his kingdome, ferit, rever- encit, and obeyit be his liegis thairof ; in respect quhairof and of the certantie and notorietie of the honestie, habilitie, qualificatioun, and sufficiency of oure said dearest brother to have the cure and regiment of oure said dearest sone, realme, and liegis foirsaidis during oure said sonnis minoritie, we have maid, namit, appointit, constitute and ordanit, and be thir oure lettres nemmis, appointis, makis, constitutis and ordanis, oure said dearest brother James Erll of Murray, Regent to oure said dearest Sone, Realme, and Liegis foirsaidis during his minoritie and les aige, and ay and

quhill he be of the aige of sevintene yeris compleit, and
that oure said dearest brother be callit during the said
space Regent to oure said Sone, Realme, and Liegis, swa
that oure said Sone eftir the completing of the yeris foirsaidis in his awin persoun may tak upoun him the said
governament, and use and exerce all and sindry privilegis,
honouris, and utheris immunities that appertenis to the
office of ane King alsweill in governing his realme and
peopill according to the lawis as in repressing the violence
of sic as wald invaid or injustlie resist him or thame or his
authoritie ryall ; with power to oure said dearest brother
James Erll of Murray in name authoritie and behalf of oure
said maist deare sone, to ressave resignationis of quhatsumevir landis haldin of him, or yit of offices, castellis,
touris, fortalices, mylnis, fischeingis, woddis, benefices, or
pertinentis quhatsumevir ; the samyn agane in oure said
sonnis name to gif, and deliver signatouris thairupoun, and
upoun the giftis of wardis, nonentressis, and relevis of landis,
mariages of airis, falland or that sal happin to fall in oure
said sonnis handis as superiour thairof ; and als upoun
presentatioun of landis, benefices, eschetis of gudis, movabill
and unmovabill, dettis, and takkis, respectis, remissionis,
supersedereis ; and upoun the dispositioun of offices
vacand, or quhen thai sal happin to vaik ; to subscrive and
caus be past the seillis ; the said office of Regentrie to use
and exerce in all thingis privilegis and commoditeis, siclike
als frelie and with als greit libertie as ony Regent or Governour to us or oure predecessouris usit in ony tymes bigane ;
and siclike as gif everie heid privilege and article concerning
the said office, wer at lenth expressit and amplifiit in this
oure lettres ; promissand to hald ferme and stabill in the
word and fayth of ane Prince to quhatsumevir thingis oure
said dearest brother in the premissis happynnis to do ;
chargeing heirfoir you, all and sindrie, oure Jugeis and
Ministeris of law, liegis, and subdittis foirsaidis, to answer
and obey to oure said dearest brother in all and sindrie
thingis concerning the said office of Regentrie as ye and
ilkane of you will declair you loving subjectis to our said

deir sone, and under all pane, charge, and offence that ye
and ilkane of you may commit and inrin aganis his Majestie
in that part. Subscrivit with oure hand, and gevin under
oure Previe Seill, at Lochlevin, the xxiiii day of Julii, and
of oure regnne the twentie fyve yeir.

Marie, be the grace of God, Quene of Scottis, to all and
sindrie oure Jugeis and Ministeris of law, liegis, and subdittis, quhome it efferis, to quhais knawlege thir oure lettres
sall cum, greting : Forsamekill as be lang, irksum, and
tedious travell takin be us in the governament of this oure
Realme and liegis thairof, we ar sa vexit and weryit that
oure body, spreit, and sences ar altogidder becum unabill
langar to travell in that rowme ; and thairfoir we have
dimittit and renunceit the office of governament of this
oure Realme and liegis thairof, in favouris of oure maist
onelie deir sone, native Prince of this oure realme ; and
becaus of his tendir youth and inhabilitie to use the said
governament in his awin persoun during his minoritie, we
have constitute oure dearest brother James Erll of Murray
Lord Abernethie, etc., Regent to oure said Sone, Realme,
and liegis foirsaidis ; and in respect that oure said dearest
brother is actualie furth of our realme, and can nocht
instantlie be present to accept the said office of Regentrie
upoun him, and use and exerce the samyn during oure said
dearest sonnis minoritie ; We quhill his returning within
oure realme, or in caise of his deceise, have maid, constitute,
namit, appointit and ordanit, and be thir oure lettres makis
constitutis namis appointis and ordanis, oure traist cousingis
and counsalouris, James Duke of Chestellarault Erll of
Arrane Lord Hammiltoun, Mathow Erll of Levenax Lord
Dernlie, etc., Archibald Erll of Ergyle Lord Campbell and
Lorne, etc., Johnne Erll of Atholl, James Erll of Mortoun,
Alexander Erll of Glencarne, and Johnne Erll of Mar,
Regentis to oure said dearest Sone, Realme, and liegis ;
and in caise our said brother James Erll of Murray cum
within oure realme, and refuise to accept the said office
of Regentrie upoun his singular persoun, we mak, constitute,

name, appoint and ordane, our traist cousingis and coun-salouris foirsaidis, and our said brother Regentis of our said deir Sone, Realme, and liegis, gevand grantand and committand to thame, or ony fyve of thame conjunctlie, full power for oure said sone, and in his name to ressave resignationis of landis, mak dispositioun of wardis, nonentressis, relevis, mariagis, benefices, eschetis, offices, and utheris casualiteis and privilegis quhatsumevir concerning the said office, signatouris thairupoun to mak subscrive and caus be past throw the seillis ; and to use and exerce the said office of Regentrie in all thingis, privilegis, commoditeis, siclike als frelie and with als greit libertie as ony Regent or Governour to us or oure predecessouris usit the samyn in ony tymes bigane ; promittand to hald ferme and stabill in the word and fayth of ane Prince to quhatsumevir thingis oure saidis dearest cousingis dois in the premissis ; chargeing heirfoir you all and sindry oure jugeis and ministeris of law, liegis, and subdittis foirsaidis, to answer and obey to oure saidis traist cousingis, Regentis foirsaidis, in all and sindrie thingis, concerning the said office of Regentrie, during oure said dearest sonnis minoritie, and ay and quhill he be of the aige of sevintene yeris compleit, as ye and ilkane of yow will declair you loving subjectis to oure said maist deir sone, your native Prince ; and under all pane, charge, and offence, that ye and ilkane of yow may commit and inrin aganis his Majestie in that part. Subscrivit with oure hand, and gevin under oure Previe Seill, at Lochlevin, the xxiiii day of Julij, and of our regnne the xxv yeir.

Reg. Privy Council, i, 539–41

CHAPTER TEN

SOCIAL AND ECONOMIC CONDITIONS

THE BURGHS

Our earliest details of the election of burgh magistrates and officials come from the records of the burgh of Aberdeen where, in 1398, the alderman (or provost) was elected at the Michaelmas head court ' cum consensu et assensu totius communitatis dicti burgi.' This seems to imply election by all the burgesses (freemen) ; but already the freemen in the burghs were distinguished as being either merchants (buyers and sellers) or craftsmen (makers),[1] and in the fifteenth and sixteenth centuries the merchants—possibly because they were the wealthier class, possibly because their trading activities brought greater benefit to the burghs and the realm, possibly because the organisation of trade and the organisation of the burgh were so closely interrelated —gradually acquired, with the aid of parliamentary enactments, complete control of burghal government. In 1469 the old retiring town-council was to choose the new town-council, and the officers of the town were to be chosen by the two councils, combined, together with a representative from each craft ; in 1474 four of the old retiring council were to sit with the new council ; and in 1504 all officers and magistrates were to be chosen from those using merchandise—i.e. merchants. By these successive acts offices and power were gradually concentrated in the hands of the merchants and, where the Act of 1469 became operative,[2] power was further concentrated in the hands of a small group

[1] ' The cheif libertie and fredome of ane fre burgh of ryaltie consistes in twa thingis, the ane in using of marchandice, the uther in using of craftes.' (1570, *Edinburgh Burgh Records*, iii, 273.)

[2] Although the Act became at once operative in Edinburgh, certain other burghs conformed with its provisions only after a wide interval of time. It does not appear to have been observed in Aberdeen (where the council had apparently continued itself in office for forty or fifty years) until the second half of the sixteenth century, and in Peebles it was not observed until the beginning of the seventeenth century.

of merchants who elected their own members to office year by year.[1] Such a monopoly of power soon led to corruption (revealed in the complaint of the inhabitants of Cupar in 1567,[2] and ably satirised by John Galt in *The Provost*) which flourished almost unchecked until the Reform Act of 1832.

The craftsmen, however, did not quietly accept their exclusion from burghal government. In the reign of James I, while the objects of the crafts' associations—to secure good workmanship, to maintain the proper training of apprentices, and to prevent unfair competition—were recognised, such associations were regarded as ' conspiracies ' to raise prices to the hurt of the lieges. Accordingly, and following the medieval concept of *justum pretium*, power was given to the town-councils to fix the prices of craftsmen's work—again giving the merchants further control. Nor was it easy for a craftsman to become a merchant, for now the dividing line had become hard : a craftsman could become a merchant only if he renounced his craft, and only if the merchants were willing to accept him in their fraternity— though occasional instances of craftsmen becoming merchants are to be found in the records.[3] Nevertheless, despite continued and continuing repressive legislation (much of which, however, was clearly ineffective) the crafts, in the latter half of the fifteenth century, had succeeded in further organising themselves (to secure ' good rule ' within the craft) by obtaining ' seals of cause ' from the burgh councils. These documents (sealed with the burgh's court seal—its ' seal of causes ') were virtually charters of incorporation. They granted disciplinary authority to the deacon

---

[1] In Aberdeen, for example, complaint was made in 1590 against the ' unlauchful usurpatioun ' of the magistracy of the burgh by ' the race of Menzeissis ' whereby the burgh was ' thrallit to serve ane raice of pepill ' (*R.P.C.*, iv, 533 ; *Recs. of the Convention of Royal Burghs*, i, 313).

[2] *Infra*, p. 203

[3] The distinction between merchant and craftsman was also regarded as a social one. In Edinburgh, in 1588, Robert Vernour, a skinner, having been admitted a member of the merchant guild, not only became bound to desist and cease from ' all tred and occupatioun in his awin persoun that is nocht comely and decent for the rank and honesty of ane guild brother,' but also bound himself that ' his wyfe and seruandis sall use and exerce na poynt of commoun cwikry outwith his awin howse ' and, *inter alia*, not ' be sene in the streitis with thair aiprounes and seruiets ' (J. D. Marwick, *Edinburgh Guilds and Crafts*, p. 151).

of the craft, and enabled the craft to organise its religious activities (usually the maintenance of an altar to the patron saint of the craft) and its charitable activities (usually through the payment of a 'weekly penny' to form a fund for the maintenance of decayed brethren, widows and orphans).[1]

The crafts were now stronger and better organised, and it is evident that they were far from content with their status in the burghs. There are many references to 'risings' and 'commotions'—reflected in the Act of 1555 [2] : though the 'dispensation' of 1556 may have been an attempt by the Queen Regent to secure support from the craftsmen since Protestantism had already found a strong hold among the merchants.

Matters came to a head with a riot in Edinburgh in 1582 at the time of the burgh elections. Following an arbitration, over which the precocious James VI himself presided, a decreet-arbitral was issued in 1583 and its terms, ratified by Parliament in 1584, provided the basis for the 'sett' of the town. The craftsmen secured representation (though still a minority one) on the town-council, and the deacons of the crafts were given a share in the management of the common good (*A.P.S.*, iii, 360–4, c. 25). And 'setts' somewhat similar to that thus established for Edinburgh were later adopted in other burghs.

Finally, in the second half of the sixteenth century, with the growth of overseas trade, the craftsmen in the different burghs were generally successful in securing local agreements with the merchants whereby the merchants contented themselves with wholesale and overseas trade ('merchandise') and the craftsmen were allowed to sell, locally, the products of the craft. About the same time such price-fixing as still continued was done in agreement between the town-councils and the crafts ; though price-fixing was fast disappearing to the regret of James VI, who wrote, in *Basilicon Doron*, 'The craftsmen thinke we should be content with their worke, howe bad and deare soever it be, and if they in any thing be controlled, up goeth the blew-blanket'—though he also added, 'The merchants think the whole common-weale ordayned for making them up, and accounting it their lawfull game and trade to enriche themselves upon the losse of all the

---

[1] See the Seal of Cause of the Skinners of Edinburgh, 1474, *infra*, p. 207
[2] *Infra*, p. 206

rest of the people. . . . They buy for us the worst wares and sell them at the dearest prices.' (See, in general, W. Mackay Mackenzie, *The Scottish Burghs*, pp. 114–37.)

Election of Burgh Officials

30 September 1398. Die lune proximo post festum beati Michaelis Archangeli anno domini millesimo ccc^{mo} nonagesimo octavo Quo die Willelmus de Camera pater cum consensu et assensu totius communitatis dicti burgi electus est in officium aldirmanni Et Robertus filius David, Simon de Benyn, Johannes Scherar ac Magister Willelmus Dicsoun electi sunt in officium ballivorum et Mauricius filius Roberti, Johannes filius Bricii, Walterus Rede et Simon de Camera electi sunt in officium serjiandorum.

MS. Burgh Records of Aberdeen

1469. Item as tuiching the electioune of alderman bailyis and utheris officiaris of burowis because of gret truble and contensione yeirly for the chesing of the samyn throw multitud & clamor of commonis sympil personis It is thocht expedient that nain officiaris na consail be continuit eftir the kingis lawis of burowis forthir than a yeir And at the chesing of the new officiaris be in this wise that is to say that the aulde counsail of the toune sall cheise the new counsail in sic noumyr as accordis to the toune And the new counsail & the aulde of the yeir before sall cheise all officiaris pertenyng to the toune as alderman bailyis dene of gild and utheris officiaris And that ilka craft sall cheise a persone of the samyn craft that sall have voce in the said electioune of the officiaris for that tyme in like wise yeir be yeir.

A.P.S., ii, 95, c. 5

1474. Item it [is] statute and ordanit in burowis nocht withstanding the actis maide of before that thair salbe of the aulde consale of the yer befor foure worthy personis chosin yeirly to the new consale at thair entre to syt with thame for that yere and have power withe thame to do justice.

A.P.S., ii, 107, c. 12

1504. Item That all officiaris provestis balyeis and utheris haifand office of jurisdictioune within burgh be changeit yeirlie and that nain have jurisdictioune within burgh bot gif thai use merchandice within the said burgh.

A.P.S., ii, 252, c. 25

1567. The auld counsale having alwayis facultie to elect the new, thay cheis men of thair factioun and swa haldis the publict offices and counsale amangis a certane of particular men fra hand to hand, usand and disponand the commoun gude of the said burgh at thair plesour.

Protest of the inhabitants of Cupar, in *R.P.C.*, i, 582

Statutes anent Crafts

1426. The king of deliverance of parliament has ordanit that the dekynnis of craftis in borowis stande to the next parliament in the maner that eftir folowis, that is to say that the dekyn of ilk craft sal hafe na correccioun of the craft na of the lafe of the men of that craft bot allanerly se at the werkmen be cunnande and the werk sufficiande the quhilk he sal assay and examyn everilk xv dais anis.

Item it is ordanit that the alderman and the consal of ilk toune sworn sal se and prise the mater of ilk craft and consider the price of the mater and the cost and the travale of the werkmen ande thareeftir prise the maid werk how it sal be sauld and that price mak knawin to the kingis commonis and be opyn cryit.

Item it is ordanit that the consal of the toune sal se and ordane quhat fee werkmen sal haf for thar handiling of

thar craft that wirkis uther menis materis as wrychtis,
masonis and uthir sic like.

A.P.S., ii, 13, cc. 2, 3, 4

1427. Since the ordinances made in preceding parliaments
anent the deacons of craftsmen in the burghs of the realm
tend to the harm and common loss of the whole realm, the
king, by deliverance of the three estates of the realm,
revoked those ordinances and completely annulled them,
making inhibition besides that such deacons be not elected
among the crafts in any burghs of the realm, that those
already elected no more exercise the office of deacons and
that they make not their accustomed meetings which are
presumed to savour of conspiracies.

A.P.S., 14, c. 4 (translated)

1428. Anentis the men of craftis in burowis, it is sene
spedfull ande the king with the hail consal has ordanit for
a yere that of every craft thare salbe chosyn a wardane be
the consal of the burgh the quhilk wardane with consale
of uthir discret men unsuspect assignyt til hym be the said
consal sal examyn ande pryse the mater ande the werk-
manschip of ilk craft and sett it to a certane price, the
quhilkis gif ony brekis the said wardane sal punyss the
brekaris in certane payn, quhame gif he punyss nocht the
alderman, balyeis and consal of the burgh sall punyss in
certane payn, quhame gif thai punyss nocht the king sal
hafe a certane payn of the burgh : the payn of the brekaris
of the price salbe the eschet of the samyn thing of the quhilk
the price beis brokyn of, . . . the payn of the prisar gif he
be negligent and punyss nocht salbe the unlaw of the borow
court, . . . the payn of the alderman, bailyeis and the
consal of the burgh that beis negligent . . . salbe in x lib.
to the king . . . : the quhilk ordinance salbe extendit to
masonis, wrychtis, smythis, talyeouris, webstaris and all
uthiris elik generally quhais feis and handilling sal be prisit
as it is befor saide. And attour to landewart in scherefdomis

ilk baron sal ger pryse in thare baronryis ande punyss the
trespassouris as the wardane dois in the borowis, ande gif
the barone dois nocht the scheref sal punyss the barone,
ande gif the scheref dois nocht thai salbe in amerciament
to the king . . .

A.P.S., ii, 15, c. 3

1467.   It is statute and ordanit that na man of craft use
merchandise be himself, his factouris or servandis, bot gif
he lefe and renunce his craft but colour or dissimulacioun.

A.P.S., ii, 86, c. 2

1487.   It is statut and ordanit that the act of parlment
tueching the craftsmen usand and deland with merchandise
micht be put to execucioun sa that he that is a craftisman
outher forbere his merchandise or ellis renunce his craift
but ony dissimulacioun or colour, under the pain of eschete
of the merchandise that he usis occupyand his craift, and
this eschete to be inbrocht be the said serchouris to our
soveran lordis use, and compt thairof to be made in his
chekker.

A.P.S., ii, 178, c. 13

1493.   Becaus it is cleirly understandin to the kingis hienes
and his thre estatis that the using of dekynnis of men of
craft in burrowis is rycht dangerous and as thay use the
samin may be the caus of greit troubill in burrowis and
convocation and rysing of the kingis lieges be statutis
making contrair the commone proffet and for thair singulair
proffet and avale, quhilk servis greit punytioun, and als
belangand masonis and uther men of craft that convenis
togidder and makis reule of thair craft sic as masonis and
wrichtis and utheris that thay sall have thair feis alsweill
on the haly dais as for work dais or els they sall nocht laubour
nor wirk, and als quhat personis of thame that wald begin
ane uther mannis werk and he at his plesur will leif the said
werk and than nane of the said craft dar nocht compleit

nor fulfill the samin wark : it is heirfoir avisit, statute and ordanit that all sic dekynnis sall ceise for ane yeir and have na uther power bot allanerly to examyn the fynace of the stuffe and werk that beis wrocht with the remanent of his craft ; and . . . that all the makaris and usaris of the said statutis [concerning holydays] salbe indictit as commone oppressouris of the kingis liegis be thir statutis ; . . . and in likewise of the makaris of the statutis [concerning completion of work].

A.P.S., ii, 234, c. 14

1555. Because it hes bene cleirlie understand to the quenis grace regent and the thre estatis that the chesing of dekinnis and men of craft within burgh hes bene rycht dangerous and as thay have usit thameselfis in tymes bygane hes causit greit troubill in burrowis commotioun and rysing of the quenis liegis in divers partis and be making of liggis and bandis amangis thameselfis and betuix burgh and burgh quhilk deservis greit punischement, Thairfoir the quenis grace regent with avise of the thre estatis foirsaidis hes statute and ordanit that thair be na dekinnis chosin in tymes cumming within burgh bot the provest baillies and counsall of the burgh to cheis the maist honest man of craft of gude conscience ane of everie craft to visie thair craft that thay laubour sufficientlie and that the samin be sufficient stuffe and wark and thir persounis to be callit visitouris of thair craft and to be electit and chosin yeirlie at Michaelmes be the provest, baillies and counsall of burgh and that thay thairefter gif thair aith in jugement to visie leililie and trewlie thair said craft without ony powar to mak gaddering or assembling of thame to ony private conventioun or making of ony actis or statutis bot all craftismen in tymes cumming to be under the provest baillies and counsall and thir visitouris chosin sworne and admittit to have voting in chesing of officiaris and uthers thingis as the dekinnis votit in of befoir and that na craftismen bruke office within burgh in tymes cumming except twa of thame maist honest and famous to be chosin yeirlie upone the counsall and thay twa to be ane part of the auditouris yeirlie to the compt of the commoun gudis according to the actis of parliament maid thairupone of befoir and quha sa ever cummis in the contrare of this act to be punist be warding of thair persounis be the space of ane yeir and tinsall of thair fredome within burgh and never to be ressaifit thairefter as fre men unto the tyme thay obtene the favour and bene-volence of the provest baillies and counsall quhair the fault is committit and the thrid part of thair gudis to be eschetit and applyit to our soverane ladyis use for thair contemptioun.

A.P.S., ii, 497, c. 26

A letter under the great seal, 16 April 1556, relating that the statute of 1555 had not been observed and ' that everything is done more carelessly among those craftsmen at this day than formerly,' granted ' dispensations to all and sundry craftsmen of our burghs and cities within our said kingdom, in regard to the said act of our last parliament ' and restored to the craftsmen ' the power of using and having deacons of crafts, who shall have suffrages and votes in electing the officers of the burghs,' with all other liberties and privileges held by them in times past, notwith-standing the act of parliament (*Records of the Convention of Royal Burghs*, ii, 469–72 ; abstract in *R.M.S.*, iv, No. 1053). This ' dispensation ' was confirmed in 1564 and 1581 (*R.M.S.*, iv, No. 1583, and v, No. 233).

Seal of Cause of the Skinners of Edinburgh

2 December 1474. Til all and sindry quhais knawlag thir present letteres sal cum The prouost bailyeis and consale of the burgh of Edinburgh greting in the Sone of the glorios Virgine : Sen it efferis to ws jugis be verteu of our office to declar schew and bere suthfast witnessing to the verite of the thingis led pronunsit determit and ordanit be ws or befor ws in jugement, sa that innocentis be nocht throu the hiding of verite hurt nor scaithit in our defaltis. Herefor it is that to your vniuersite we mak it knawin and declaris that the daye of the makin of thir

207

presentis, in the chawmer of the Tolbuth of the said burgh comperit befor ws we sittand in jugement the craftismen of the Skinnaris of the self burgh, that is to saye John of Cranston dekin, Robert Haithwy, William Ramsaye, Thomas Salmund, Thomas Grahame, Thomas Frew, Robert of Duscon, Alane Skinnar, John Mathe, James Tod, William Trumbule, Henry Haswele, James Greg, Robert Lauerok, John Scot, Thom of Harlawbankis, Robert Wilschot, Thomas Evinson, Alexander Red and William Craufurd for thaim and in the name of the hale craft present to us thair bill of complaynt of certane thingis that was vsit amangis the craftismen, quharthrou the tone had a sclander and lak, the craft sustenit gret scaith and hurt and the commounis dissauit, and als that diuine seruice and sufferage of Sant Cristoforis alter is mynist, and reparatioun of the said alter nocht beildit nor helpit efter the avis statutis and ordinance of the tone and of the said craft vsit of befor ; and als anentis the dissobeying of thair dekin in the cumming and gaddering befor hym and the craft quhen thai ar warnit, for the comonning and avising for the gude of the hale craft, and for stanching of deformaris and babillaris of the werk baith in kirkis and in tone and for the reformatioun to be had of thir thingis and diuers wtheris concerning and rying [referying] to the hale craft. The quhilk bill beand in presens of us and diuerse of the craft red, herd, and thair desire resonable considerit to the fortifeing and obseruing of the said desiris and statutis vnderwritten we have assentit : In the first, as tuiching the rasing of the Monundais penny of hym or thaim at werkis thair awin laubor, it is statut and ordanit be the dekin and the laif of the craft witht awis of ws that the said penny be rasit wolkly on the Monundaye outhir be the dekin or ony at beis ordanit to gidder it, of al personis lauborand thair awin werk and quha that dissobeyis the gadderar to pund hym thairfor quhil it be pait. Alswa that all personis of the craft sal compere before the dekin and the craft quhen thai ar warnit for the gude of the sammin and quha that dissobeyis and absentis hym in the tym withoutin leif or a resonable assonye he sal paye to Sant Cristoforis alter half a pund of wax. And alswa quha that beis fundin or attayntit brekand schepe skinnis on the ryme sidis outher for poyntis or for gait leddir, or at sellis the samin poyntis for raphell outhir in priue or in aperth fenyeit and fals stuf the committer sal be brouch and the stuf at is fundin takin witht him befor the prouost bailyeis and consale of the tone, and thai sal witht avis and ordinance of the dekin and four or five of the worthiest and best of the craft mak the said persone or personis to be pvnyst as efferis ; and richt swa of the bauchlaris of the said laubour, outhir in the opin gate or in the kirk, quha at beis tayntit tane thairwitht on halidais or werkdais the dekin sal rais on him for the first falt half a pund of wax, the secund falt a pund of wax but fauour to the reparatioun of the said alter of Sanct Cristofor, and the thrid tym the dekin sal bring him and the werk befor the consale of the tone, and thair the prouost bailyeis and consale sal pvnis it witht avis of the dekin and the best of the craft. The quhilkis articlis and desiris we appruf ratifeis and for us and our successouris in sa fer as afferis us or sa fer as we haf power confermys ; and this til all thame quham it efferis we mak knawin be thir oure presentis ; and for the mare witnessing hereof the commoun sele of cause of our said burgh is to hungin togidder witht the subscripcione manuale of oure common clerc William Farnely at Edinburgh the secund day of the moneth of December the yer of our Lord a thousand foure hundreth sevinty and four yere.

Edinburgh Burgh Records, i, 29–30

TRADE AND COMMERCE

Until the close of the sixteenth century Scottish exports were almost wholly confined to wool, woolfells, hides, skins, salmon, trout, dried fish and a little coarse cloth. Imports included essential materials, such as iron, timber, salt (rock-salt for fish-curing), pitch and manufactured goods, and luxuries such as fine cloths, jewellery, spices of many kinds (though these might be regarded as essential to make the 'high' or salted meat more palatable) and much wine.

Our earliest ledger of foreign trade, that of Andrew Halyburton, covering the period 1492–1503, contains interesting accounts of his transactions and shows the general nature of Scotland's foreign trade at that time. The following copy of a letter from Halyburton to a correspondent in Scotland is inserted in his ledger.

1503. *Letter from Andrew Halyburton*

Richt worschipfull schir,—I commend me to yow with all my hert. And ye sall resaiv, God willing, furth of Gilbert Edmestouns schipe, a boit of Malwesy, markit with your mark ; cost at the first bying, v li. xii s. Item, for cran gilt,[1] scout hyr and pynour [2] fee, xii grotis ; soum of this wyne with the costis, v li. xiii s. Item, sall ye resave furth of the sammyne schipe, God willing, a roundale in the first ii steikis of Risillis claith, ane broune and ane blak, of the gret seill, cost xvii li. Item, a steik of Rouane tanny,[3] quhilk was berterit with ane sek of woll of youris ; cost v s. ilk ell, haldand xxxi$\frac{1}{2}$ ell, $\frac{1}{2}$ ane ell to bait ; soume of that steik is vii li. xv s. Item, ii copill [4] of fustiane, cost ii li. ii grotis. Item, ii breddis of bughe,[5] ane better and ane slychtare ; cost ii li. xii s. Item, ii steikis of lawne ; ane cost xxxvi s., the tother xxi s. ; soum of thir ii steikis, ii li. xvi s. Item, half ane pund of fyne gold, cost xix s. Item, i^c and lvi ellis of canvess, cost xxiiii s. the i^c ; soum of the canwess, xxxvii s. ii grotis. Soume of all the gudis in this roundale at the first bying, is xxxv li. iiii grotis. Item, for the roundale, nalis and packing, xxvi grotis. Item, for toll in Berre, viii grotis ; for the pynour fee and scout hyre to the Were, vii grotis ; soume of this roundale with the costis is xxxv li. iii s. ix grotis. Soume of the gudis ye have in this schipe with the boit of Malwesy, is

---

[1] crane charges   [2] labourers
[3] tawney   [4] a measure of cloth
[5] quantities of lambskin fur ; ' breddis ' are the usual measurement of this fur.

xl li. xvi s. ix grotis. Item, thar standis yit ii sekkis of woll of youris unsauld ; and quhen thai are sauld I sall send yow your rekyning of all thingis betuix us. And ony uther that ye have ado in this cuntre I am at your command. And forther plesit yow to wit that here is ane evill mercat, sa help me God, except yowr woll, the best woll that I sauld to yere I couth nocht get xxi mark for it. Youris have I sauld, ane sek for xxii mark, ane uther for xxiii markis. Hydis, I trow, salbe the best merchandice that cumis her at Pasche, for thar is mony folkis that speris about thaim. It were bot a sport to yow to cum oure this somer tyme in this cuntre, and mak yow blyth, and lat us talk of auld fernyeris,[1] and thairefter mak your Jubile, and syne ye may pass hame at Witsonday. And our Lord Jhesu be your keper in saule and body. Writtin at Middilburgh the xxiii day of Januarr 1502.

Youris at power
Androw Halyburtoun

Andrew Halyburton's Ledger, Intro., xxi-xxii

Act for the building of fishing boats

Increasing foreign trade and the demand for imported goods stimulated the fishing industry which was the source of one of Scotland's main exports. This legislation of 1493 and other similar acts endeavoured to combine encouragement of the herring industry with a solution of the constant problem of ' the poor.'

1493.

Anent the greit innumerable ryches that is tint in fault of schippis and buschis to be disponit for fischeing siclyke as utheris realmes hes that ar merchand with the sey, and for the policy and conquest that may be had heirintill, and to cause idill men, vavengeouris, to laubour for thair leving for the eschewing of vicis and idilnes and for the commoun proffeit and universall weill of the realme, it is thocht

---

[1] past years

expedient be the lordis of the articlis and als statute and ordanit in this present parliament that thair be schippis and buschis maid in all burrowis and townis within the realme and at the leist of the said schippis and buschis be of xx tun and at the townis and burrowis have the said schippis and buschis according to the substance of ilk towne and to the maner as eftir followis weill abeilyeit with all necessar graith for the said schippis and buschis and with marynaris, nettis and uther graith convenient for the taking of greit fische and small, and all the said schippis and buschis to be reddy maid and furneist to pas to fisching be fastrenisevin [1] nixt tocum, and in ilk burgh of the rialtie that the officiaris of the burgh mak all the stark idill men within thair boundis to pass with the said schippis for thair wagis, and gif the said idill men refusis to pas that thay baniss thame the burgh and into burgh of barronis quhilk ar neir upone the sey that the scheref of the schire compell the idill men within his boundis to pas to the said schippis for thair wagis and gif thay refuse in lykewyse to baneis thame his schire and gif the officiaris of the burrowis or schereffis of the schiris beis fundin negligent othir in the putting furth of the said schippis and buschis or compelling the idill men to pas in thame for thair wagis or banissing of thame of thair burrowis or schiris gif thai refuse as said is thai sall pay to the king ane unlaw of xx pund ilk ane of thame, that is to say the officiar of the burgh for the tyme and the schiref of the schire, for the quhilk thai salbe chargeit in the checkar and gif compt yeirlie thairupoun.

A.P.S., ii, 235, c. 20

The Jurisdiction of the Scottish Conservator in the Netherlands

Some time after its establishment, the Scottish trading colony in the staple Flemish port (Bruges, Middelburg and finally Veere) [2] gained a conservator ' to pursue, procure, request or defend the goods . . . rights and actions ' of the Scottish merchants trading there. Originally there was close Flemish control, and disputes

[1] Shrove Tuesday   [2] cf. vol. i, p. 213

between the merchants themselves had to be settled in Flemish courts and according to Flemish law ; but, stage by stage, the colony became self-governing and finally attained a status similar to that of the late nineteenth-century Treaty Ports in China. The Act of 1504, whereby the Scottish parliament confirmed the Conservator's exclusive jurisdiction in disputes between Scottish traders, represents an important stage in that development. This jurisdiction was exercised with the help of six, or four, merchants acting as assessors, and control over the Conservator was maintained by concurrent legislation compelling him to visit Scotland once a year to answer any charges made against him.

1504.

It is statute and ordanit for the wele of merchandis and for the gret exorbitant expensis maid be thaim apon pleis in the partis beyond sey that tharefore the conservatour of this realme have jurisdiction to do justice amangis the said merchandis our soverane lordis liegis that is to say betuix merchand and merchand in tha partis beyond se and the said conservatour proceid nocht apon ony materis amang the said merchandis bot gif thare sit vi of the best and honeste merchandis of maist knawlage of the realme that sall syt and have powar with him gif sa mony canne be gottin, and gif thair be nocht to the nomer of sax that thar sit foure merchandis with him at the lest that sall have sik like powar with him to ministre justice and that na merchand persew ane other before ony other juge beyond se nor do in contrare this act under the pain of v li. to be pait to the king of the persewar and payment of the expense to the partii persewit.

A.P.S., ii, 244, c. 32

Act of Council against the Overloading of Ships
1508.

It is statut and ordanit be our soverane lord and his lordis of consale that because thare has bene grete skath and hurt done in tymes bigain to his merchandis liegis and to

the common wele of his realme throu the oureladin of the
schippis passand fortht and cumand in his realme with
merchandice (throu the quhilk grete quantite of gudis
has been cast and spilt, and diverse schippis with thair
hale merchandis and gudis pericht and tynt), and for the
eschewin of sic skath and inconvenientis in tyme to cum,—
that na skippar, master, nor awnar of ony schip . . . fure
nor laid thair schippis forther na thai may gudelye bere ;
and that thai fure nor stow na merchandice abon the
ourloftis of thair schippis without that thai indent with
the awnaris of thar gudis, and tak thair writing . . . ; and
gif thar gudis be castin, na man to haf skath tharof bot he
that aw the samyn.

MS. Acta Dominorum Concilii, xix, f. 170

FINANCE

In common with the rest of Europe, Scotland was affected by the
bullion scarcity of the fifteenth and early sixteenth centuries, and
her position had been aggravated by the drain of bullion to meet
the ransom of David II and part of the ransom of James I.
Legislation dealing with monetary affairs begins in the fourteenth
century, and increases in volume and frequency until the sixteenth.
There were several popular methods of overcoming the difficulty
—debasement of the coinage, stringent regulation of the export
of money, and a series of devices for fostering its import. None
proved effective. The first had wide repercussions both at home
and abroad since each recoinage not only proved inflationary but
also involved a revaluation in terms of foreign currencies. The
second conflicted with the interests of the church, for churchmen
were recognised as the greatest exporters of bullion[1]; moreover
any regulation was extremely difficult to enforce, and open to
innumerable forms of evasion. The third method was generally
unsuccessful, since every country in western Europe was endeavouring to encourage the inflow of bullion into its own coffers.

Monetary difficulties became particularly acute during the
reign of James III, which was in every way a period of ' expanding

[1] cf. *supra*, p. 82

economy.' The 'blak' pennies were a source of widespread grievance, and the measures to combat constant debasement of the coinage provided a source of difference between Parliament and Council. The following series of parliamentary pronouncements on the subject is an indication of the extent to which the question of 'the money' occupied the attention of both government and Parliament—and is an interesting commentary on the efficacy of fifteenth-century legislation.

1424.

Item it is ordanit that na man haf out of the realme golde nor silver bot he pay xl d. of ilk punde of custum to the king under the payne of tynsal of all gold and silver at beis fundyn and x lib. to the king for the unlawe.

A.P.S., ii, 5, c. 16

1430.

Item that ilk gret baral of salmond sal brynge hame in bulyoune xl d. and ilka smal baral xxx d. of the mone now ryngande.

Scot. Hist. Rev., xxix, p. 11

1431.

The King and the haill parliament has statute and ordanit that na salmonde be saulde nor barteryt with ony man at has it oute of the realme bot for Inglis mone alanerly that is to say golde or silver for the tane halfe and gascone wyne or siclyk gude penny worthis for the tother half.

A.P.S., ii, 20, c. 2

1451.

Item that na catal be sauld in Inglande or to Ingliss men bot for redy gold or silver under the payn of eschete of sa mekil as is saulde to be distribute betuix the king and the wardane of the marche.

A.P.S., ii, 40, c. 16

1458.

Item as to the mone thir ar the lordis that ar chosyne thar apone [*thirteen persons named*] And thir personis to be chargyt be the kingis lettres to convene in the tyme of the nixt chekar in the place quhare the chekare is haldin or ony uther place sene speidfull till our souerane lorde to commone and provyde apon the mater of the mone for the profet of the realme And in the meyn tyme it is sene speidfull that the strikin of the cunye cese quhill uther provisione be maide tharfor.

A.P.S., ii, 48, c. 7

1466.

It is statute for the mater of the money ande for the haldin of the samyn within the realme it is statute that na persone spirituale nor temporale liegis to our soverane lorde have nore sende na money oute of the realme undir the payne of ten pundis unremittable to the king for amerciament and als mekil money as he takis or sendis oute of the realme . . . safyng moderate expensis to the avale of ane Inglis noble for ilk persone. Ande that clerkis sailing or passing oute of the realme sal cum before thare ordinar or his official and mak athe that thai sal nouther have nor sende na money oute of the realme bot his said expensis ande that secularis sal cum befor the kingis depute to be lymmit at ilk havin and mak faith in lyke wis. . . .

A.P.S., ii, 86, c. 10

1466.

For the inbringing of the moneye in the realme it is statute that ilk merchiande having wol skyn or hyde oute of the realme sal bring of ilk sek of birnt silver twa unce to the cunyeoure for the quhilkis he sal have ix s. ij d. efter the forme of the Act maid in the last parliament therupone and the pain contenit in the samyn And this to indure to the next parliament.

A.P.S., ii, 86, c. 11

1466.

It is statute for the eise and sustentatioun of the kingis liegis and almous deide to be done to pure folk that thare be cunyeit coppir money four to the penny having in prent on the ta parte the crois of Saint Androu and the croune on the tother parte with superscripcione of Edinburgh on the ta parte and ane R with James on the tother parte And that thare be cunyet thre thousand pundis countande to the silver. And that thai pas in payment for brede and ale and uther merchiandice and in grete merchiandice to be takin xii d. in the punde. And that all uther money gold and silver have course as it had of befor except that the new Inglis grote of Edwardis [1] cunye have course amang the kingis liegis for x d. and na derrare. Ande the new noble of the Rose for xxv s.

And the lordis that salbe lymmit til have the strenth of the parliament in uther causis as is before writtin have power to mak and set reulis and statutis of the vi d. grot of the floure delice as thai sal think expedient for the gude of the realme.

A.P.S., ii, 86, c. 12

1467.

Item, our soverane lorde the king and the thre estatis in this present parliament fyndis his hieness and the haill body of the realme gretumly hurt and skathit in the mone of this realme haifande lawer course than uther realmis about us has, throu the quhilk the mone of this realme is born out in gret quantite and the realme puryt of the sammyn, for the quhilk our said soverane lorde and his thre estatis in this present parliament has statute ande ordanit that the mone of uther realmis, that is to say, the Ingliss noble Henry and Edwarde with the rose, the franche crown, the salute,[2] the lewe [3] and the ridar [4] sall haif course in this

---

[1] Edward IV   [2] a French gold coin
[3] louis   [4] a gold coin

realme of our mone to the valour and equivalence of the course at thai haf in Flandris. . . .

And the striking of the blak pennyis to be cessyt that thar be nane strikyn in tyme to cum under payne of dede. . . .

A.P.S., ii, 88, c. 1

1471.

As twechin the mater of the mone : sen the mater is gret and twechis the hail body of the realme in gret nernes, and the lordis heir present can nocht hastely be avisit to tak a final determinacioun tharof, it is statut and ordanit that the mone have course as it dois now unto the continuatioun of this parlyament, and the lordis that sal have the power in al uther materis for the comon gude of the realme at that tyme to avise, determyn and conclude apone the said mater of the mone that now rynnis. . . .

A.P.S., ii, 100, c. 8

1473.

As anentis the brynging in of bulyoun within the realm the lordis thinkis that thare is mony and sindry actis maid be the kingis progenitouris and himself in diverse parliaments apone the bringing in of bulyoun the quhilkis actis war profittable to be sene and put to execucioun. And, thai beand duely execut, thai traist that thare suld sudanly cum bullioun in the realme in gret quantite. And inlikewise to ger the actis and statutis maid apone the keiping of money within the realme be duely keipit and sic sercheouris and inquisitouris set therupon that will execut the said actis without corrupcioun or dissimul[acioun] for the commoun proffit of the realme.

Anent the conye, because of the skantnes of bullioun that is in the realme the lordis prelatis thinkis expedient that the goldin pennyis have the sammyn course that thai war wont to haf and now has. . . .

A.P.S., ii, 105, cc. 11, 12

1473.

Alsa the lordis barounis remembris that thare was a statute maid in our soverane lordis tyme quham god assolye that thare sulde nane Ingliss claith cum within his realme be na merchandice, considering quhare thai myt have gude money baith gold and silver for thare salmound keling and utheris fisches, thai have alanerly now bot claith quhilk is gret hurt and skaith to his hienes in his custume and to his liegis that are bare of money. Tharefor thai counsale our soverane lorde that thare be ane inhibicioun gevin in this present parliament that na merchand Ingliss nor Scottis bryng in sic merchandice under the pane of escheting of the claith and punicioun of the person that bryngis it at the kingis will.

A.P.S., ii, 105, c. 15

1478.

Alssua becaus our soverain lord is informit that his realme is parit and wastit of money in default of the cunye that has bene strikin in tymes bigain, and the auld money that had course in this realme baith of the realme self and utheris has bene translatit and put to fyre and maid bulyeoun to uther moneye that is strikin of new incontrare the avisement of the last parliament throu the quhilk thar is litle or nane alde moneye of this cuntre nor utheris gangande, nouther demyis, lyounis, Ingliss nobillis, lewis, Franche crounis, Ingliss grotis, floure de lise, grotis, xiiij d. grotis, bot of the maist part baith gold and silver put to fyre, oure soverane lord at the raquest of his thre estatis has grantit now to mak the actis of his parliament, baith in his progenitouris tymes and his awin, of the inbringing of bulyeoun, be put in execucioun and be observit and kepit, and in likewise the actis maid uppoun the sercheing and keping in of the money in the realme be put to scharp execucioun and gud serchearis sett tharuppon at all portis and places neidfull and, gif it nedis, scharpe reuyllis tharuppone be counsale and avise of his lordis of counsale.

And in the meyntyme quhill the realme may be stuffit of bulyeone that it may be sene and knawin quhareof that new money may be strikin his hienes wil of his grace as said is ger cess all cunyeing and stryking of moneye gold, silvyr gret or small, and ger tak the irnys fra the cunyeouris incontinent and put thaim in sour keping sua that thar cum na mare hurt to the realme throu the stryking of moneye in tyme cumming. And quhat tyme that his hienes thinkis that the realme be stuffit of bulyeoune he sall than, God willing, with the avise of the lordis of his counsale mak a sett and reuyle of his moneye baith gold and silver of the wecht and finance that it sal hald, the course that it sal haf, and mak and ordane a wardain and a master of his cunye of substans and knaulege that salbe responsable to his hienes upon ther lifis and honour for the keping of the ordinans and statutis that salbe maid.

A.P.S., ii, 118, c. 3

1487.

Anent the mater of the inbringin of bulyeoun and keping of gold and silver within the realme and punycioun of the merchandice that bringis nocht in bulyeoun, and als the punycioun of thame that has gold and silver furth of the realme, it is statute and ordanit that the actis and statutis of parliament made tharuppoun of before be put to scharp execucioun.

A.P.S., ii, 182, c. 11

Feu-ferme Tenure

With the increasing expenses of government and, in particular, with the increasing expense of waging war in defence of the realm—owing to the development of artillery and the growth of navies—the ' money income ' of the state was proving wholly insufficient for new needs. Land, which was still the main source of wealth, was still largely held for feudal returns—of a knight, or an archer, or even in blencheferme for, say, a rose in midsummer or a pound of pepper—and taxation was still ' extra-ordinary ' income, a source to be drawn upon only upon extra-ordinary occasions. In the reign of James IV the accounts of the Comptroller and the Treasurer show steadily mounting deficits ; the government was heavily ' overdrawn ' when James V succeeded to the throne ; and the troubles of Albany's regency were not conducive to sound finance. There might be occasional ' wind-falls,' like the forfeiture of the Black Douglases in 1455 and the forfeiture of the Red Douglases in 1528 ; with the Act of 1455 lands were to be ' annexed ' to the crown to help to meet crown finances (*supra*, p. 16) ; and there was a steady debasement of the coinage (*supra*, p. 214). But there was still an ever-pressing need for *money*.

Money was found in two ways : (i) by exploiting the wealth of the church—as, for example, by abusing the Indult of 1487 (see *supra*, pp. 89–91), or by extorting finance from the church for state purposes, as in the establishment of the College of Justice (*supra*, pp. 47–9) ; and (ii) by developing a new ' money economy ' through the encouragement of feuing—that is, ' setting ' lands on a perpetual heritable tenure in return for an annual fixed money-rent (the *feu-duty*).

The feu system had already developed in the burghs and in holdings of church lands (despite such a permanent alienation being contrary to canon law), for the burghs were naturally dependent upon a money-economy and the churchmen were in constant need of money for their many payments to Rome. But now the system is widely extended to the holdings of crown lands. The Act of 1457/8 is the first indication of an endeavour to encourage tenure in feu ; in 1504 the king is given power to set the crown lands, both annexed and unannexed, in feu ; in 1541 a similar act speaks of feuing as being ' to the great profit of the crown ' ; and finally, in 1584, parliament declares that lands which have fallen, or shall in future fall, into the hands of the crown by forfeiture, are to be annexed and set in feu, and that any other disposition of such lands is to be null and void.

Henceforward, through the feuing of the crown lands, the king obtains (i) capital payments for the granting of feu-charters which, conferring a permanent tenure of the lands, are much sought after ; and (ii) a steady annual income in hard cash from feu-duties.

Legislation

1457/8. Item anentis feuferme, the lordis thinkis speidfull that the king begyne and gif exempill to the laif and quhat prelate barone or frehaldare that can accorde with his tenande apone setting of feuferme of his awin lande in all or in part our soverane lorde sall ratify and appreif the said assedacioun sa that gif the tenandry happynnis to be in warde in the kingis handis the saide tenande sall remane with his feuferme unremovyt payande to the king siklik ferme endurande the warde as he did to the lorde sa that it be set to a competent avail without prejudice to the king.

A.P.S., ii, 49, c. 15

1503/4. It is statute and ordanit be our soverane lord and his thre estatis in this present parliament that it salbe lefull to his hienes to sett all his propir landis, baith annext and unannext, in fewferme to ony persone or personis as he plesis sa that it be nocht in diminutioun of his rentale grassoumis nor uther dewites, and to sett thame with sic clausis as he thinkis expedient according to the conditioun aforesaid. And that the landis that he settis in his tyme as said is to stand perpetualy to the airis eftir the forme of thair conditioun. . . .

A.P.S., ii, 253, c. 36

1540/1. Becaus it is thocht be the kingis grace and the hale thre Estatis of his realme that the setting of his lands baith annext and unannext in few is to the grett proffitt of his croun swa the samin be maid in augmentatioun of his rentale it is tharefore statute and ordanit . . . [*exactly as in 1503*].

A.P.S., ii, 376, c. 35

1584. . . . [*Parliament considering*] the daylie incresce of the chargeis and expensis of his hienes hous and the diminutioun of the rentis of his maiesties proprietie quharon his said hous aucht to be intertenyit, hes thairfoir thocht convenient, statute and ordinit that the landis, lordshipis baroneis and utheris rentis alreadie fallin or how sone the same sall happin to fall and becum in his hienes handis be vertew of the eschaet throw the processis and domis of foirfalture . . . salbe annext unto his maiesties croun, and presentlie, now as then, and then as now, annexis the same thairto, followand the guid exemple of his predecessouris, for the honorable support of his estate. And the saidis landis lordshippis baroneis and utheris rentis heirefter specifeit to remane perpetuallie with the croun, may nather be gevin away in fie, franktenement,[1] in pensioun or ony uther disposition to ony persoun of quhat estate or degrie that ever they be of without avise decreit or deliverance of the haill parliament and for great reasounable causis concerning the weilfair of the realme. . . . And that alwayis sic infeftmentis as sall happin to be maid or grantit be his hienes of ony of the saidis landis and lordshippis salbe onlie in fewferme for pament of sic yeirlie fewferme as his hienes and his counsell sall think reasounable. . . . And albeit it sall happin our soverane lord that now is or ony of his successouris kingis of Scotland to annalie or dispone the saidis lordshippis, landis, castellis . . . annext to the croun as said is, utherwayis that the same alienationis and dispositionis sall be of nane availl. . . .

A.P.S., iii, 307, c. 25

The Benefits of Feu-ferme Tenure

The expected, and appreciated, benefits of feu-ferme tenure are to be seen in the opening words of many feu-ferme charters. Thus, Walter Young, chaplain of the altar of St Michael in the diocese of Dunkeld, begins his charter of feu-ferme (1540) of the lands of Wester Balnagard, to Thomas Lindsay and his wife, with the style :

Because divers kings of the realm of Scotland in times past in their parliaments, with the three estates of their

[1] i.e. liferent

223

realm, taking into their joint consideration the welfare of the same, have decreed by divers statutes and acts of parliaments, which are observed as law among us in Scotland, that the lands of the king and of prelates, temporal lords, earls, barons, and all others whomsoever holding lands in heritage should be set in emphiteusis or feu-ferme, without diminution of their rents or issues, as could be agreed with the tenants, judging that thereby, from the assured hope to them and their heirs of enjoying and holding a tenure in perpetuity, some reasonable advantages in the increase of ' improvement ' would accrue—in suitable buildings, lands put under new cultivation, the recovery of ' waste,' the planting of trees, the raising of fish in fresh waters and by means of stanks, the construction of dove-cots, orchards, pleasaunces and warrens, together with the enrichment in moveable goods of the tenants holding the same lands thus set in emphiteusis or feu-ferme, and the provision of arms and military equipment for the defence of the king and kingdom against the ' old enemy ' or any other invaders, all being of advantage to the king and kingdom and of especial profit to the welfare of the commonweal, Know, therefore [*that I have set my lands of Wester Balnagard in feu-ferme to Thomas Lindsay and Margaret Cochrane, his wife, etc. . . .*]

Fraser's *Red Book of Grandtully*, i, No. 46

The rapid and widespread extension to church lands of the practice of feuing dates from the finance connected with the erection of the College of Justice (see *supra* pp. 49–50). Confronted by the necessity of raising £72,000 in four years, the churchmen had to resort to transactions which would yield large lump sums. According to Canon Law alienation was forbidden and transactions in church lands had to be ' to evident advantage.' But it was possible to argue that feu charters, yielding as initial payments the sums which the church required towards the payment of the £72,000 and specifying a feu duty slightly in excess of the rent for which the land had previously been set, were ' to evident advantage.' The fallacy, of course, was that the feu duty was fixed in perpetuity, whereas when lands were leased the rent could be increased on renewal.

Many feu charters were in this way granted to members of the nobility, who thereby obtained a grasp of church lands (cf. *supra* p. 142)—which, having been well administered in the past, proved fruitful and gave the nobility an appetite for more. The tenants on these lands, however, had enjoyed easy conditions from the church as a landlord ; many, indeed, enjoyed ' kindly tenancy ' or heritable tenure. Now, however, the nobility, as their new landlords, proceeded not only to the raising of rents, but also to eviction. Complaints soon began to pour into the Lords of Council, who appear to have been either powerless or unwilling to intervene. Thus arose a social discontent which aggravated the ' Reformation.'

CONDITIONS OF WORK

Holidays

1469. Forsamekle as the Setterday and uthir vigillis ar nocht of law biddin haly day bot fra evinsang to evinsang, that thairfor masonis wrichtis and uthir craftismen that ar set for lang tyme or schort for the werk sall wirk on the Settirday and uthir festuale evinnis quhil foure houris eftir none undir pain of tynsail of his wolkis [1] fee and that [they] keip na ma haly days na is biddin of halykirk of gret solempnit festis, and gif ony dois in the contrare that the ordinar led processis of cursing upone thame.

A.P.S., ii, 97, c. 15

Hours of Work

The following extract from the *Edinburgh Burgh Records* of January 1491/2 prescribes the hours to be worked by the masons engaged on the kirk of St Giles.

1492.

The quhilk day, the provest dene of gild baillies and counsale of the burgh of Edinburgh thinkis expedient and als ordanis

---

[1] week's

that thair maister masoun and the laif of his collegis and servandis of thair kirk wark that now ar and sall happin to be for the tyme sall diligentlie fulfill and keip thair service at all tymes and houiris as after followes : That is to say, The said maister and his servandis sall begyn to thair werk ilk day in somer at the straik of v houris in the morning, and to continew besylie into thair lawbour quhill viij houris thairafter, and than to pas to thair disione[1] and to remane thairat half ane hour, and till enter agane to thair lawbouris at half hour to ix houris before none, and swa to wirk thairat quhill that xj houris be strikken, and afternone to forgather agane to thair wark at the hour of ane, and than to remayne quhill iiij houris after-none, and than to gett a recreatioun in the commoun luge be the space of half ane hour, and fra thine furth to abyde at thair lawbour continually quhill the hour of vij be strikkin : And in winter to begyn with day licht in the morning kepand the houris abovewritten, and to haif bot thair none shanks[2] allanerly afternone, and to remayne quhill day licht be gane. And gif the said maister quhat-sumevir or his collegis and servandis faillis in ony poyntis abovewritten, or remainis fra his said service ony tyme, he to be correctit and punist in his wages at the plesour of the dene of gild that sall happin to be for the tyme, as the said dene will ansuer to God and to the guid towne thairupoun.

Edinburgh Burgh Records, i, 61–2

Apprenticeship

1489.

Johne Stewart, with the consent and assent of George Stewart, his brother, is becummyn printis to the said William Androsone to lere the cutlar craft for the termes of 7 yeris, the entere at Witsonday that last wes and ther-after till endoir to the full end of the said 7 yeris etc., and

---

[1] *disjeune* : breakfast   [2] interval

that the said Johne sal be lell and trew to his master etc.,
and he sal teich and schaw him al the poyntis of his craft
and consele nain fra him and gif him met and drinke
endorand the said 7 yeris ; and the said Johne sal fynd
him self bedding and claithis, for the quhilk the said
William, his master, giffis him full liciens and leif to
wyrk his aune werk ilke Setterday efter nowne, that
is to say the fyrst 2 yeris fra sex houris efter nowne
furtht and the tother last 5 yeris fra thre houris efter
nowne etc.

Protocol Book of James Young (Scot. Rec. Soc.), No. 237

PLANTING AND POLICY

1504.

It is statute and ordanit anent policy to be haldin in the
cuntre that everilk lord and lard mak thame to have parkis
with dere stankis, cunyngaris, dowcatis, orchartis, heggis
and plant at the leist ane aker of wod quhare thair is na
greit woddis nor forestis.

A.P.S., ii, 251, c. 19

1535. Item for polecy to be had within this realme in
planting of woddis making of heggies orchartis yardis and
sawing of browme It is statute and ordanit be the kingis
grace and his thre estatis of parliament that . . . every
man spirituale and temporal within this realme havand
ane hundreth pund land of new extent be yeir, and may
expend samekle, quhar thar is na woddis nor forestis plant
wod and forest and mak hedgis and hanyng for him self
extending to thre aikir of land, and abone or under as his
heretage is mare or less, in placis maist convenient and
that thai cause every tennent of thair landis that hes the
samin in tak and assedacioun to plant upoun thare onsett
yerelie for every merk land ane tree ; Ilk lord of ane

hundreth pund land under the pane of x li. and less or mare efter the rait and quantite of thair landis And that inquisitioun be maid yerelie herupoun as the kingis grace sall think maist expedient. . . .

A.P.S., ii, 343, c. 7

1541.

Thir ar the claussis divisit be the Comptrollar and commissaris chosin be the kingis grace for setting of his landis of Fiffe and Stratherne in few and takkis, to be insert in thair charteris and to be observit and kepit be thaim and thair successouris in tyme to cum.

In the first, that all and sindry quhatsumevir tenentis of our soverane lordis landis of Fiffe that hes tane his landis for ferme sall have ane gud, large yard, weil dykit and heggeit with hawthorne, sawch, allir or esp,[1] with planting of eschis, planis, and elme, that is to say, for ilk mark of silvir thre treis, and for ilk chalder of ferme quheit and beir yerlie to plant xx treis, and for ilk chalder of aitis ten treis, for the compleit circuling of thair yardis, with sawing of brome, wphalding of woddis and schawis, quhar ony ar at this tyme, or hes bene, or may be had be diking and haning ; and to saw hemp and lint outwith thair caleyard, and nane within ; and that na tenant sall analy nor wedsett ony of his few landis, in all nor in part, without speciale avise and consent of the kingis grace, and that be resignatioun of the samin maid in his hienes handis ; and that every tenent big, wphald, and sustene honest and sufficient houssis efferand to the quantite of thair maling.

And quhar ony man hes fewis seperat be thaimselfis, for silvir or ferme or part of baith [he] sall have [ane] honest mansioun, with hall, chalmer, pantry, kiching, and uthir

---

[1] aspen

office houssis substantiously biggit, efferand to the quantite of thair maling, berne, byre, dowcat, planting of treis, orchardis, or yardis, wele dikit, heggit or fowseit and sett about with treis precedand, and with uthir clausis as is above writtin ; and to hayne medowis in all placis quhair thai may be had, with planting of allir, sawch and hesill in boggis and humyde placis convenient thairfor, and to have stankis and pondis for fische, quhar the samin may be gudly had, with cunyngaris.

Item, that every ane of the saidis tenentis be honestlie and sufficientlie armit, and conforme to the actis of parliament to pas with our soverane lord in his army or uthir particular radis, as thai sall be chargit at all tymes.

Royal Rentals (*E.R.*, xvii, 719)

TAVERNS

1436.

Item the king and the thre estatis has ordanyt that na man in burghe be fundyn in tavernys at wyne aile or beir eftir the straik of ix houris and the bell that salbe rongyn in the said burghe The quhilkis beande fundyn the alderman ande bailyies sall put thame in the kingis presone The quhilk gif thai do nocht thai sall pay for ilk tyme at thai be fundyn culpabill befor the chawmerlane l s.

A.P.S., ii, 24, c. 8

1552.

. . . That na maner of tavernaris tak upone hand to mak ony mixtioun with ony auld wynis and new wynis of this yeir or put ony watter in the samin under the pane of escheting of the punschoun that sic auld wyne or watter salbe put into togidder with the rest of all and sindrie the wynis being the awnaris of sic ane taverne and tinsall of thair fredome for ever And in lyke maner that nane of our soverane ladyis liegis byaris of sic wynis [i.e. *wines of*

229

Bordeaux and Rochelle] and havaris of tavernis tak upone hand to huird or hyde ony sic wynis coft be thame in thair housis and privie placis bot that thay put the samin in thair commoun tavernis and woltis thairof to be sauld indifferentlie to our soverane ladyis liegis. . . .

A.P.S., ii, 483, c. 1

PRINTED IN GREAT BRITAIN AT
THE PRESS OF THE PUBLISHERS